Quartz Job Scheduling Framework

Quartz Job Scheduling Framework

Building Open Source

Enterprise Applications

PRENTICE
HALL

Chuck Cavaness

Upper Saddle River, NJ • Boston• Indianapolis • San Francisco
New York • Toronto • Montreal • London • Munich • Paris • Madrid
Capetown • Sydney • Tokyo • Singapore • Mexico City
Many of the designations used by manufacturers and sellers to distinguish

their products are claimed as trademarks. Where those designations appear in this book, and the publisher was aware of a trademark claim, the designations have been printed with initial capital letters or in all capitals.

The author and publisher have taken care in the preparation of this book, but make no expressed or implied warranty of any kind and assume no responsibility for errors or omissions. No liability is assumed for incidental or consequential damages in connection with or arising out of the use of the information or programs contained herein.

The publisher offers excellent discounts on this book when ordered in quantity for bulk purchases or special sales, which may include electronic versions and/or custom covers and content particular to your business, training goals, marketing focus, and branding interests. For more information, please contact:

U.S. Corporate and Government Sales
(800) 382-3419
corpsales@pearsontechgroup.com

For sales outside the United States, please contact:

International Sales
international@pearsoned.com

 This Book Is Safari Enabled

The Safari® Enabled icon on the cover of your favorite technology book means the book is available through Safari Bookshelf. When you buy this book, you get free access to the online edition for 45 days. Safari Bookshelf is an electronic reference library that lets you easily search thousands of technical books, find code samples, download chapters, and access technical information whenever and wherever you need it.

To gain 45-day Safari Enabled access to this book:

Go to http://www.prenhallprofessional.com/safarienabled

Complete the brief registration form

Enter the coupon code BJLL-EMRM-XZDB-1XMN-1JNS

If you have difficulty registering on Safari Bookshelf or accessing the online edition, please e-mail customer-service@safaribooksonline.com.

Visit us on the Web: www.prenhallprofessional.com

Library of Congress Cataloging-in-Publication Data

Cavaness, Chuck.
    Quartz job scheduling framework : building open source enterprise
applications / Chuck Cavaness.
        p. cm.
    ISBN 0-13-188670-3 (pbk. : alk. paper)
    1. Quartz (Electronic resource) 2. Production scheduling. 3. Open
source software.   I. Title.
    TS157.5.C38 2006
    658.5'3—dc22

                                            2006007504

ISBN 0-13-188670-3
Text printed in the United States on recycled paper at R.R. Donnelley in Crawfordsville, Indiana.
First printing, June 2006

DEDICATION

This book is dedicated to the Quartz user community. I hope you find both the project and this book helpful in your work life. Quartz is a great tool and can make your job easier. Learn it—live it—love it. James, you should be proud of what you created.

Chuck Cavaness

CONTENTS

FOREWORD

The event-driven programming paradigm has been popular for a number of decades, and although the term is not among the current industry buzzwords, it is one of the most popular and useful ways in which a software system can be built. Operating systems, word processors, Web applications, and games are all event driven: The software waits until it receives notification of some event (such as a system interrupt, key stroke, or mouse click) and then changes the control of program flow based on some interpretation of the event.

Quartz enables programs to take advantage of the event-driven paradigm without any human interacting with the system. More specifically, it lets applications define events that should occur at certain trigger points in time. Running a small subprogram (or job) based upon a date in time is commonly called job scheduling.

Job scheduling is found in nearly every class of software application and service, from large e-commerce systems, to simple stand-alone GUI applications, to system-maintenance and monitoring tools, to even games—virtually anywhere the event-driven paradigm is useful.

Indeed, before building Quartz, I found myself continually working on projects that needed scheduling functionality. The Java Platform provided by Sun Microsystems offered reasonably good support for threading but provided little else to cause events to occur within a system at certain times or on regular intervals. Because of this, I found myself frequently creating components to provide rudimentary scheduling capabilities. Some of the projects I worked on during the "dotcom" heydays enabled me to see some of the scheduling functionality provided by various higher-level platforms, such as EAI tools, manufacturing process–control systems, and even a few of the first J2EE application servers that included some basic scheduling features. And, of course, I had been familiar with UNIX cron for a number of years.

Although scheduling wasn't the focus of any of my projects (I concentrated on a service needed by each), my mind began to take interest in the problem of scheduling, and I found myself spending time thinking of various designs for a Java-based scheduling service. I created a few proofs-of-concept and then, having seen that that the open source community at that time had no offering in the way of a scheduler, in 2001 I registered a project with the name of Quartz on SourceForge. I decided it was my turn to pay back the community for other people's great work that I had been benefiting from freely.

I was quickly surprised by the number of people interested in using Quartz, as well as how many other open source projects were including Quartz in their distribution. But most of all, I began to see that Quartz was destined to become far more feature rich than I had ever planned it to be. Although it had been designed with a fair amount of extensibility and customization in mind, several more hooks for providing plug-ins and the like were added—and growing pains have become a bit evident in the code base. One of the most major changes for the Quartz project came in 2004 when it joined the OpenSymphony family of projects and moved its source code repository from SourceForge to java.net.

The community around Quartz has grown well, and I owe many thanks to dozens of people who have contributed in the user forums, mailing lists, and, of course, the source code itself. I now know firsthand that no open source project can be successful without a contributing user base. As you learn to use Quartz, please consider contributing back to the open source community because you yourself are benefiting from the work of others. Or, in the words of Benjamin Franklin, "Live usefully."

I have found job scheduling to be a field that is simple in concept but very challenging in certain areas of implementation. Many ways exist for integrating and making use of Quartz with your stand-alone and J2EE applications. I am regularly surprised by hearing about some way in which someone has put job scheduling to work. I hope that this book will aid you in not only learning how to use Quartz, but also identifying the ways in which you can put the (schedule-based) event-driven paradigm to use in the applications you build.

James House

PREFACE

I first came across Quartz in 2004 when I was looking for a job scheduler while designing a medical claims–processing engine. I was initially skeptical about the framework because it seemed to so exactly fit what I was looking for. Very quickly that skepticism turned into kidlike joy as I realized what I had stumbled upon.

During the course of writing other books and articles and while doing the presentation circuit at various Java User's Groups across the country, I had not once come across the Quartz framework. I probably had looked at and researched hundreds—possibly even thousands—of other open source frameworks. I was just dumbfounded by how this framework could have escaped my attention and the detection of the user community.

Many things about the framework remind me of the early days with Apache Struts, including some of the internal design approaches that the creator of Quartz chose, as well as the way in which the user community has grown as word has spread. Although it's true that the number of users who need job scheduling will likely never be as high as those who need a Web framework, Quartz offers much to be excited about.

ACKNOWLEDGMENTS

It's important that I thank many people for helping me get this book finished. The book started fast and was easy to write, but as most book projects (and most things in life) go, it was hard to keep the motivation all the way through to the end.

I need to thank the editors for having so much patience with me. To the technical editors, James House and Doug Barth, I appreciate your time and feedback to make the book as good as it can be. To Greg and Mary Kate, I know that I was difficult to work with and worked more slowly than you wanted, but I do appreciate the understanding and calmness you always presented to me.

It would be criminal to not personally thank James House for the immense amount of time that he has given to the Quartz project and to the user community. Many of us think about creating stuff like Quartz, but people like James make it happen and make it possible for people like me to write these books. Without him, none of this would be possible. I hope that life rewards him tenfold.

Next, I would like to acknowledge the team of Quartz users and developers that provided advice and feedback on the book's content and direction. Your help was very much appreciated. I only hope I've done justice to your input and given something back to the community.

I would be remiss if I didn't thank the OpenSymphony folks as well. They are doing a great service to users like me, and much of it goes unnoticed. Thanks for the help from you during this project.

And finally, I would be kicked out of my house and left homeless if I didn't thank my wonderful wife of 16 years and our three boys, Josuha, Benjamin, and Zachary. What a sacrifice they made to provide me with the time that I needed to complete this. I love all of you and thank you for indulging my selfishness during this time.

About the Author

Chuck Cavaness is the Chief Technology Officer at Cypress Care, Inc. and a software technologist with more than 10 years of technical management, software engineering, and development experience. Chuck has spent time in the travel, health-care, banking, and B2B/B2C sectors, and has spent the past several years building large enterprise J2EE systems for the financial and health-care industries.

Chuck is a published author of five books on popular technologies, including books on Java J2EE and many open source technologies such as Apache Struts. He has also written for *JavaWorld*, O'Reilly, OnJava, and InformIt.com and has taught courses on programming and software development at Georgia Institute of Technology.

## CHAPTER 1

SCHEDULING IN THE ENTERPRISE

What Is Job Scheduling?

The concept of a "job" in the technical sense dates back to mainframe days when users/programmers submitted a deck of punched cards or paper tape (which represented a job) to an operator who was responsible for running the job. The user then waited for the job to finish or came back later to pick up the printout and cards from the user bin.

Because not every job demands immediate execution, jobs can be scheduled to be executed in the future. For example, a system administrator might have a job list that he follows every night:

- 10:00 PM: Run patient upload job
- 11:00 PM: Run sales data report
- 11:59 PM: Run database backup

Job scheduling is often referred to as running batch jobs or batch processing. These batch jobs typically run in the background and normally don't involve much user interaction. The variety of tasks that are now considered as potential batch jobs has grown significantly: It's not uncommon for larger organizations to run hundreds of jobs per hour, every hour of every day. And as the size and complexity of organizations continues to grow, so does the demand for batched jobs and a job scheduler.

Why Job Scheduling Is Important

As the saying goes, "Time is money." Devoting highly paid resources to menial tasks is a waste of money and resources. As the complexity of the business processes increases, so does the benefit of automating the process. This is indicated in Figure 1.1.

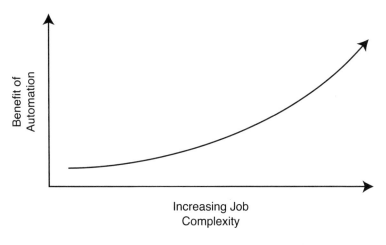

FIGURE 1.1
The bigger, more complex, and more frequent the task is, the more value can be gained from automation.

Humans are, well, human. We make mistakes far more frequently than computers do. By automating a series of tasks into a job and then creating a schedule for when that job should be executed, we can eliminate much of the chance for errors by simply removing humans from the equation.

Another advantage of job scheduling is scalability. We might be able to manually accommodate 10 or 20 jobs per hour, but the higher we go in job count, the harder it is to keep up without introducing errors in the jobs. With job scheduling, we are limited only by hardware resources.

So we can safely say that automation through job scheduling offers at least these three advantages over a similar manual approach:

- Resource efficiency
- Fewer errors
- More scalability

Uses for Job Schedulers in the Enterprise

The term *enterprise* is used so often—and so carelessly—today that it's hard to know which definition is being referred to. We have one meaning in mind when we use it in this book: the software systems and processes that are part of an organization. These systems might be legacy mainframes, a client/server architecture, or J2EE applications—it doesn't matter. Real-world examples of where job schedulers can be used are plentiful. The following scenarios, although obviously not exhaustive, present some common uses in applications today.

Scenario #1: Sending E-Mails, Reminders, and Alerts

Many Web sites (both commercial and otherwise) allow users to register an account that includes a username and password. For security reasons, it's a good idea to expire the user's passwords regularly—say, every 90 days. You might create a job that runs every night at midnight and sends an e-mail to a list of users when their passwords will expire in three days. This is great use of a job scheduler. Figure 1.2 illustrates the password reminder job.

FIGURE 1.2   The password expiration job sends e-mails nightly to remind users that their passwords will expire soon.

Besides expiring passwords, Web sites can send other alerts and reminders (not to mention spam). A job scheduler can be used for those in a similar way.

Scenario #2: Performing File-Transfer Operations

Many businesses need to integrate information with their vendors and clients. One method of performing this integration is to exchange data files. Businesses can use real-time methods such as SOAP, but many don't need to operate in real time and instead choose asynchronous methods such as File Transfer Protocol (ftp) to drop and pick up files.

Picture a worker's compensation company that receives files every morning containing patient/accident information. This company could hire someone to manually check the ftp site every morning for the file. Alternatively, someone could write a job that executes every morning to scan the ftp site and insert the files into the patient database. With a scheduled job, the employee no longer has to perform the manual checks and can do something more valuable for the company. Figure 1.3 illustrates the file-transfer operation.

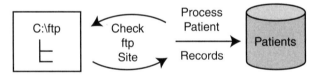

FIGURE 1.3   The file-transfer job checks the ftp site for patient files to process to the database.

Scenario #3: Creating Sales Reports

Companies are driven on profit and loss, and it's important to have the latest revenue and margin data for executives and the finance team to analyze. Pulling the data for sales reports can be very slow and resource intensive because it usually involves searching thousands of records and joining many database tables. A better approach involves running a job every night after the billing and invoicing is updated to create temporary tables or views that then can be used to run reports against. Creating temp tables or views makes the reports more dynamic, and users won't get frustrated while waiting for a report to generate. Some reporting packages, such as Crystal Reports XI, include a job scheduler (see Figure 1.4).

FIGURE 1.4   The sales data report is executed to generate revenue and margin information for the sales team.

Uses for Job Schedulers in Non-Enterprise

Quartz also can be helpful in plenty of non-Enterprise situations. For example, suppose you had a stand-alone application with events based on time, not on mouse clicks. You could build Quartz into the application and schedule events to occur periodically within the application.

As another example, you might just want to query a database and send e-mails to mail recipients based on the data.

Job Scheduling Versus Workflow

It's important to understand that job scheduling is not workflow. The two are often used as part of the same solution, but they are distinct solutions, and each can stand on its own. A job generally consists of several steps. Consider the password expiration job mentioned earlier. Essentially three distinct steps make up the job:

1. Get a list of users about to expire

2. Generate an e-mail for each user in the list

3. Update the record so we know an e-mail has already been sent for next time

This job can take advantage of a workflow in which each part of the job is a step in the workflow. This doesn't mean that job scheduling without a workflow component is bad. It's just a very common next step. As long as the job-scheduling framework can integrate with a third-party workflow solution as Quartz easily does, all is good. More on Quartz and workflow comes in Chapter 14, "Using Quartz with Workflow."

What About Alternative Solutions?

You know that this book is about Quartz, but what about alternatives to the Quartz framework? Other approaches are often mentioned when comparing job scheduling solutions, so it's worthwhile to briefly mention them.

Java SDK Timer and TimerTask Classes

The java.util.Timer and java.util.TimerTask classes were added to the Java SDK in Version 1.3. These new classes are ideal as the basis of a scheduler, but they are only a fraction of what is needed with a complete job-scheduling framework. Any serious job-scheduling framework has functionality for selecting the execution time, storing job information in various places, and using hooks for customization, just to name a few. Two classes in the Java SDK don't make a job scheduler: The Java Timer has no way to organize jobs and triggers, uses one thread per task instead of a pool of threads, and has several other deficiencies that keep it from performing as a full job scheduler.

Home-Grown Solution

As with the Timer and TimerTask classes just mentioned, it's easy to underestimate the effort involved in creating a flexible and feature-rich job scheduler. Creating a job scheduler is not a trivial task, either. It requires expertise in not only Java threads, but many other complicated topics as well. Job scheduling is not something to build from scratch if it's not your specialty.

Commercial Solutions

Quite a few commercial job schedulers are available on the market. We make no attempt in this book to review or evaluate these commercial solutions. Table 1.1 lists several of the more popular solutions and URLs where you can get more information.

Table 1.1   Commercial Job Schedulers

Name	URL
Flux Scheduler	www.fluxcorp.com/
Enterprise Batching Queuing	www.argent.com/p/qe/qe.html
Unicenter AutoSys Job Management 4.5	www.ca.com
BMC Software Control-M	www.bmc.com
Cybermation ESP Espresso 4.2	www.cybermation.corly;9'm
Vexus Consulting Avatar Job Scheduling Suite 4.5.5	www.vexus.ca
Argent Software The Argent Job Scheduler 4.5A	www.argent.com
Tidal Enterprise Scheduler	www.tidalsoftware.com

## CHAPTER 2

GETTING STARTED WITH QUARTZ

This chapter gives you a quick introduction to the modest beginnings of the Quartz framework. It also attempts to point you in the proper direction for downloading, building, and installing the framework.

History of the Quartz Framework

As with many other open source projects in use today, Quartz started out as a simple solution for one individual. With the rise of open source initiatives and the generosity of key individuals, Quartz has become a very public framework that many people use to help solve a much larger problem.

Quartz was created by James House, who envisioned the first conceptual pieces of the framework in 1998. These included the concept of a queue of jobs and a pool of threads to process the jobs, although probably in an unrecognizable form by most of today's Quartz users.

Over the next several years, House noted that he kept running into the same requirement: the need for a flexible job-scheduling tool. His search for a cheap but feature-rich job-scheduling framework for Java led him to several alternatives:

- A costly commercial tool
- An embedded solution tied to a larger (and unneeded) framework
- UNIX Cron or Windows Scheduler
- A custom solution of his own

House's limited choices and interest in the problem prompted him to create an open source project for job scheduling. In spring 2001, he created the project and registered it on SourceForge. The site is still viewable today at http://sourceforge.net/projects/quartz, but it is no longer maintained there.

Since Quartz first was developed, numerous contributors and developers have added to the project. It's safe to say, however, that the framework exists as it does today thanks to House and his interest in the job scheduling problem. His determination to solve the problem in the public arena is commendable.

Downloading and Installing Quartz

The download link for Quartz is located on the main Quartz page (www.opensymphony.com/quartz), which is hosted by OpenSymphony. Here you can get the latest version as well as several earlier versions. Quartz is available as a full distribution download, which includes source as well as a prebuilt deployable JAR file. The Quartz JARs are also available via the ibiblio maven repository, in case you want to integrate it with build systems such as Maven or Ivy.

The download file is in a ZIP format, so you need a zip utility such as WinZip. You can also use Java's jar command to unzip the distribution file:

```
jar -xvf quartz-1.5.0-rc1.zip
```

The contents of the Quartz distribution are extracted to the current directory.

The extracted Quartz zip file contains several subdirectories. Table 2.1 describes the directories that are part of the Quartz download.

Table 2.1   Quartz Directory Structure and Contents

Directory Name	What's in There
Docs	
docs/api	Javadocs for the Quartz framework
docs/dbTables	Database scripts for creating the Quartz database
docs/wikidocs	The main documentation for Quartz (start with index.html)

Directory Name	What's in There
Examples	Examples of using various aspects of the framework
Lib	Third-party libraries used by the framework
src/java/org/quartz	Source code for the client-side (public) API of the scheduler
src/java/org/quartz/core	Source code for the server (private) API of the scheduler
src/java/org/quartz/simpl	Simple implementations provided by the framework that have no dependencies on third-party products
src/java/org/quartz/impl	Implementations of support modules that might have dependencies on third-party products
src/java/org/quartz/utils	Helper and utility components used throughout the framework
src/jboss	Quartz features that are specific for use with Jboss
src/oracle	Quartz features that are specific for use with Oracle
src/weblogic	Quartz features that are specific for use with WebLogic

Installing the Necessary JAR Files

If you are in a hurry to get Quartz working, the fastest way is to grab the prebuilt Quartz JAR, located in the root directory of the download, and add it to the classpath of your application. You also need to grab the dependent JARs Quartz requires. Table 2.2 lists the JAR files that are required for a basic Quartz installation.

Table 2.2   JARs Required for a Basic Quartz Installation

Name	Location	Notes
Commons BeanUtils	<quartz-download>/ lib/optional	Depends on how you use Quartz. It's best to just include it.
Commons Collections	<quartz-download>/ lib/cor	Yes.

Table 2.2   JARs Required for a Basic Quartz Installation *(continued)*

Name	Location	Notes
Commons Digester	`<quartz-download>/lib/optional`	Depends on how you use Quartz. It's best to just include it.
Commons Logging	`<quartz-download>/lib/core`	Yes.

As with the Quartz JAR, you should also put the dependent JARs in the classpath for your application.

BE CAREFUL OF VERSION CONFLICTS

Quartz is built and tested with specific third-party versions. Many other projects, including some very well-known application servers, use these third-party libraries. In some cases, the libraries already are part of the application server. Class loaders are a strange and wonderful entity. If you're installing Quartz into an application server environment, be careful not to use duplicate libraries, or you're likely to get strange results. With the libraries mentioned in Table 2.1, you should be fine if those libraries exist in other parts of the server. However, libraries such as `servlet.jar` and `ejb.jar` could give you troubles if there are duplicates in the `classpath`. In those cases, you might want to leave out your copy and see if the application still functions.

The `quartz.properties` File

Quartz includes a configuration file called `quartz.properties` that enables you to configure many aspects of Quartz. A default `quartz.properties` file exists within the Quartz JAR, but if you need to modify any of the defaults, you must include a copy of this file in your classpath.

The next chapter goes into detail about which settings are configurable from this file and how to do it. You will most likely need to configure one or more of these settings, so you should copy the default `quartz.properties` file to your classpath.

Building Quartz from Source

The Quartz download includes the source code as well as a deployable JAR file. One of the benefits of having the source code is that you can look inside and figure out how it does what it does. The source is included as a convenience for developers who want to take a peek inside. It's also necessary if you want to step through the code in an IDE such as Eclipse.

The Quartz CVS Repository

The CVS repository for the Quartz project, along with the other OpenSymphony projects, is hosted on Java.net. To download anything from the CVS repository, you must have an account. You can view the source tree anonymously from xwork.dev. java.net/source/browse/quartz, but you need an account to download the entire tree.

CREATING A JAVA.NET ACCOUNT

You can create a free Java.net account by signing up at www.dev.java.net/servlets/Join. Besides getting access to the Quartz CVS repository, you can find plenty of good information and tips available on the site (see www.java.net).

After you have created your account, you can download the necessary files to build Quartz. To do this, open a command prompt in a directory where you want to put the projects. The download creates two subdirectories in the directory where you run the command: quartz and opensymphony.

From the command prompt, type

```
cvs -d :pserver:[username]@cvs.dev.java.net:/cvs login
cvs -d :pserver:[username]@cvs.dev.java.net:/cvs checkout
quartz
```

and

```
cvs -d :pserver:[username]@cvs.dev.java.net:/
cvs checkout opensymphony
```

Substitute your account name (without the brackets) in the username field.

After you have downloaded the two modules, change the directory to the quartz module and type this:

```
ant -projecthelp
```

This gives you a list of targets with descriptions. The default target for the Quartz build file is jar; you can just type ant from the command line, and it will build a deployable Quartz JAR.

BUILDING FROM SOURCE IN AN IDE

It's worth pointing out that several of the Quartz packages are dependent on third-party products such as JBoss and WebLogic. When building from source using the Ant build file, these necessary flags are set to ignore attempts to build these components. If you include the entire source from Quartz in your development environment and you don't have these third-party products in your environment, you will get compile errors. The easiest way around this is to not include these Quartz source files in your environment. Fortunately, the Quartz source hierarchy is structured so that you can choose not to include these at a directory/package level.

Getting Help from the Quartz Community

One of the key aspects that is often used to judge the health of an open source project is its user community. Because participation is voluntary and no paychecks are issued, users must feel somewhat passionate about a project to put in their time. Thus it makes sense that if a project has an adequate user community, those users believe in the value of the project.

The user community for Quartz is rather active. As with many other open source projects, the majority of members simply anonymously view the lists and messages; fewer users post and answer questions. In the six months that Quartz has been recording user's posts, the user forum has received more than 1,500 messages on 500 different topics and an amazing 25,000 people having viewed threads. This doesn't even include the messages and views of the developer list. If you track these numbers over six months, you can actually see an increasing trend. In terms of the number of downloads, Quartz is downloaded an average of 2,000 to 3,000 per month. These numbers can go higher when a new version is released.

You can find the links to both the user and developer forum at http://forums.opensymphony.com, or you can get to it by going to the Quartz home page at www.opensymphony.com/quartz. You are encouraged to sign up for e-mail from the lists; when you feel comfortable, you can then join in and help the project in any way you can.

Who's Using Quartz?

One of the questions that is often asked of open source software is, "Who's using it?" The idea is that if others are using the software, it must be okay and safe for use. Although Quartz has been around for quite a while, it's just recently starting to get the attention it deserves from the development community.

The list of users and projects that are using Quartz is quite impressive. You can find the list on the Quartz Wiki at http://wiki.opensymphony.com/display/QRTZ1/Quartz+Users. Probably what's most impressive is the number of other well-known open source projects that include Quartz as part of their software: Among them are JIRA, Spring, and several Jakarta projects.

There's no real way to gauge how many users are actively using Quartz in "real" projects. But judging from the download numbers and some of the high-profile projects that are currently using Quartz, it looks like the number of users is many thousands—and on the rise.

## CHAPTER 3

HELLO, QUARTZ

Most readers will benefit from a small but realistic walkthrough of an example. As a writer, it takes some restraint to keep from unloading everything in a single chapter; as a reader, it takes some patience and a little leap of faith that the material is relevant and should be read, regardless of the simplicity of the example.

With those thoughts in mind, this chapter introduces a simple Quartz application that is representative of the type of applications that you'll create with the Quartz framework. This example walks you through the steps necessary to create and execute the sample application. When you're finished with this chapter, you should have a solid foundation to build upon for the rest of the book.

The "Hello, World" Quartz Project

This example application is a little more interesting than the proverbial System.out.println("Hello World from Quartz"). When Quartz executes a job, we expect it to perform some interesting and useful task on our behalf. That's what we are going to do here—something useful and interesting.

This chapter shows you how to create a Quartz job that, when told to do so by our Quartz application, will scan a specified directory and look for XML files. If it finds one or more XML files within the specified directory, it will print some cursory information about the file. How is this useful and interesting, you say? Hopefully, you can make the leap that after your job detects certain files in a directory, it can do many interesting things with those files. You might want to ftp them to a remote host or e-mail them as attachments. Perhaps the files are orders that were sent from a customer and need to be inserted into your database. Infinite possibilities exist; we discuss some of the more interesting ones later in the book.

All attempts have been made to keep this new material straightforward and to cover only the essentials. However, we also investigate some of the common configuration settings that affect the runtime behavior of a Quartz application. It's expected that you know the Java language well; we spend very little time explaining the standard aspects of it.

Finally, this chapter wraps up with a brief discussion of how to package the example application. Apache Ant is our choice for building and packaging Java projects: Quartz applications are no exception.

Setting Up the Quartz Project

The first step is to set up your development environment for this project. You can choose any development tool or IDE that makes you feel warm and fuzzy; Quartz won't hold it against you. If you're part of the growing mass of Java developers that have realized just how great Eclipse is, you'll be extra warm and fuzzy: We use that IDE throughout the examples in the book.

If you haven't already done so, you can download Eclipse from http://eclipse.org. You can choose any of the 3.x. For Eclipse documentation, check www.eclipse.org/eclipse/index.html; you should find everything you need to help you get started with Eclipse.

Configuring Quartz Within Eclipse

For the examples throughout this book, we create an Eclipse Java project; each chapter contains a separate source directory. Figure 3.1 illustrates the Quartz Java project in Eclipse.

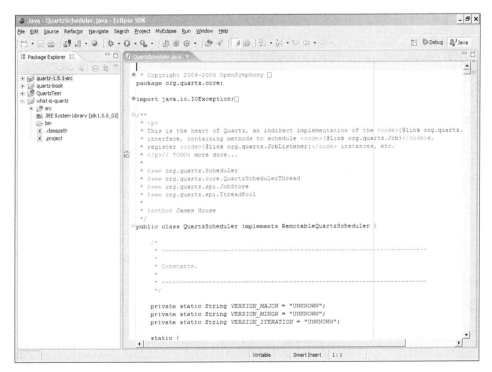

FIGURE 3.1   Creating a Quartz Java project in Eclipse

You need to import several JARs into the project to build them successfully. To start, you need the Quartz binary, which is named `quartz-<version>.jar`. Quartz also requires several third-party libraries to work; the ones you need depend on which features of the framework you're using. For now, you should include the Commons Logging, Commons Collections, Commons BeanUtils, and Commons Digester libraries, found in the `<QUARTZ_HOME>/lib/core` and `<QUARTZ_HOME>/lib/optional` directories. Table 3.1 provides more information on the dependent JARs for Quartz.

It's also a good idea to pull the Quartz source code into Eclipse. This does two things for you. First, it enables you to set breakpoints and step from the code into Quartz source. Second, it helps you learn the framework from the inside out. If you need to see how something is (or isn't) working, you have the actual code right there at your fingertips. Try that with commercial software!

Difference Between a Quartz Application and a Job

It's worth pausing for a moment here to explain a potentially confusing point. We use the phase "Quartz application" to refer to any software application that uses the Quartz framework as one of its included libraries. Many other libraries generally are used within the application, but if Quartz is present, we consider it a Quartz application for the purposes of the discussions throughout this book. On the other hand, when we talk about a Quartz job, we're actually talking about a specific Java class that performs some task. Normally many different types of jobs exist within a Quartz application, each one with a concrete Java class. The two terms are not used interchangeably.

Creating the Quartz Job Class

Every Quartz job must have a concrete Java class that implements the `org.quartz.Job` interface. The Quartz job interface has a single method, `execute()`, that you must implement in your job. The `execute()` method signature is shown here:

```
public void execute(JobExecutionContext context)
*➥throws JobExecutionException;
```

When the Quartz Scheduler determines that it's time to fire a job, it instantiates the job class and invokes the `execute()` method. The Scheduler calls the `execute()` method with no expectations other than that you throw an `org.quartz.JobExecutionException` if there's a problem with the job.

---

*Code continuation characters ➥ are used throughout the book to represent continuous code lines that are broken due to the restrictions of the printed page.

You can perform whatever business logic you need within the execute() method: For example, you might instantiate and call a method on another class, send an e-mail, ftp a file, invoke a Web Service, call an EJB, execute a workflow, or, in the case of our example, check to see if files exist in a particular directory.

Listing 3.1 shows our first Quartz job, which is designed to scan a directory for files and display details about the files.

Listing 3.1   The Example ScanDirectoryJob

```
package org.cavaness.quartzbook.chapter3;


import java.io.File;
import java.util.Date;

import org.apache.commons.logging.Log;
import org.apache.commons.logging.LogFactory;
import org.quartz.Job;
import org.quartz.JobDataMap;
import org.quartz.JobDetail;
import org.quartz.JobExecutionContext;
import org.quartz.JobExecutionException;

/**
 * <p>
 * A simple Quartz job that, once configured, will scan a
 * directory and print out details about the files found
 * in the directory.
 * </p>
 * Subdirectories will filtered out by the use of a
 * <code>{@link FileExtensionFileFilter}</code>.
 *
 * @author Chuck Cavaness
 * @see java.io.FileFilter
 */
public class ScanDirectoryJob implements Job {
    static Log logger = LogFactory.getLog(ScanDirectoryJob.class);

    public void execute(JobExecutionContext context)
            throws JobExecutionException {

        // Every job has its own job detail
        JobDetail jobDetail = context.getJobDetail();

        // The name is defined in the job definition
        String jobName = jobDetail.getName();

        // Log the time the job started
        logger.info(jobName + " fired at " + new Date());

        // The directory to scan is stored in the job map
        JobDataMap dataMap = jobDetail.getJobDataMap();
                String dirName = dataMap.getString("SCAN_DIR");
```

Listing 3.1   Continued

```
    // Validate the required input
    if (dirName == null) {
        throw new JobExecutionException("Directory not configured");
    }

    // Make sure the directory exists
    File dir = new File(dirName);
    if (!dir.exists()) {
     throw new JobExecutionException("Invalid Dir " + dirName);
    }

    // Use FileFilter to get only XML files
    FileFilter filter = new FileExtensionFileFilter(".xml");

    File[] files = dir.listFiles(filter);

    if (files == null || files.length <= 0) {
        logger.info("No XML files found in " + dir);

        // Return since there were no files
        return;
    }

    // The number of XML files
    int size = files.length;

    // Iterate through the files found
    for (int i = 0; i < size; i++) {

        File file = files[i];

        // Log something interesting about each file.
        File aFile = file.getAbsoluteFile();
        long fileSize = file.length();
        String msg = aFile + " - Size: " + fileSize;
        logger.info(msg);
    }
  }
}
```

Let's take a closer look at what's going on in Listing 3.1.

When Quartz calls the execute() method, it passes it an org.quartz.JobExecutionContext, which wraps many things about the Quartz runtime environment and currently executing job. From the JobExecutionContext, you can access information about the Scheduler, the job, the trigger information for the job, and much, much more. In Listing 3.1, the JobExecutionContext is used to access the org.quartz. JobDetail class. The JobDetail class holds the detailed information about a job, including the name given to the job instance, the group that the job belongs to, whether the Job is persistent (volatility), and many other interesting properties.

The `JobDetail` has a reference to `org.quartz.JobDataMap`. The `JobDataMap` holds user-defined properties configured for the particular job. For example, in Listing 3.1, we get the name of the directory to scan from the `JobDataMap`. We could have hard-coded the directory in the `ScanDirectoryJob`, but we would have had a tough time reusing the job for other directories. In the later section "Scheduling a Quartz Job Programmatically," you'll see exactly how the directory is configured in the `JobDataMap`.

The rest of the code in the `execute()` method is just standard Java: It gets the directory name and creates a `java.io.File` object. It does a little bit of validation on the directory name to make sure it's a valid directory and that it exists. It then calls the `listFiles()` method on the `File` object to retrieve the files from the directory. `java.io.FileFilter` is created and passed in as an argument to the `listFiles()` method. `org.quartzbook.cavaness.FileExtensionFileFilter` implements the `java.io.FileFilter` interface to weed out directories and return only XML files. By default, the `listFiles()` method returns everything it finds, whether it's a file or a subdirectory, so the list must be filtered because we are interested only in XML files.

> **NOTE**
>
> The `FileExtensionFileFilter` is not part of the Quartz framework; it's a subclass of the `java.io.FileFilter`, which is part of core Java. We have created the `FileExtensionFileFilter` as part of our example to filter out everything but XML files. This is quite handy—you should think about building a set of file filters for your application and reusing them for your various Quartz jobs.

Listing 3.2 shows the `FileExtensionFileFilter`.

Listing 3.2   The FileExtensionFileFilter Used in ScanDirectoryJob.java

```
package org.cavaness.quartzbook.chapter3;

import java.io.File;
import java.io.FileFilter;
```

Listing 3.1   Continued

```
/**
 * A FileFilter that only passes Files of the specified extension.
 * <p>
 * Directories do not pass the filter.
 *
 * @author Chuck Cavaness
 */
public class FileExtensionFileFilter implements FileFilter {

    private String extension;

    public FileExtensionFileFilter(String extension) {
        this.extension = extension;
    }

    /*
     * Pass the File if it has the extension.
     */
    public boolean accept(File file) {
        // Lowercase the filename for easier comparison
        String lCaseFilename = file.getName().toLowerCase();

        return (file.isFile() &&
                    (lCaseFilename.indexOf(extension) > 0)) ? true:false;
    }
}
```

The FileExtensionFileFilter is used to block any file that doesn't contain the string ".xml" as part of its name. It also blocks any subdirectories, which would normally be returned as well from the listFiles() method. Using file filters is a very convenient way of selectively choosing inputs to your Quartz jobs when they involve files as input.

DECLARATIVE VERSUS PROGRAMMATIC CONFIGURATION

With Quartz, there are two approaches to configuring the runtime aspects of an application: declarative and programmatic. For some aspects of the framework, it makes sense to use external configuration files: We all have learned that hard-coding settings within our software has its limitations.

For other aspects of your Quartz application, you will have to make some decisions based on the requirements and functionality you need from Quartz. The next section highlights when you must use a declarative and a programmatic approach. Because much of the Java industry is moving toward a declarative approach, this is our preference.

In the next section, we discuss how to configure the job for scheduling and how to run the ScanDirectoryJob.

Scheduling the Quartz
ScanDirectoryJob

So far, we've created a Quartz job but haven't determined what
to do with it. We obviously need a way to set a schedule for the
job to run. The schedule could be a one-time event, or we might
need the job to run at midnight every night except Sunday. As
you'll shortly see, the Quartz Scheduler is the heart and soul of
the framework. All jobs are registered with the Scheduler; when
necessary, the Scheduler also creates an instance of the Job
class and invokes the execute() method.

SCHEDULER CREATES NEW JOB INSTANCES FOR EACH EXECUTION

The Scheduler creates a new instance of the Job class for every execution. This means that
any state that you have in instance variables is lost between job executions. You can choose
to make a job stateful to persist job state between executions. The name *stateful* (especially in the J2EE world) has somewhat of a negative connotation associated with it, but
with Quartz, a stateful job doesn't have the overhead and is quite easy to configure. When
you are making a Quartz job stateful, however, a few things are unique to Quartz. Most
important is that no two instances of the same stateful job class may execute concurrently.
This could affect the scalability of the application. These issues and more are discussed in
detail in the next chapter.

Creating and Running the Quartz Scheduler

Before we talk about the ScanDirectoryJob specifically, let's
discuss in general how to instantiate and run an instance of the
Quartz Scheduler. Listing 3.3 illustrates the basic steps necessary
to create and start a Quartz Scheduler instance.

Listing 3.3   Running a Simplified Quartz Scheduler

```
package org.cavaness.quartzbook.chapter3;

package org.cavaness.quartzbook.chapter3;

import java.util.Date;

import org.apache.commons.logging.Log;
import org.apache.commons.logging.LogFactory;
import org.quartz.Scheduler;
import org.quartz.SchedulerException;
import org.quartz.impl.StdSchedulerFactory;
```

Listing 3.3   Continued

```
public class SimpleScheduler {
    static Log logger = LogFactory.getLog(SimpleScheduler.class);

    public static void main(String[] args) {
        SimpleScheduler simple = new SimpleScheduler();
        simple.startScheduler();
    }

    public void startScheduler() {
        Scheduler scheduler = null;

        try {
            // Get a Scheduler instance from the Factory
            scheduler = StdSchedulerFactory.getDefaultScheduler();

            // Start the scheduler
            scheduler.start();
            logger.info("Scheduler started at " + new Date());

        } catch (SchedulerException ex) {
            // deal with any exceptions
            logger.error(ex);
        }
    }
}
```

If you run the code in Listing 3.3 and you are logging the output, you should see something like the following output:

```
INFO [main] (SimpleScheduler.java:30) - Scheduler
➥started at Mon Sep 05 13:06:38 EDT 2005
```

TURNING OFF QUARTZ INFO LOG MESSAGES

If you are using the Commons Logging framework along with Log4J, as the examples throughout this book do, you might need to turn off info log messages for everything but the examples in this book. This is because Quartz logs a sizable amount of debug and info messages. When you understand what Quartz is doing, the messages that you care more about can get lost in the volumes of log messages. You can do this by creating a `log4j.properties` file that logs only ERROR messages, and setting the messages that come from the examples in the book to show INFO messages. Here's an example `log4j.properties` file that will accomplish this:

```
# Create stdout appender
log4j.rootLogger=error, stdout

# Configure the stdout appender to go to the Console
log4j.appender.stdout=org.apache.log4j.ConsoleAppender

# Configure stdout appender to use the PatternLayout
log4j.appender.stdout.layout=org.apache.log4j.PatternLayout
```

```
# Pattern output the caller's filename and line #
log4j.appender.stdout.layout.ConversionPattern=%5p [%t] (%F:%L) - %m%n

# Print messages of level INFO or above for examples
log4j.logger.org.cavaness.quartzbook=INFO
```

This `log4j.properties` file will log only ERROR messages to stdout, but any INFO messages coming from the package org.cavaness.quartzbook will appear. This is due to the last line in the properties file.

Listing 3.3 shows just how simple it is to startup a Quartz scheduler. When the Scheduler is up and running, you can do much with it and obtain a great deal of information from it. For example, you might need to schedule a few jobs or change the execution times of jobs already scheduled. You might need to put the Scheduler in stand-by mode and then later restart it so that it begins executing scheduled jobs again. While the Scheduler is in stand-by, no jobs are executed, even if they are supposed to be based on their scheduled times. Listing 3.4 shows how to put the Scheduler in stand-by mode and then unpause it so the Scheduler picks up where it left off.

Listing 3.4   Putting the Scheduler in Stand-By Mode

```java
private void modifyScheduler(Scheduler scheduler) {

    try {
        if (!scheduler.isInStandbyMode()) {
            // pause the scheduler
            scheduler.standby();
        }

        // Do something interesting here

        // and then restart it
        scheduler.start();

    } catch (SchedulerException ex) {
        logger.error(ex);
    }
}
```

The partial fragment in Listing 3.4 is just a quick illustration that when you have a reference to a Quartz Scheduler, you can do some pretty interesting things with it. Of course, the Scheduler doesn't have to be in stand-by mode for interesting things to

happen. For example, you can schedule new jobs and unschedule existing jobs, all with the Scheduler still running. We add to
our repertoire of possibilities with a scheduler throughout the
book.

As simple as these examples seem to be, there is a catch.
We haven't specified any jobs to be executed or times for those
jobs to execute. Although the Quartz Scheduler did start up and
run in Listing 3.3, we didn't specify any jobs to be executed.
That's what we discuss next.

Scheduling a Quartz Job Programmatically

All jobs that you want Quartz to execute must be registered
with the Scheduler. In most situations, this should be done
before the Scheduler is started. As promised earlier in this chapter, this is one area in which you get to choose either a declarative or a programmatic approach. First we show you how to do
it programmatically; later in this chapter, we repeat this exercise
with the declarative version.

For each job that is to be registered with the Scheduler, a
JobDetail must be defined and associated with a Scheduler
instance. This is shown in Listing 3.5.

Listing 3.5   Scheduling a Job Programmatically

```
package org.cavaness.quartzbook.chapter3;

import java.util.Date;

import org.apache.commons.logging.Log;
import org.apache.commons.logging.LogFactory;
import org.quartz.JobDetail;
import org.quartz.Scheduler;
import org.quartz.SchedulerException;
import org.quartz.Trigger;
import org.quartz.TriggerUtils;
import org.quartz.impl.StdSchedulerFactory;

public class Listing_3_5 {
    static Log logger = LogFactory.getLog(Listing_3_5.class);

    public static void main(String[] args) {
        Listing_3_5 example = new Listing_3_5();

        try {
            // Create a Scheduler and schedule the Job
            Scheduler scheduler = example.createScheduler();
            example.scheduleJob(scheduler);
```

Listing 3.5   Continued

```
                // Start the Scheduler running
                scheduler.start();

                logger.info( "Scheduler started at " + new Date() );

        } catch (SchedulerException ex) {
            logger.error(ex);
        }
    }

    /*
     * return an instance of the Scheduler from the factory
     */
    public Scheduler createScheduler() throws SchedulerException {
        return StdSchedulerFactory.getDefaultScheduler();
    }

    // Create and Schedule a ScanDirectoryJob with the Scheduler
    private void scheduleJob(Scheduler scheduler)
        throws SchedulerException {

        // Create a JobDetail for the Job
        JobDetail jobDetail =
                    new JobDetail("ScanDirectory",
                Scheduler.DEFAULT_GROUP,
                    ScanDirectoryJob.class);

        // Configure the directory to scan
        jobDetail.getJobDataMap().put("SCAN_DIR",
                "c:\\quartz-book\\input");

        // Create a trigger that fires every 10 seconds, forever
        Trigger trigger = TriggerUtils.makeSecondlyTrigger(10);
        trigger.setName("scanTrigger");
        // Start the trigger firing from now
        trigger.setStartTime(new Date());

        // Associate the trigger with the job in the scheduler
        scheduler.scheduleJob(jobDetail, trigger);
    }
}
```

The program in Listing 3.5 provides a good example of how to programmatically schedule a job. The code first calls the createScheduler() method to obtain an instance of the Scheduler from the Scheduler factory. When a Scheduler is obtained, it is passed into the schedulerJob(), which takes care of all the details of associating a job with a Scheduler.

First, a JobDetail object is created for the job that we want to run. The arguments in the constructor for the JobDetail include a name for the job, a logical group to assign the job to,

and the fully qualified class that implements the `org.quartz.`
`Job` interface. We could have used several different versions of
the `JobDetail` constructor:

```
public JobDetail();
public JobDetail(String name, String group, Class
jobClass);
public JobDetail(String name, String group, Class jobClass,
    boolean volatility, boolean durability, boolean
recover);
```

NOTE

A job should be uniquely identifiable by its name and group within a Scheduler instance. If
you add two jobs with the same name and group, an `ObjectAlreadyExistsException` will
be thrown.

As stated earlier in this chapter, the `JobDetail` acts as a
definition for a specific job. It contains properties for the job
instance and also can be accessed by the `Job` class at runtime.
One of the most important uses of the `JobDetail` is to hold the
`JobDataMap`, which is used to store state/parameters for a job
instance. In Listing 3.5, the name of the directory to scan is
stored in the `JobDataMap` in the `scheduleJob()` method.

Understanding and Using Quartz Triggers

Jobs are only part of the equation. Notice from Listing 3.5 that
we don't set the execution date and times for the job within the
`JobDetail` object. This is done by using a Quartz trigger. As the
name implies, triggers are responsible for triggering a job to be
executed. You create a trigger and associate it with a job when
registering the job with the Scheduler. Four types of Quartz triggers are available, but two main types are used most often and,
thus, are used for the next several chapters: `SimpleTrigger`
and `CronTrigger`.

A `SimpleTrigger` is the simpler of the two and is used primarily to fire single event jobs. This trigger fires at a given
time, repeats for *n* number of times with a delay of *m* between

each firing, and then quits. `CronTriggers` are much more complicated and powerful. They are based on the common Gregorian calendar and are used when you need to execute a job with a more complicated schedule—for example, every Monday, Wednesday, and Friday at midnight during the months of April and September.

To make working with triggers easier, Quartz includes a utility class called `org.quartz.TriggerUtils`. `TriggerUtils` provides many convenience methods for simplifying the construction and configuration of triggers. The examples throughout this chapter use the `TriggerUtils` class; `SimpleTrigger` and `CronTrigger` are used in later chapters.

As you can see from Listing 3.5, the `TriggerUtils` method called `makeSecondlyTrigger()` is used to create a trigger that fires every 10 seconds (`TriggerUtils` actually produces an instance of `SimpleTrigger` in this case, but our code doesn't care to know that). We must also give the trigger instance a name and tell it when to start firing; in Listing 3.5, this starts immediately because `setStartTime()` is set to the current time.

Listing 3.5 illustrates how to register a single job with the Scheduler. If you have more than one job (and you probably do), you will need to create a `JobDetail` for each job. Each one must be registered with the Scheduler via the `scheduleJob()` method.

If you are reusing a job class to run multiple instances of the same job, you need to create a `JobDetail` for each one. For example, if you wanted to reuse the `ScanDirectoryJob` to check two different directories, you would need to create and register two instances of the `JobDetail` class. Listing 3.6 shows how this could be done.

NOTE
Go back to Listing 3.1 and look at the code where the scan directory property is retrieved from the JobDataMap. Based on Listing 3.5, you can see how it gets set.

Listing 3.6   Running Multiple Instances of `ScanDirectoryJob`

```
package org.cavaness.quartzbook.chapter3;

import java.util.Date;

import org.apache.commons.logging.Log;
import org.apache.commons.logging.LogFactory;
import org.quartz.JobDetail;
import org.quartz.Scheduler;
import org.quartz.SchedulerException;
import org.quartz.Trigger;
```

Listing 3.6   Continued

```
import org.quartz.TriggerUtils;
import org.quartz.impl.StdSchedulerFactory;

public class Listing_3_6 {
    static Log logger = LogFactory.getLog(Listing_3_6.class);

    public static void main(String[] args) {
        Listing_3_6 example = new Listing_3_6();

        try {
            // Create a Scheduler and schedule the Job
            Scheduler scheduler = example.createScheduler();

            // Jobs can be scheduled after Scheduler is running
            scheduler.start();

            logger.info("Scheduler started at " + new Date());

            // Schedule the first Job
            example.scheduleJob(scheduler, "ScanDirectory1",
                    ScanDirectoryJob.class,
                               "c:\\quartz-book\\input", 10);

            // Schedule the second Job
            example.scheduleJob(scheduler, "ScanDirectory2",
                    ScanDirectoryJob.class,
                               "c:\\quartz-book\\input2", 15);

        } catch (SchedulerException ex) {
            logger.error(ex);
        }
    }

    /*
     * return an instance of the Scheduler from the factory
     */
    public Scheduler createScheduler() throws SchedulerException {
        return StdSchedulerFactory.getDefaultScheduler();
    }

    // Create and Schedule a ScanDirectoryJob with the Scheduler
    private void scheduleJob(Scheduler scheduler, String jobName,
            Class jobClass, String scanDir, int scanInterval)
            throws SchedulerException {

        // Create a JobDetail for the Job
        JobDetail jobDetail =
                new JobDetail(jobName,
                        Scheduler.DEFAULT_GROUP, jobClass);

        // Configure the directory to scan
        jobDetail.getJobDataMap().put("SCAN_DIR", scanDir);

        // Trigger that repeats every "scanInterval" secs forever
        Trigger trigger =
                TriggerUtils.makeSecondlyTrigger(scanInterval);
```

Listing 3.6   Continued

```
        trigger.setName(jobName + "-Trigger");

        // Start the trigger firing from now
        trigger.setStartTime(new Date());

        // Associate the trigger with the job in the scheduler
        scheduler.scheduleJob(jobDetail, trigger);
    }
}
```

Listing 3.6 is very similar to the program from Listing 3.5, with a few small differences. The main difference is that Listing 3.6 has been refactored to allow multiple calls to the schedulerJob() method. The settings for things such as the job name and the scan interval are being passed in. So after the Scheduler instance is obtained from the createScheduler() method, two jobs (of the same class) are scheduled using different arguments.

SCHEDULING JOBS BEFORE OR AFTER THE SCHEDULER IS STARTED

In the example in Listing 3.6, we called the start() on the Scheduler before we scheduled the jobs. Back in Listing 3.5, we did it the other way around: We called start() after the jobs were scheduled. Jobs and triggers can be added to and removed from the Scheduler at any time (except after shutdown() has been called on it).

Running the Program in Listing 3.6

If we execute the Listing_3_6 class, we should get output similar to the following:

```
INFO [main] (Listing 3 6.java:35) - Scheduler started at Mon Sep 05 15:12:15 EDT
➥2005
 INFO [QuartzScheduler_Worker-0] ScanDirectory1 fired at Mon Sep 05 15:12:15 EDT
➥2005
 INFO [QuartzScheduler_Worker-0] - c:\quartz-book\input\order-145765.xml - Size: 0
 INFO [QuartzScheduler_Worker-0] - ScanDirectory2 fired at Mon Sep 05 15:12:15 EDT
➥ 2005
 INFO [QuartzScheduler_Worker-0] - No XML files found in c:\quartz-book\input2
 INFO [QuartzScheduler_Worker-1] - ScanDirectory1 fired at Mon Sep 05 15:12:25 EDT
➥ 2005
 INFO [QuartzScheduler_Worker-1] - c:\quartz-book\input\order-145765.xml - Size: 0
 INFO [QuartzScheduler_Worker-3] - ScanDirectory2 fired at Mon Sep 05 15:12:30 EDT
➥ 2005
 INFO [QuartzScheduler_Worker-3] - No XML files found in c:\quartz-book\input2
```

Scheduling a Quartz Job Declaratively

As discussed earlier, we would like to handle configuring our software declaratively rather than programmatically as much as possible. Looking back at Listing 3.6, if we needed to change the time or frequency at which the jobs started, we would have to modify the source and recompile. This is fine for small example applications, but with a system that is large and complex, this quickly becomes a problem. So if there's a way to schedule Quartz jobs declaratively and your requirements allow for it, you should choose that approach every time.

Before we can discuss how to schedule your jobs declaratively, we need to talk about the `quartz.properties` file. This properties file enables you to configure the runtime environment of Quartz and, more important, tell Quartz to get the job and trigger information from an external resource, such as an XML file.

Configuring the `quartz.properties` File

> **NOTE**
>
> The Quartz framework sets defaults for almost all of these properties.

The `quartz.properties` file defines the runtime behavior of the Quartz application and contains many properties that can be set to control how Quartz behaves. Only the basics are covered within this chapter; we save the more advanced settings for later. We also do not go into detail about the valid values for each setting at this point.

Let's look at a bare-bones `quartz.properties` file and discuss some of the settings. Listing 3.7 shows a stripped-down version of the `quartz.properties` file.

Listing 3.7   Basic Quartz Properties File

```
#==============================================================
# Configure Main Scheduler Properties
#==============================================================
org.quartz.scheduler.instanceName = QuartzScheduler
org.quartz.scheduler.instanceId = AUTO


#==============================================================
# Configure ThreadPool
#==============================================================
org.quartz.threadPool.threadCount =  5
org.quartz.threadPool.threadPriority = 5
```

Listing 3.7   Continued

```
org.quartz.threadPool.class = org.quartz.simpl.SimpleThreadPool

#================================================================
# Configure JobStore
#================================================================
org.quartz.jobStore.class = org.quartz.simpl.RAMJobStore

#================================================================
# Configure Plugins
#================================================================
org.quartz.plugin.jobInitializer.class =
org.quartz.plugins.xml.JobInitializationPlugin

org.quartz.plugin.jobInitializer.overWriteExistingJobs = true
org.quartz.plugin.jobInitializer.failOnFileNotFound = true
org.quartz.plugin.jobInitializer.validating=false
```

In the `quartz.properties` file in Listing 3.7, the properties
are logically separated into four sections. The properties don't
have to be grouped or listed in any order. The lines with the #
are comments.

> **NOTE**
>
> This discussion does not list every possible setting. Here we discuss only the basic settings
> that you need to be familiar or that are necessary to get the declarative example working.
> These properties are discussed throughout the book in the chapters that pertain to the rele-
> vant sections of the properties file.

SCHEDULER PROPERTIES

The first section contains two lines and sets the `instanceName`
and `instanceId` for the Scheduler. The value for the property
`org.quartz.scheduler.instanceName` can be any string that
you like. It's used to distinguish a particular scheduler instance
when multiple schedulers are being used. Multiple schedulers
are normally used within a clustered environment. (Quartz clustering is discussed in Chapter 11, "Clustering Quartz.") For now,
a string such as this one is fine:

```
org.quartz.scheduler.instanceName =
➥QuartzScheduler
```

In fact, that is the default when none is provided in the
properties file.

The second Scheduler property shown in Listing 3.7 is
`org.quartz.scheduler.instanceId`. As with the
`instanceName` property, the `instanceId` property can be any
string value you want. The value should be unique across all
Scheduler instances, especially within a cluster. You may use
the value `AUTO` if you want the value to be generated for you.
The generated value will be `NON_CLUSTERED` if this is running in
a nonclustered Quartz environment. If you're using Quartz in a
clustered environment, the value will be the hostname of the
machine plus the current date and time. For most situations,
setting the value to `AUTO` is fine.

THREADPOOL PROPERTIES

The next section sets the necessary values for the threads that
run in the background and do the heavy lifting in Quartz. The
`threadCount` property controls how many worker threads are
created and available to process jobs. In principal, the more jobs
that you have to process, the more worker threads you'll need.
The number for the `threadCount` must be at least 1. Quartz
imposes no maximum on the number of worker threads, but
setting this value to greater than 100 on most machines
becomes quite unwieldy, especially if your jobs have long-running logic in them. There is no default, so you must specify a
value for this property.

The `threadPriority` property sets the priority that the
worker threads run with. Threads with higher priorities are typically given preference over threads with a lower priority. The
minimum value for the `threadPriority` is the constant
`java.lang.Thread.MAX_PRIORITY`, which equates to 10. The
minimum value is `java.lang.Thread.MIN_PRIORITY`, which
equals 1. The typical value for this property is `Thread.
NORM_PRIORITY`, which is 5. For most situations, you'll want to
set this to the value of 5, which is the default if the property
isn't specified.

The final threadpool setting is for the property `org.
quartz.threadPool.class`. The value for this class should be
a fully qualified name of the class that implements the
`org.quartz.spi.ThreadPool` interface. The threadpool that
ships with Quartz is `org.quartz.simpl.SimpleThreadPool`,

and it should meet the needs of most users. This threadpool has simple behavior and is well tested. It provides a fixed-size pool of threads that survive the lifetime of the Scheduler. You can create your own threadpool class, if you want. For example, you might need to do this if you want a threadpool that grows and shrinks with demand. There is no default specified, so you must provide a value for this property.

JOBSTORE SETTINGS

The properties within the JobStore section describe how job and trigger information is stored during the lifetime of the Scheduler instance. We haven't yet talked about the JobStore and its purpose; we save that for later because it's not necessary for the current example. For now, all you need to know is that we are storing Scheduler information in memory instead of a relational database.

Storing Scheduler information in memory is fast and the easiest to configure. When the Scheduler process is halted, however, all job and trigger state is lost. Job storage in memory is accomplished by setting the `org.quartz.jobStore.class` property to `org.quartz.simpl.RAMJobStore`, as we've done in Listing 3.7. If we don't want to lose our Scheduler state when the JVM is halted, we could use a relational database to store that information. This requires a different JobStore implementation that we discuss later. Chapters 5, "Cron Triggers and More," and 6, "JobStores and Persistence," cover the various types of JobStores and when you should use them.

PLUG-IN SETTINGS

The final section in the simple `quartz.properties` file is the one that specifies any Quartz plug-ins that you want to configure. A plug-in is used by many other open source frameworks, such as Struts from Apache (see http://struts.apache.org).

The idea is to declaratively extend the framework by adding classes that implement the `org.quartz.spi.SchedulerPlugin` interface. The `SchedulerPlugin` interface has three methods that are called by the Scheduler.

> **NOTE**
> Plug-ins for Quartz are discussed in detail in Chapter 8, "Using Quartz Plug-Ins."

To declaratively configure the Scheduler information for our example, we will be using a plug-in called `org.quartz.plug-ins.xml.JobInitializationPlugin` that comes with Quartz.

By default, this plug-in searches for a file called `quartz_jobs.xml` in the classpath and loads job and trigger information from the XML file.

The next section discusses the `quartz_jobs.xml` file, which we informally refer to as the job definition file.

NOTE

By default, the `JobInitializationPlugin` looks for a file called `quartz_jobs.xml` on your classpath. You can override this and force it to look for and use a file with a different name. To do this, you must set the filename in the `quartz.properties` file that we discussed in the previous section. For now, we are going to just rely on the default filename `quartz_jobs.xml` and show you how to modify the `quartz.properties` file later in this chapter.

Using the `quartz_jobs.xml` File

Listing 3.8 shows the job-definition XML file for the Scan Directory example. It configures job and trigger information using a declarative approach exactly like the example from Listing 3.5.

Listing 3.8   The quartz_ jobs.xml file for the ScanDirectory Job

```xml
<?xml version='1.0' encoding='utf-8'?>

<quartz>

  <job>
    <job-detail>
      <name>ScanDirectory</name>
      <group>DEFAULT</group>
      <description>
        A job that scans a directory for files
      </description>
      <job-class>
          org.cavaness.quartzbook.chapter3.ScanDirectoryJob
      </job-class>
      <volatility>false</volatility>
      <durability>false</durability>
      <recover>false</recover>
```

Listing 3.8   Continued

```
    <job-data-map allows-transient-data="true">
        <entry>
        <key>SCAN_DIR</key>
        <value>c:\quartz-book\input</value>
        </entry>
    </job-data-map>
    </job-detail>

    <trigger>
     <simple>
       <name>scanTrigger</name>
       <group>DEFAULT</group>
       <job-name>ScanDirectory</job-name>
       <job-group>DEFAULT</job-group>
       <start-time>2005-06-10 6:10:00 PM</start-time>
       <!-- repeat indefinitely every 10 seconds -->
       <repeat-count>-1</repeat-count>
       <repeat-interval>10000</repeat-interval>
     </simple>
    </trigger>

  </job>
</quartz>
```

The `<job>` element represents a job that you want to register with the Scheduler, just as we did earlier in the chapter with the `scheduleJob()` method. You can see the `<job-detail>` and `<trigger>` elements, which we programmatically passed into the `schedulerJob()` method in Listings 3.5. This is essentially what is happening here, but in a declarative fashion. You can also see in Listing 3.8 that we set the SCAN_DIR property into the `JobDataMap`, as we also did in the Listing 3.5 example.

The `<trigger>` element is also very intuitive: It simply sets up a `SimpleTrigger` with the same properties as before. So Listing 3.8 is just a different (arguably, better) way of doing what we did in Listing 3.5. You obviously can support multiple jobs as well. We did this in Listing 3.6 programmatically, and we can also support it declaratively. Listing 3.9 shows the comparable version of Listing 3.6.

Listing 3.9   You Can Specify Multiple Jobs in the quartz_jobs.xml File

```
<?xml version='1.0' encoding='utf-8'?>

<quartz>
  <job>
    <job-detail>
     <name>ScanDirectory1</name>
```

Listing 3.9   Continued

```
        <group>DEFAULT</group>
        <description>
            A job that scans a directory for files
        </description>
        <job-class>
            org.cavaness.quartzbook.chapter3.ScanDirectoryJob
        </job-class>
        <volatility>false</volatility>
        <durability>false</durability>
        <recover>false</recover>

        <job-data-map allows-transient-data="true">
        <entry>
          <key>SCAN_DIR</key>
            <value>c:\quartz-book\input1</value>
        </entry>
        </job-data-map>
      </job-detail>

    <trigger>
      <simple>
        <name>scanTrigger1</name>
        <group>DEFAULT</group>
        <job-name>ScanDirectory1</job-name>
        <job-group>DEFAULT</job-group>
        <start-time>2005-07-19 8:31:00 PM</start-time>
        <!-- repeat indefinitely every 10 seconds -->
        <repeat-count>-1</repeat-count>
        <repeat-interval>10000</repeat-interval>
      </simple>
    </trigger>
</job>

<job>
  <job-detail>
    <name>ScanDirectory2</name>
    <group>DEFAULT</group>
    <description>
        A job that scans a directory for files
    </description>
    <job-class>
        org.cavaness.quartzbook.chapter3.ScanDirectoryJob
    </job-class>
    <volatility>false</volatility>
    <durability>false</durability>
    <recover>false</recover>

    <job-data-map allows-transient-data="true">
      <entry>
        <key>SCAN_DIR</key>
        <value>c:\quartz-book\input2</value>
      </entry>
    </job-data-map>
  </job-detail>

  <trigger>
    <simple>
```

Listing 3.9   Continued

```
    <name>scanTrigger2</name>
    <group>DEFAULT</group>
    <job-name>ScanDirectory2</job-name>
    <job-group>DEFAULT</job-group>
    <start-time>2005-06-10 6:10:00 PM</start-time>
    <!-- repeat indefinitely every 15 seconds -->
    <repeat-count>-1</repeat-count>
    <repeat-interval>15000</repeat-interval>
    </simple>
  </trigger>
 </job>
</quartz>
```

Modifying the `quartz.properties` File for the Plug-In

Earlier in this chapter, you were told that the `JobInitializationPlugin` looks for the file `quartz_jobs.xml` to get the declarative job information. If you want to change that file, you need to modify the `quartz.properties` file and tell the plug-in which file to load. For example, if you wanted Quartz to load job information from an XML file called *my_quartz_jobs.xml*, you would have to give the plug-in that filename. Listing 3.10 shows how this can be accomplished; we are only repeating the plug-in section here.

Listing 3.10   Modifying `quartz.properties` for `JobInitializationPlugin`

```
org.quartz.plugin.jobInitializer.class =
org.quartz.plugins.xml.JobInitializationPlugin

org.quartz.plugin.jobInitializer.fileName = my_quartz_jobs.xml

org.quartz.plugin.jobInitializer.overWriteExistingJobs = true
org.quartz.plugin.jobInitializer.validating = false
org.quartz.plugin.jobInitializer.overWriteExistingJobs = false
org.quartz.plugin.jobInitializer.failOnFileNotFound = true
```

In Listing 3.10, we add the property `org.quartz.plugin.jobInitializer.fileName` and set the value to the name of our file. It must be available to the classloader, which means somewhere on the classpath.

When Quartz starts up and reads the `quartz.properties` file, it initializes the plug-in. It passes all of these properties to the plug-in, and the plug-in gets notified to look for a different file.

Packaging the Quartz Application

Let's finish off this early chapter by briefly discussing the process of packaging an application that utilizes the Quartz framework.

Quartz Third-Party Dependencies

Starting with the 1.5 distribution, you will see a <QUARTZ_HOME>\lib directory. Underneath this directory, you'll find several subdirectories:

- <QUARTZ_HOME>\lib\core
- <QUARTZ_HOME>\lib\optional
- <QUARTZ_HOME>\lib\build

For deployment, you absolutely need the Quartz JAR file, as well as some of the other dependent libraries. Which third-party libraries are required is somewhat dependent on whether you are running in a stand-alone environment or as part of a J2EE distribution. Typically, the Jakarta Commons libraries (commons-logging, commons-beanutils, and so on) are needed regardless. However, when deploying into an application server environment, you need to be sure not to copy JARs that are already present; if you do, you will generally get very strange results.

Table 3.1 lists the included third-party libraries and information to help you decide whether you need to include them.

Table 3.1   Quartz Third-Party Libraries Required/Optional

Name	Required/Notes	Where to Find More Information
activation.jar	Primarily used by JavaMail	http://java.sun.com/products/javabeans/glasgow/jaf.html
commons-beanutils.jar	Yes	http://jakarta.apache.org/commons/beanutils
commons-collections.jar	Yes	http://jakarta.apache.org/commons/collections
commons-dbcp-1.1.jar	Yes, if using a database for job storage	http://jakarta.apache.org/commons/dbcp

Table 3.1   Quartz Third-Party Libraries Required/Optional

Name	Required/Notes	Where to Find More Informatio
commons-digester.jar	Yes	If you are using some of the plug-ins, you'll need it.
commons-logging.jar	Yes	http://jakarta.apache.org/commons/logging/
commons-pool-1.1.jar		http://jakarta.apache.org/commons/pool/
javamail.jar	Sending e-mails	http://java.sun.com/products/javamail/
jdbc2_0-stdext.jar	Yes, if using a database for job storage	http://java.sun.com/products/jdbc/
jta.jar	Yes, if using a database for job storage	http://java.sun.com/products/jta/
quartz.jar	Yes	Core Quartz Framework
servlet.jar	If using a Servlet container, but it should already be present	http://java.sun.com/products/servlet/
log4j.jar	Come on, who is not using this?	http://logging.apache.org/

Configuration and Properties Files

You also must include `quartz.properties` with your application. If you are deploying your application in an exploded format, you should place the `quartz.properties` file in a directory that is loaded by the classloader. (An "exploded" format is one that is not contained within a JAR, WAR, EAR, or other Java archive, but that is laid on the file system in individual files.) For example, if you have a `classes` directory (such as a Web application's `WEB-INF/classes` directory), store the `quartz.properties` file there. If you are deploying in one of Java's archived formats, put the properties file in the root of the archive file. This same rule applies when using the `quartz_jobs.xml` file.

SCHEDULING JOBS

In the last chapter, you got your first real taste of using Quartz to schedule jobs. Admittedly, the jobs were not very complex, but that wasn't the point. You should have walked away with a fair understanding of how to construct and schedule jobs and, more important, a desire and excitement to learn more. That's where this chapter picks up.

Chapter 4 moves into the core of the Quartz framework. Arguably, this is the most important chapter for you to read and understand. The `Scheduler` is the heart of the framework. This chapter focuses on how to use the Scheduler to manage your jobs, how to create and associate triggers so the jobs will fire, and how to choose the calendar to provide more flexibility for a given schedule.

"For a moment, nothing happened. Then, after a second or so, nothing continued to happen."

—*Douglas Adams*, Hitchhiker's Guide to the Galaxy

The Quartz Scheduler

The Quartz framework contains many classes and interfaces separated into approximately 11 packages. Much of the interaction that you'll have with the framework will take place with the org.quartz package. This package contains the public API of the Quartz framework.

We don't attempt to cover every class and interface within the framework. Instead, we present a subset of the components that will help you understand how Quartz does what it does. Figure 4.1 shows a compacted class diagram for the essential Scheduler components.

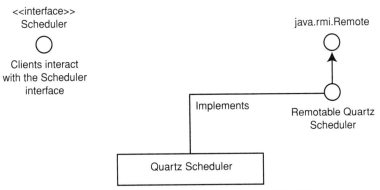

FIGURE 4.1 Quartz class diagram (only major components shown)

The Scheduler is the primary API of Quartz. For Quartz users, most of the interaction with the framework takes place with the Scheduler. Clients interact with the Scheduler through the org.quartz.Scheduler interface. The Scheduler implementation, in this case, is a proxy, and the calls are forwarded to an instance of the QuartzScheduler. The QuartzScheduler is not visible to the client, and there's no direct interaction with the instance.

The QuartzScheduler is at the root of the framework and is the engine that drives the entire framework. Not all of the

functionality is built directly into the `QuartzScheduler`, however. The framework has been designed to be flexible and configurable so that many of the important functions are carried
out by separate components and subframeworks. This means
that Quartz users can substitute their own versions of certain
key features for the default ones. Still, even though the
`QuartzScheduler` delegates some of its responsibility, it is still
in charge of the overall process of scheduling.

The Quartz Scheduler Hierarchy

Clients can interact with two types of Schedulers, shown in
Figure 4.2. Both implement the `org.quartz.Scheduler`
interface.

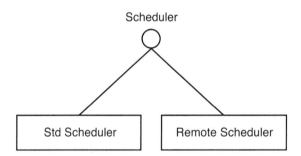

FIGURE 4.2   The `org.quartz.Scheduler` hierarchy

As a Quartz user, you interact with the classes that implement the `org.quartz.Scheduler` interface. Before you can
invoke any of its API, you need to know how to create an
instance of the Scheduler.

The Quartz `SchedulerFactory`

Regardless of the type of Scheduler you use, you should never
create an instance of the Scheduler directly. Instead, you should
use one of the factory methods to ensure that all facets of the
Scheduler are instantiated and initialized properly. (The factory
design pattern is referred to as a *factory pattern* because it is

responsible for "manufacturing" an object. In this case, it man-
ufactures a Scheduler instance) The Quartz framework provides
the `org.quartz.SchedulerFactory` interface for this purpose.
The role of the `SchedulerFactory` is to produce Scheduler
instances. When created, the instances are stored in a repository
(`org.quartz.impl.SchedulerRepository`) that provides
lookup facilities within a class loader. To use the Scheduler
instances, the client must retrieve them from the factory (and
subsequent repository) by using a separate method call. In other
words, creating a Scheduler instance through the factory and
getting the instance of that Scheduler takes two method calls.
Some convenience methods encapsulate those two calls, as
you'll see shortly.

You can use two different types of the `SchedulerFactory`
to create Schedulers (see Figure 4.3).

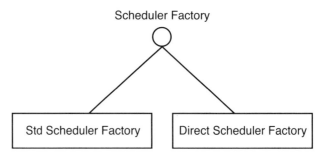

FIGURE 4.3 All Scheduler instances should be created by
using the `SchedulerFactory`.

The two Scheduler factories are `org.quartz.impl.`
`DirectSchedulerFactory` and `org.quartz.impl.`
`StdSchedulerFactory`. Let's examine each one.

Using the `DirectSchedulerFactory`

The `DirectSchedulerFactory` is designed for those who want
absolute control over how a Scheduler instance is manufac-
tured. Listing 4.1 shows that the easiest way to use the
`DirectSchedulerFactory` to create a Scheduler instance.

Listing 4.1   Using the `DirectSchedulerFactory`

```
public class Listing_4_1 {
    static Log logger = LogFactory.getLog(Listing_4_1.class);

    public static void main(String[] args) {
        Listing_4_1 example = new Listing_4_1();
        example.startScheduler();
    }

    public void startScheduler() {
        DirectSchedulerFactory factory =DirectSchedulerFactory.getInstance();

        try {
            // Initialize the Scheduler Factory with 10 threads
            factory.createVolatileScheduler(10);

            // Get a scheduler from the factory
            Scheduler scheduler = factory.getScheduler();

            // Start the scheduler running
            logger.info("Scheduler starting up...");
            scheduler.start();

        } catch (SchedulerException ex) {
            logger.error(ex);
        }
    }
}
```

When using the `DirectSchedulerFactory`, there are three basic steps. First, you must acquire an instance of the factory using the static `getInstance()` method. When you have the factory instance, you need to initialize it by calling one of the `createXXX` methods. For example, Listing 4.1 used the `createVolatileScheduler()` method to tell the factory to initialize itself with ten worker threads (we talk more about worker threads later in this chapter). The third and final step is to retrieve an instance of a Scheduler from the factory with the `getScheduler()` method.

CALL ONE OF THE `createXXX` METHODS BEFORE CALLING `getScheduler()`

The `createVolatileScheduler()` method doesn't return an instance of a Scheduler. The `createXXX()` methods tell the factory how to configure the Scheduler instances they create. You must call the `getScheduler()` method to retrieve the instance produced by the `createXXX()` method from the factory. In fact, before calling the `getScheduler()` method, you must have called one of the `createXXX()` methods; otherwise, you will get a `SchedulerException` error because no Scheduler will exist.

You can choose from several different `createXXX()` methods, depending on what type of Scheduler you want to use and how you need it configured. Listing 4.1 used the `createVolatileScheduler()` method to create a Scheduler. The `createVolatileScheduler()` method takes a single argument: the number of threads to create. In Figure 4.2, you saw that there is also a `RemoteScheduler` class. You must use a different `createXXX()` method to create a `RemoteScheduler` instance. Two versions are available:

```
public void createRemoteScheduler(String rmiHost, int rmiPort)
  throws SchedulerException;

protected void createRemoteScheduler(String schedulerName,
  String schedulerInstanceId, String rmiHost, int rmiPort)
  throws SchedulerException;
```

`RemoteSchedulers` are discussed in Chapter 10, "Using Quartz with J2EE." If you just need a standard Scheduler, you can use one of these versions:

```
public void createScheduler(ThreadPool threadPool, JobStore jobStore)
  throws SchedulerException;

public void createScheduler(String schedulerName,
  String schedulerInstanceId, ThreadPool threadPool, JobStore jobStore)
  throws SchedulerException;

public void createScheduler(String schedulerName,
  String schedulerInstanceId, ThreadPool threadPool,
  JobStore jobStore, String rmiRegistryHost, int rmiRegistryPort,
  long idleWaitTime, long dbFailureRetryInterval)
  throws SchedulerException;
```

In the last chapter, we used a properties file to initialize the Scheduler. To create a Scheduler instance with `DirectSchedulerFactory`, you must pass configuration parameters through one of the `createXXX()` methods. In the next section, we discuss the `StdSchedulerFactory`, a version of `SchedulerFactory` that relies on a set of properties to configure the Scheduler instead of passing them in as arguments to the `createXXX` method. It thus avoids hard-coding Scheduler configuration settings within your code.

Using the StdSchedulerFactory

In contrast to the DirectSchedulerFactory, the
org.quartz.impl.StdSchedulerFactory relies on a set of
properties to determine how to manufacture the Scheduler
instance. You can supply these properties to the factory in one
of three ways:

- By supplying a java.util.Properties instance
- By supplying an external properties file
- By supplying a java.io.InputStream that has the
  contents of a properties file

JAVA PROPERTIES FILES

We use the phase "properties file" here in the traditional Java sense: a set of key=value
pairs that are typically specified in an external file as key=value, one per line.

Listing 4.2 demonstrates the first approach, supplying the
properties through a java.util.Properties instance.

Listing 4.2   Creating a StdSchedulerFactory Using a java.util.Properties Instance

```
public class Listing_4_2 {
    static Log logger = LogFactory.getLog(Listing_4_2.class);

    public static void main(String[] args) {
        Listing_4_2 example = new Listing_4_2();
        example.startScheduler();
    }

    public void startScheduler() {

        // Create an instance of the factory
        StdSchedulerFactory factory = new StdSchedulerFactory();

        // Create the properties to configure the factory
        Properties props = new Properties();

        // required to supply threadpool class and num of threads

        props.put(StdSchedulerFactory.PROP_THREAD_POOL_CLASS,
                "org.quartz.simpl.SimpleThreadPool");
```

Listing 4.2   Continued

```
props.put("org.quartz.threadPool.threadCount", "10");

try {

    // Initialize the factory with properties
    factory.initialize(props);

    Scheduler scheduler = factory.getScheduler();

    logger.info("Scheduler starting up...");
    scheduler.start();

} catch (SchedulerException ex) {
    logger.error(ex);
}
    }
}
```

Listing 4.2 provides a very simple example of using the StdSchedulerFactory to create an instance of a Scheduler. The two properties passed into the factory in the example are the name of a class that implements the org.quartz.spi.ThreadPool interface and the number of threads that the Scheduler should use to process jobs. These two properties are required because no defaults are set for them (we talk more about these shortly).

With the DirectSchedulerFactory from Listing 4.1, we called one of the createXXX() methods to initialize the factory. With the StdSchedulerFactory, you use one of the available initialize() methods. After the factory has been initialized, you can call the getScheduler() method to acquire the instance of the Scheduler. Passing the properties to the factory using the java.util.Properties object is just one way of configuring the SchedulerFactory. Hard-coding configuration properties is hardly recommended and should be avoided when possible. If you needed to modify the number of threads in this example, you would need to change the code and recompile.

Fortunately, the StdSchedulerFactory provides other ways to supply the necessary properties. The factory can also be initialized by passing in the name of an external file that contains these configuration settings. This alternate form of the initialize() method is shown here:

```
public void initialize(String filename) throws
➡SchedulerException;
```

For the file and properties to be loaded successfully, the file must be available to the classloader. This means that it should be in the classpath of your application. If you would rather use an java.io.InputStream to load the file, you can use this alternate form of the initialize() method:

```
public void initialize(InputStream propertiesStream) throws
➥SchedulerException;
```

In Chapter 3, "Hello, Quartz," you saw an example that used an external file called quartz.properties to load the settings for the SchedulerFactory. This external properties file is just a special use of the previous method signatures. If you don't specify where to get the properties using one of the initialize() methods, the StdSchedulerFactory attempts to load them from a file called quartz.properties. This is the behavior you saw in Chapter 3.

CREATING A SCHEDULER USING THE DEFAULT quartz.properties FILE

If you use the no-argument version of the initialize() method, the StdSchedulerFactory performs the following steps to attempt to load the properties for the factory:

1. Checks for a different filename using System.getProperty("org.quartz.properties");
2. Otherwise, uses the name quartz.properties as the file to load
3. Tries to load the file from the current working directory
4. Tries to load the file from the system classpath

DEFAULT quartz.properties IN THE QUARTZ JAR FILE
Step 4 always succeeds because a default quartz.properties file is stored within the Quartz JAR. If you want to use an alternate file, you must create one and make sure it's within the classpath.

Using the StdSchedulerFactory for creating a Scheduler instance is so common that the StdSchedulerFactory includes a static convenience method called getDefaultScheduler() that uses the previous steps outlined to instantiate the factory. This is shown in Listing 4.3.

Listing 4.3   Using the Static getDefaultScheduler() Method to Create a Scheduler

```
public class Listing_4_3 {
    static Log logger = LogFactory.getLog(Listing_4_3.class);

    public static void main(String[] args) {
        Listing_4_3 example = new Listing_4_3();
        example.startScheduler();
    }

    public void startScheduler() {

        try {
            // Create a default instance of the Scheduler
            Scheduler scheduler =
                        StdSchedulerFactory.getDefaultScheduler();

            logger.info("Scheduler starting up...");
            scheduler.start();

        } catch (SchedulerException ex) {
            logger.error(ex);
        }
}}
```

The static getDefaultScheduler() method calls the empty constructor. If none of the initialize() methods has been previously invoked, the no-argument initialize() method is called. This sets in motion the load file sequence mentioned earlier. In the default case, the quartz.properties file is located, and the properties are loaded from that file.

Scheduler Functionality

Most of the material in this chapter so far has focused on obtaining an instance of the Scheduler. So when you have a Scheduler instance, what can you do with it? Well, to start, the examples have shown that you can call the start() method on it. The Scheduler API includes approximately 65 different methods. We don't enumerate all of them here, but you need to understand a little more about the Scheduler API.

The Scheduler API can be grouped into three categories:

- Managing the Scheduler
- Managing jobs
- Managing triggers and calendars

Managing the Scheduler

Besides starting the Scheduler, you might need to perform a few other operations on the Scheduler during your application's lifetime. These Scheduler operations include querying, putting the Scheduler in standby mode, resuming, and stopping. For many situations, when a Scheduler is started, you don't need to do anything except let it run. In certain circumstances, you might need to temporarily halt the Scheduler using the standby mode.

Starting the Scheduler

Starting the Scheduler couldn't be more straightforward. When you have an instance of a Scheduler that has been properly initialized and your jobs and triggers have been registered, simply call the `start()` method:

```
// Create an instance of the Scheduler
Scheduler scheduler =
  StdSchedulerFactory.getDefaultScheduler();

// Start the scheduler
scheduler.start();
```

When the `start()` method is called, the Scheduler starts looking for jobs that need to be executed. You use the `start()` method when you have a new Scheduler instance and when the Scheduler has been placed into standby mode. After `shutdown()` has been called, you can no longer call `start()` on that Scheduler instance.

DON'T CALL start() AFTER shutdown() HAS BEEN CALLED

You can't use the start() method on a Scheduler instance that has been shut down. This is because the shutdown() method destroys all the resources (threads, database connections, and so on) that were created for the Scheduler. A SchedulerException will be thrown if you call start() after shutdown().

Standby Mode

Putting the Scheduler in standby mode causes the Scheduler to temporarily stop looking for jobs to execute. As an example, suppose your Scheduler gets its job information from a database and you need to restart the database. You could either restart Scheduler when the database is back online or just put the Scheduler in standby mode. You can put a Scheduler in standby mode by calling the standby() method:

```
public void standby() throws SchedulerException;
```

In standby mode, the Scheduler does not attempt to execute jobs because the thread that searches for jobs that need executing is paused.

Stopping the Scheduler

You can use two versions of the shutdown() method to stop the Scheduler:

```
public void shutdown(boolean waitForJobsToComplete)
throws SchedulerException;

public void shutdown() throws SchedulerException;
```

The only difference between these two methods is that one version takes a Boolean argument that doesn't let the Scheduler stop until all currently executing jobs have finished executing. The shutdown() method without the argument is similar to calling shutdown(false).

Managing Jobs

Previous chapters took a cursory look at Quartz jobs, but now we go through a more formal discussion of Quartz jobs and how to use them.

What Is a Quartz Job?

Quite simply, a Quartz job is a Java class that performs a task on your behalf. This task can be anything that you can code in Java. Here are a few examples to make the point:

- Use JavaMail (or another Mail framework, such as Commons Net) to send e-mails
- Create a remote interface and invoke a method on an EJB
- Use HttpClient and invoke a URL for a Web application
- Get a hibernate session and query and update data in a relational database
- Use OSWorkflow and invoke a workflow from the job

These examples are just a few; you surely can come up with your own. Anything that you can do in Java can become a job.

The `org.quartz.Job` Interface

The only requirement that Quartz puts on your Java class is that it must implement the `org.quartz.Job` interface. Your job class can implement any other interfaces that it wants or extend any class that it needs, but it or a superclass must implement the job interface. The job interface defines a single method:

```
public void execute(JobExecutionContext context)
    throws JobExecutionException;
```

When the Scheduler determines that it is time to run the job, the `execute()` method is called, and a `JobExecutionContext` object is passed to the job. The only contractual obligation that

Quartz puts on the execute() method is that if there's a serious problem with the job, you must throw an org.quartz.JobExecutionException.

JobExecutionContext

When the Scheduler calls a job, a JobExecutionContext is passed to the execute() method. The JobExecutionContext is an object that gives the job access to the runtime environment of Quartz and the details of the job itself. This is analogous to a Java Web application in which a servlet has access to the ServletContext. From the JobExecutionContext, the job can access everything about its environment, including the JobDetail and trigger that were registered with the Scheduler for the job. Listing 4.4 shows a job called PrintInfoJob that prints some information about the job.

As you can see from Listing 4.4, Quartz jobs can be very basic. The PrintInfoJob gets the JobDetail object, which is stored in the JobExecutionContext, and prints some basic details about the job. The JobDetail class deserves a little more discussion.

Listing 4.4   The PrintInfoJob Shows How to Access the JobExecutionContext

```
public class PrintInfoJob implements Job {
    static Log logger = LogFactory.getLog(PrintInfoJob.class);

    public void execute(JobExecutionContext context)
            throws JobExecutionException {

        // Every job has its own job detail
        JobDetail jobDetail = context.getJobDetail();

        // The name and group are defined in the job detail
        String jobName = jobDetail.getName();
        logger.info("Name: " + jobDetail.getFullName());

        // The name of this class configured for the job
        logger.info("Job Class: " + jobDetail.getJobClass());

        // Log the time the job started
        logger.info(jobName + " fired at " + context.getFireTime());

        logger.info("Next fire time " + context.getNextFireTime());
    }
}
```

JobDetail

You first saw the `org.quartz.JobDetail` class back in
Chapter 3. A `JobDetail` instance is created for every job that is
scheduled with the Scheduler. The `JobDetail` serves as the definition for a job instance. Notice in Listing 4.5 that the job isn't
the object registered with the Scheduler; it's actually the
`JobDetail` instance.

Listing 4.5   A `JobDetail` Is Registered with the Scheduler, Not the Job

```
public class Listing_4_5 {
    static Log logger = LogFactory.getLog(Listing_4_5.class);

    public static void main(String[] args) {
        Listing_4_5 example = new Listing_4_5();
        example.runScheduler();
    }

    public void runScheduler() {

        try {

            // Create a default instance of the Scheduler
            Scheduler scheduler =
                        StdSchedulerFactory.getDefaultScheduler();

            logger.info("Scheduler starting up...");
            scheduler.start();

            // Create the JobDetail
            JobDetail jobDetail =
                    new JobDetail("PrintInfoJob",
                    Scheduler.DEFAULT_GROUP,
                            PrintInfoJob.class);

                // Create a trigger that fires now and repeats forever
            Trigger trigger = TriggerUtils.makeImmediateTrigger(
                    SimpleTrigger.REPEAT_INDEFINITELY, 10000);
            trigger.setName("PrintInfoJobTrigger");

            // register with the Scheduler
            scheduler.scheduleJob(jobDetail, trigger);

        } catch (SchedulerException ex) {
            logger.error(ex);
        }
    }
}
```

You can see in Listing 4.5 that the `JobDetail` gets added to the Scheduler, not the job. The job class is part of the `JobDetail` but is not instantiated until the Scheduler is ready to execute it.

JOB INSTANCES ARE NOT CREATED UNTIL EXECUTION TIME

Job instances are not instantiated until it's time to execute them. Each time a job is executed, a new job instance is created. One implication of this is that your jobs don't have to worry about thread safety because only one thread will be executing a given instance of your job class at a time—even if you execute the same job concurrently.

Setting Job State Using the `JobDataMap` Object

You can define state for a job using `org.quartz.JobDataMap`. The `JobDataMap` implements `java.util.Map` through its superclass, `org.quartz.utils.DirtyFlagMap`. You can store key/value pairs within the `JobDataMap`, and those data pairs can be passed along and accessed from within your job class. This is a convenient way to pass configuration information to your job. Listing 4.6 illustrates this approach using a job we created especially for this purpose, called `PrintJobDataMapJob`.

Listing 4.6   Use the `JobDataMap` to Pass Configuration Information to Your Job

```
public class Listing_4_6 {
    static Log logger = LogFactory.getLog(Listing_4_6.class);

    public static void main(String[] args) {
        Listing_4_6 example = new Listing_4_6();
        example.runScheduler();
    }

    public void runScheduler() {
        Scheduler scheduler = null;

        try {
            // Create a default instance of the Scheduler
            scheduler = StdSchedulerFactory.getDefaultScheduler();
            scheduler.start();
            logger.info("Scheduler was started at " + new Date());

            // Create the JobDetail
            JobDetail jobDetail =
                    new JobDetail("PrintJobDataMapJob",
                    Scheduler.DEFAULT_GROUP,
```

Listing 4.6   Continued

```
                                PrintJobDataMapJob.class);

        // Store some state for the Job
        jobDetail.getJobDataMap().put("name", "John Doe");
        jobDetail.getJobDataMap().put("age", 23);
        jobDetail.getJobDataMap().put("balance",
                                new BigDecimal(1200.37));

        // Create a trigger that fires once
        Trigger trigger =
                    TriggerUtils.makeImmediateTrigger(0, 10000);
        trigger.setName("PrintJobDataMapJobTrigger");

        scheduler.scheduleJob(jobDetail, trigger);

    } catch (SchedulerException ex) {
        logger.error(ex);
    }
  }
}
```

In Listing 4.6, the information that we want to pass to the
PrintJobDataMapJob is stored in the JobDataMap within the
JobDetail. Because the JobDataMap implements the
java.util.Map interface, we store state there using a key/value
pair configuration. The JobDataMap includes niceties to make it
easier to deal with object conversion. Normally with maps, you
have to explicitly convert from object to the known type. The
JobDataMap includes methods that do this on your behalf.

When the Scheduler eventually calls the job, the job can use
the JobDetail to access and use the key/value pairs from the
JobDataMap. Listing 4.7 shows the PrintJobDataMapJob.

**Listing 4.7   The Job Can Access the JobDataMap Through the JobExecutionContext
Object**

```
public class PrintJobDataMapJob implements Job {
    static Log logger = LogFactory.getLog(PrintJobDataMapJob.class);

    public void execute(JobExecutionContext context)
            throws JobExecutionException {

        logger.info("in PrintJobDataMapJob");

        // Every job has its own job detail
        JobDataMap jobDataMap =
                context.getJobDetail().getJobDataMap();

        // Iterate through the key/value pairs
        Iterator iter = jobDataMap.keySet().iterator();
```

Listing 4.7 Continued

```
        while (iter.hasNext()) {
            Object key = iter.next();
            Object value = jobDataMap.get(key);

            logger.info("Key: " + key + " - Value: " + value);
        }
    }
}
```

When you obtain the JobDataMap, you can use its methods as you might any map instance. Normally, you access the data within the JobDataMap using a predefined key of your choice. You can also iterate through the map itself, as Listing 4.7 shows.

For jobs such as PrintJobDataMapJob, the properties within the JobDataMap become an informal contract obligation between the client scheduling the job and the job itself. Job creators should document very carefully which properties are required and which are optional. This helps ensure that jobs get reused by other members of your team.

SINCE QUARTZ 1.5, A JobDataMap IS AVAILABLE ON TRIGGERS

As of Quartz 1.5, a JobDataMap is also available at the trigger level. This one is used similar to the one at the job level, except that it can support multiple triggers for the same JobDetail. Along with this enhancement added during version 1.5, a new convenience method on the JobExecutionContext can be used to get a merged map of values from the job and trigger level. This method, called getMergedJobDataMap(),can be used within a job. From Quartz 1.5 forward, this method should be considered a best practice for retrieving the JobDataMap.

Stateful Versus Stateless Jobs

You learned from the previous section that information can be inserted into the JobDataMap and accessed by your jobs. For every job execution however, a new instance of the JobDataMap is created with the values that have been stored (for example, in a database) for the particular job. Therefore, there's no way to hold that information between job invocations—that is, unless you use a stateful job.

In the same way that stateful session beans (SFSB) in J2EE keep their state between calls, the Quartz StatefulJob can hold its state between job executions. However, just like SFSBs, Quartz stateful jobs have some downsides when compared with their stateless counterparts.

USING STATEFUL JOBS

The Quartz framework offers the org.quartz.StatefulJob interface when you need to maintain state between job executions. The StatefulJob interface extends the standard job interface and adds no methods that you have to implement. You simply implement the StatefulJob interface using the same execute() method as the job interface. If you have an existing job class, all you have to do is change the job interface to org.quartz.StatefulJob.

Two key differences exist between a job and StatefulJob as they are used by the framework. First, the JobDataMap is repersisted in the JobStore after each execution. This ensures that changes that you make to the job data are kept for the next execution.

CHANGING THE JobDataMap FOR STATEFUL JOBS

You can modify the JobDataMap within Stateful Jobs by simply calling the various put() methods on the map. Any data that was present will be overwritten with the new. You can also do this for stateless jobs, but because the JobDataMap is not repersisted for stateless jobs, the data will not be saved. Changes are also not saved for JobDataMaps on triggers and the JobExecutionContext.

The other important difference between stateless and stateful jobs is that two or more stateful JobDetail instances can't execute concurrently. Say that you have created and registered a stateful JobDetail with the Scheduler. You also have set up two triggers that fire the job: one that fires every minute and another that fires every five minutes. If the two triggers tried to fire the job at the same time, the framework would not allow that to occur. The second trigger would be blocked until the first one completed.

This requirement has to do with the JobDataMap storage. Because the JobDataMap is stored along with the JobDetail that defines the job instance, thread-safety issues must be taken into consideration. Only one thread can run and update the JobDataMap storage at a time. Otherwise, the data would be erroneous because the second trigger could try to execute the job before the first had a chance to update the storage. Even stranger results could occur if the second execution completed before the first, which is possible, depending on what your job does.

Because of these differences, you should use the StatefulJob carefully. When you need to prevent concurrent executions of a job, the stateful job is your easiest bet. In the J2EE world, *stateful* has developed a somewhat negative connotation, but this is not true for Quartz.

Volatility, Durability, and Recoverability

All three of these attributes are similar in that they affect the runtime behavior of a job. Each one is discussed in turn.

Job Volatility

A volatile job is one that is not persisted between program shutdowns. A job is set to be volatile by calling the setVolatility(true) method on the JobDetail.

RamJobStore SHOULDN'T BE USED WHEN YOU NEED PERSISTENT JOBS

RamJobStore uses volatile memory, and all knowledge about jobs and triggers is lost when the application is shut down. Storing jobs in RAMJobStore effectively makes them volatile. If you need your job information to be persisted across application restarts, you should consider one of the other JobStore types, such as JobStoreTX or JobStoreCMT. These are discussed in Chapter 6, "JobStores and Persistence."

The default value for job volatility is false.

Job Durability

A durable job is one that should remain in the JobStore, even if there are no longer any triggers that can fire for the job. Let's say that you set up a single-fire trigger that fires and is therefore moved to the STATE_COMPLETE state. No more firing times exist, but the trigger was scheduled to execute only once. The job that this trigger pointed to is now orphaned because it no longer has any triggers associated with it.

If you set a job to be durable, it will not be removed from the JobStore when it becomes orphaned. This keeps it available for further scheduling whenever your program decides to add another trigger for it. If the setDurability(false) method was invoked on the JobDetail, the job would be removed from the JobStore when all triggers have fired. The default value for durability is false. Hence, the default behavior of jobs and triggers is to be automatically removed from the JobStore—the trigger when it completes all its firing and the job when it has no associated triggers.

Job Recoverability

When the Scheduler experiences an unexpected shutdown and a job is executing, a recoverable job is re-executed when the Scheduler is restarted. The job starts executing again right from the beginning. The Scheduler has no way of knowing where the job was during execution when the program was stopped and, therefore, must start all over again.

To set a job to be recoverable, use the following method:

```
public void setRequestsRecovery(boolean shouldRecover);
```

By default, the value is set to false and the Scheduler does not try to recover the jobs.

Removing Jobs from the Scheduler

You can remove a job that has been scheduled in several ways. One way is to remove all the triggers associated with the job; if the job is durable, it will be removed from the Scheduler. An easier way is just to remove the job directly. You can use the deleteJob() method to do this:

```
public boolean deleteJob(String jobName, String groupName)
throws SchedulerException;
```

Interrupting Jobs

It's sometimes necessary to be able to interrupt a job, especially if it takes a long time to execute. For example, suppose you have a job that takes an hour to run, and you realize five minutes into the job that it's going to need to run again because of some uncontrollable error. You might as well interrupt the job, fix the problem, and then rerun it.

Quartz includes an interface called org.quartz. InterruptableJob that extends the normal job interface and offers an interrupt() method:

```
public void interrupt() throws
UnableToInterruptJobException;
```

You can call the interrupt() method on the Scheduler by providing the name of the job and the group that was used when the job was scheduled:

```
public boolean interrupt(SchedulingContext ctxt, String
jobName, String groupName) throws
UnableToInterruptJobException;
```

Listing 4.8 shows an example InterruptableJob called CheckForInterruptJob.

The Scheduler will invoke the interrupt() method on your job. It's up to you and your job to determine how to interrupt the job. Although there are several acceptable approaches, Listing 4.8 provides one of the more common. The Quartz framework can signal to a job that an interrupt has been requested for it, but here you have control over the job and, therefore, are responsible for the approach.

Listing 4.8   An `InterruptableJob` Can Be Used to Determine Whether `interrupt()` has Been Called on the Scheduler

```java
public class CheckForInterruptJob implements InterruptableJob {
    static Log logger = LogFactory.getLog(CheckForInterruptJob.class);

    private boolean jobInterrupted = false;

    private int counter = 5;

    private boolean jobFinished = false;

    public void interrupt() throws UnableToInterruptJobException {
        jobInterrupted = true;
    }

    public void execute(JobExecutionContext context)
            throws JobExecutionException {

        while (!jobInterrupted && !jobFinished) {

            // Perform a small amount of processing
            logger.info("Processing the job");
            counter-;

            if (counter <= 0) {
                jobFinished = true;
                }

            // Sleep and wait for 3 seconds
            try {
                Thread.sleep(3000);
            } catch (InterruptedException e) {
                // do nothing
            }
        }

        if (jobFinished) {
            logger.info("Job finished without interrupt");
        } else if (jobInterrupted) {
            logger.info("Job was interrupted");
        }
    }
}
```

Jobs Provided by the Framework

The Quartz framework provides several jobs that you can use within your applications with little work. Table 4.1 lists the jobs and their usage.

Table 4.1   Jobs Provided by the Quartz Framework

Job Class	Job Usage
`org.quartz.jobs.FileScanJob`	A job that checks for changes to a specified file and then informs a listener that the file has changed.
`org.quartz.jobs.FileScanListener`	A listener that tells `FileScanJob` when a file has been modified.
`org.quartz.jobs.NativeJob`	A job that is used for executing native programs (such as .exe files under Windows).
`org.quartz.jobs.NoOpJob`	A job that doesn't do anything but that might be useful for testing listeners. Some users even use this just to cause a listener to run.
`org.quartz.jobs.ee.mail.SendMailJob`	A job that sends an e-mail using the JavaMail API.
`org.quartz.jobs.ee.jmx.JMXInvokerJob`	A job that invokes a method on a JMX bean.
`org.quartz.jobs.ee.ejb.EJBInvokerJob`	A job that invokes a method on an EJB.

Quick Java Thread Overview

Consider this a small but very necessary diversion from our discussion of the Quartz framework. Threads play an important role in the Quartz framework—for that matter, in Java in general. Without threads, Java (and, subsequently, Quartz) would have to use heavy-weight processes to perform simultaneous tasks (jobs, in the Quartz vernacular). This material might be basic for those who understand how threads work in Java. If you do, bear with us. If you haven't yet had the opportunity to learn about Java threads, this is a perfect time for a quick overview. Although the discussion focuses on Java threads in general, we tie it all together at the end with a discussion on how threads are used in Quartz.

Threads in Java

Threads allow a program to do many tasks simultaneously—or, at least, it seems that the tasks are running simultaneously.

Excluding parallel processing for this discussion, only a single thread executes at any particular moment, but the CPU gives each thread a little bit of time to run and then switches (through time-slicing) back and forth between threads very quickly. It can give the appearance of multiple running threads.

The Java language includes built-in support for threads with the Thread class. When a thread is told to run, the thread's run() method is executed. Just because you create a thread instance and call the start() method does not mean that the run() method will be executed immediately; the thread instance must wait until the JVM tells it that it can run.

Life Cycle of a Thread

A thread can be in one of several possible states during its lifetime. It can be in only one state at a time, and these states are dictated by the JVM, not the operating system. The thread states are listed here:

- New
- Runnable
- Blocked
- Waiting
- Timed Waiting
- Terminated

When a new thread is created, it is assigned to the New state. No system resources are allocated to a thread in this state. To move the thread to the Runnable state, the start() method must be called.

When the start() method is called on a new thread, the thread enters the Runnable state and is considered to be running. This doesn't mean that the thread is actually executing instructions. Even though the state is set to Runnable and the thread is scheduled to run, it might have to wait until other executing threads finish or are temporarily suspended. The JVM decides which thread should get a chance to run next. The manner in which the JVM determines the next thread depends on several factors, including the operating system, the particular JVM, and thread priority, among others. Figure 4.4 shows the life cycle of a Java thread.

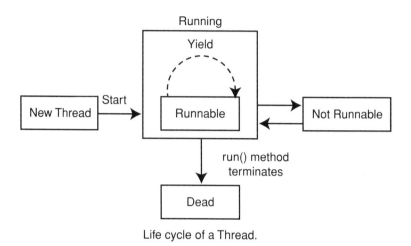

Life cycle of a Thread.

FIGURE 4.4   The life cycle of a Java thread

The Blocked and Waiting states are a little beyond the discussion for this book and tie into some topics that we don't need to explore here. If you want more information on this topic, see the Java tutorial on threads at the Sun site, http://java.sun.com/docs/books/tutorial/essential/threads/index.html.

Processes Versus Threads

Each Java program is assigned a *process.* The program then breaks up its tasks into threads. Even when you write a simple "Hello, World" program that consists of only a single `main()` method, the program still uses threads, albeit just one.

Sometimes the term *lightweight process* is used to refer to a thread. This is in contrast to the term *heavyweight,* which refers to an actual operating system process. If you are using the Windows operating system, you can look at the Task Manager and see the heavyweight processes running, but you won't see threads. Figure 4.5 illustrates how multiple threads operate within a Java application.

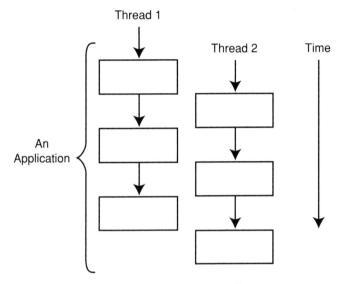

Two Threads Within a Program

FIGURE 4.5   Two threads running within a program

As you can see from Figure 4.5, threads don't usually run concurrently. Putting aside multiple CPUs and parallel processing here, only one thread at a time gets attention from the CPU to execute. Each JVM and operating system might handle this differently, however. Sometimes the thread might get to run to completion and then another thread can then run. This is known as *non-preemptive*. Other times, a thread is interrupted so that the others can do their thing. This is called *preemptive*. In general, threads must compete with one another for the CPU, and this competition is often based on thread priority.

Understanding and Using Thread Priorities

We have mentioned several times that it's up to the JVM to determine which Runnable thread should get the next opportunity to run. The JVM supports a scheduling scheme known as *fixed-priority scheduling* that schedules threads based on their priority, compared to other Runnable threads.

The priority is an integer value that gets assigned to a new thread based on the priority of the parent thread that created it. The value ranges from `Thread.MIN_PRIORITY`, which equates to 1, up to `Thread.MAX_PRIORITY`, which equates to 10. The constants are defined in the `java.lang.Thread` class.

The larger the integer value (up to the `MAX_PRIORITY`), the higher the priority the thread will have. Unless otherwise specified, most of the threads created in a Java application run at `Thread.NORMAL_PRIORITY`, which is right in the middle at a value of 5. You can modify the priority of the thread by calling the `setPriority()` method.

In general, a running thread continues to run until one of several conditions occurs:

- The thread yields (possibly by calling the `sleep()` method, `yield()` method, or `Object.wait()` method).
- The thread's `run()` method finishes.
- If the OS supports time slicing, its time is up.
- Another higher-priority thread becomes Runnable.

Daemon Threads

Daemon threads are sometimes referred to as service threads becomes they usually run at a very low priority (in the background) and do the dull yet essential tasks. For example, the garbage collector in Java is an example of a daemon thread. This thread runs in the background and looks for and reclaims memory that the application no longer is using.

You can make a thread a daemon by setting `true` in the `setDaemon()` method. Otherwise, the thread will be a *user* thread. You can make a thread a daemon thread only before the thread is started. Daemon threads are special, in that the JVM exits if only daemon threads are running and no nondaemon threads are still alive.

Java ThreadGroups and ThreadPools

ThreadGroups in Java are implemented by the
java.lang.ThreadGroup class and represent a group of threads
that can be acted upon as a single entity. Every Java thread is a
member of a thread group. In a thread group, you can stop and
start all of the threads that are members of the group. You can
set priorities and perform other common thread functions.
Thread groups are very useful for building multithreaded applications such as Quartz.

When a Java application starts, it creates a ThreadGroup
called main. Unless specified, all threads that are created
become members of this group. When a thread is assigned to a
specific ThreadGroup, it can't be changed.

JAVA ThreadPools

Java 1.5 introduced a new concept to the Java language called
thread pools. At first glance, these might seem similar to thread
groups, but they actually are used for different purposes.
Whereas multiple threads can belong to the same ThreadGroup,
groups don't share the qualities of a typical pooled resource.
That is, thread groups are only used for membership.

Thread pools are shared resources and are a managed col-
lection of threads that can be used to perform tasks. Thread
pools (and resource pools, in general) provide several benefits
over nonpooled resources. First and foremost, resource pools
provide performance improvements by reducing the overhead of
object creation. If you instantiate ten threads and use these
threads repeatedly instead of creating a new one every time you
need one, you improve the performance of the application. This
concept permeates Java and J2EE. Other benefits include being
able to limit the number of resources, which can help the stabil-
ity and scalability of the application—a greatly desired feature,
no matter what language or application this is.

Thread Usage in Quartz

Threads are extremely important to Quartz because Quartz is designed to support multiple Jobs running simultaneously. To perform this feat, Quartz relies heavily on the thread support built into the Java language and augments it with a few of its own classes and interfaces. You have already seen some of this in the examples in this chapter and the previous one.

When a Quartz Scheduler is first created through one of the factory methods, the factory configures several important resources that the Scheduler will need throughout its lifetime. A few of those important resources have to do with threads.

The Main Processing Thread: QuartzSchedulerThread

When a Quartz application is first launched, the `main` thread starts the Scheduler. The `QuartzScheduler` is created and creates an instance of the `org.quartz.core.QuartzSchedulerThread` class. The `QuartzSchedulerThread` contains the processing loop for determining when the next job should be triggered. As the name implies, the `QuartzSchedulerThread` is a Java thread. It runs as a nondaemon thread with a normal priority.

The main processing loop for the `QuartzSchedulerThread` method is illustrated here:

1. While the scheduler is running:

   A. Check to see if standby mode has been requested.

      1. If the standby method has been called, wait for the signal to continue.

   B. Ask the `JobStore` for the next trigger to fire.

      1. If no trigger is ready to fire, wait for a small amount of time check again.

2. If there's a trigger available, wait for the exact time for it to fire.

   D. When it's time, get the `TriggerFiredBundle` for the trigger.

E. Create a `JobRunShell` instance for the job using the Scheduler and `TriggerFiredBundle`.

F. Tell the `ThreadPool` to run the `JobRunShell` when possible.

This logic exists within the `run()` method of the `QuartzSchedulerThread`.

The `QuartzSchedulerResources`

When the factory creates the Scheduler instance, it also passes the Scheduler an instance of an `org.quartz.core.QuartzSchedulerResources`. The `QuartzSchedulerResources` contains, among others things, a `ThreadPool` instance that provides a pool of worker threads that are responsible for executing jobs. In Quartz, a `ThreadPool` is represented by the `org.quartz.spi.ThreadPool` interface (because Quartz was invented before JDK 1.5, it needed to create its own `ThreadPool` class—to ensure backward compatibility, Quartz still utilizes its `ThreadPool` instead of Java's) and includes a concrete implementation called `org.quartz.simpl.SimpleThreadPool`. The `SimpleThreadPool` has a fixed number of worker threads and doesn't shrink or grow based on load. Figure 4.6 shows the sequence of steps that the framework undergoes during startup as it relates to threads.

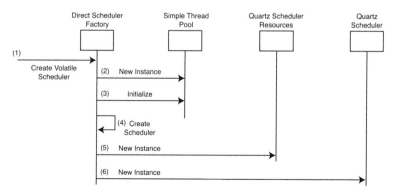

FIGURE 4.6 Several thread-related resources are created at Quartz startup.

What Are Quartz Worker Threads?

Quartz doesn't process your jobs on the main thread. If it did, it would severely reduce the scalability of the application. Instead, Quartz delegates the thread-management responsibilities to a separate component. For the generic Quartz setup, which most users employ, the SimpleThreadPool class handles thread management. The SimpleThreadPool creates a number of WorkerThread instances that are responsible for processing a job on a separate thread. The WorkerThread is an inner class defined within the SimpleThreadPool class and is essentially a thread. The number of WorkerThreads that are created and the priority for these threads are specified by the configuration settings in the quartz.properties file or are passed into the factory.

When the QuartzSchedulerThread asks the ThreadPool to run a JobRunShell instance, the ThreadPool checks to see if a worker thread is available. If all the configured worker threads are busy, the ThreadPool waits until one becomes available. When a worker thread is available and a JobRunShell is waiting to be executed, the worker thread calls the run() method on the JobRunShell class.

CONFIGURING ALTERNATIVE ThreadPools

The Quartz framework enables you to change the ThreadPool implementation that is used. The alternative must implement the org.quartz.spi.ThreadPool interface, but the framework supports this through the use of configuration files. For example, you can use more advanced ThreadPool implementations that change the number of threads based on demand or even get the worker threads from an application server. For most users, the default implementation will suffice.

The JobRunShell run() Method

Although WorkerThreads are indeed Java threads, the JobRunShell class implements Runnable as well. That means that it can act as a thread and contains a run() method. As discussed earlier in the chapter, the purpose of the JobRunShell is to call the `execute()` method on a job. It does this and also notifies the job and trigger listeners, and it finishes by updating trigger information about the execution.

Understanding Quartz Triggers

Jobs contain the logic for the task to perform, but a job knows nothing about the time that it should be executed. This knowledge is left for the trigger. A Quartz trigger extends the abstract `org.quartz.Trigger` class. Currently, three Quartz triggers are available:

- `org.quartz.SimpleTrigger`
- `org.quartz.CronTrigger`
- `org.quartz.NthIncludedDayTrigger`

There is a fourth trigger, called `UICronTrigger`, but it has been deprecated in Quartz 1.5. It was primarily used by the Quartz Web application and is not used within Quartz itself.

Using the `org.quartz.SimpleTrigger`

Appropriately named, the `SimpleTrigger` is the simplest Quartz trigger to set up and use. It's designed to be used for jobs that need to start at a particular date/time and to repeat *n* number of times with a possible delay between each execution. Listing 4.9 provides an example that uses a `SimpleTrigger`.

Listing 4.9   Using a `SimpleTrigger` to Schedule a Job

```
public class Listing_4_9 {
    static Log logger = LogFactory.getLog(Listing_4_9.class);

    public static void main(String[] args) {
        Listing_4_9 example = new Listing_4_9();
        example.startScheduler();
    }

    public void startScheduler() {
        try {
            // Create and start the scheduler
            Scheduler scheduler =
                        StdSchedulerFactory.getDefaultScheduler();
            scheduler.start();
```

Listing 4.9 Continued

```
        logger.info("Scheduler has been started");

        JobDetail jobDetail =
                new JobDetail("PrintInfoJob",
                    Scheduler.DEFAULT_GROUP,
                        PrintInfoJob.class);

        /*
         * Create a SimpleTrigger that starts immediately,
         * with a null end date/time, repeats forever and has
         * 1 minute (60000 ms) between each firing.
         */
        Trigger trigger =
                new SimpleTrigger("myTrigger",
                        Scheduler.DEFAULT_GROUP, new Date(), null,
                            SimpleTrigger.REPEAT_INDEFINITELY,
                            60000L);

        scheduler.scheduleJob(jobDetail, trigger );

    } catch (SchedulerException ex) {
        logger.error(ex);
    }
  }
}
```

Several variations of the SimpleTrigger constructor exist. They range from the no-argument version all the way to one that takes a full set of arguments. This code fragment shows a simple constructor that takes just the name and group for the trigger:

```
// No Argument Constructor
SimpleTrigger sTrigger =
    new SimpleTrigger("myTrigger", Scheduler.DEFAULT_GROUP);
```

This trigger will execute immediately and will not repeat. There's also a constructor that takes several arguments and configures the trigger to fire at a particular time, repeat multiple times, and delay between each firing.

```
public SimpleTrigger(String name, String group,
    String jobName, String jobGroup, Date startTime,
    Date endTime, int repeatCount, long repeatInterval);
```

Using the org.quartz.CronTrigger

The CronTrigger allows for a much more complex firing schedule. Whereas you might have to use two or more

SimpleTriggers to meet your firing needs, you might need just a single CronTrigger instance.

As the name implies, the CronTrigger is based on UNIX cron-like expressions. For example, you might have a job that needs to be executed every five minutes between 8:00 AM and 9:00 AM on Monday and Friday. If you tried to implement this with a SimpleTrigger, you would probably end up with several triggers for the job. However, you can use an expression like this to produce a trigger that will fire on this schedule:

```
"0 0/5 8 ? * MON,FRI"

try {
    CronTrigger cTrigger = new CronTrigger("myTrigger",
            Scheduler.DEFAULT_GROUP, "0 0/5 8 ? *
MON,FRI");
} catch (ParseException ex) {
ex.printStackTrace();
}
```

Because CronTriggers have so much flexibility built into them by the nature of the almost limitless expressions that can be created, the next chapter focuses exclusively on everything you wanted to know about CronTriggers and cron expressions. Chapter 5, "CronTriggers and More," also presents a set of cookbook examples of how to create CronTriggers for specific firing schedules.

Using the org.quartz.NthIncludedDayTrigger

The org.quartz.NthIncludedDayTrigger is one of the newest triggers the Quartz development team added to the framework. It's designed to be used to execute a job on an *n*th day of every interval type. For example, if you needed to execute a job that performs invoicing on every 15th of the month, you could use NthIncludedDayTrigger to perform this feat. A Quartz Calendar can also be associated with the trigger to take weekends and holidays into account and move the days forward if necessary. The following fragment illustrates how to create a NthIncludedDayTrigger.

```
NthIncludedDayTrigger trigger =
    new NthIncludedDayTrigger(
        "MyTrigger", Scheduler.DEFAULT_GROUP);
            trigger.setN(15);

trigger.setIntervalType(
    NthIncludedDayTrigger.INTERVAL_TYPE_MONTHLY);
```

Using Multiple Triggers for a Job

You are not forced to live with just a single trigger per job. If you need a more complex firing schedule, you can create multiple triggers and assign them to the same job. The Scheduler determines the proper execution schedule based on all the triggers for the job. Using multiple triggers for the same JobDetail is shown in the following method fragment:

```
try {
    // Create and start the scheduler
    Scheduler scheduler =
        StdSchedulerFactory.getDefaultScheduler();
    scheduler.start();
    logger.info("Scheduler has been started");

    JobDetail jobDetail =
        new JobDetail("PrintInfoJob",
            Scheduler.DEFAULT_GROUP,
            PrintInfoJob.class);

    // A trigger that fires every 5 seconds
    Trigger trigger1 =
        TriggerUtils.makeSecondlyTrigger("trigger1",
            5000, SimpleTrigger.REPEAT_INDEFINITELY);

    // A trigger that fires every 10 minutes
    Trigger trigger2 =
        TriggerUtils.makeMinutelyTrigger("trigger2", 10,
            SimpleTrigger.REPEAT_INDEFINITELY);

    // Schedule job with first trigger
    scheduler.scheduleJob(jobDetail, trigger1);

    // Schedule job with second trigger
    scheduler.scheduleJob(jobDetail, trigger1);

} catch (SchedulerException ex) {
    logger.error(ex);
}
```

> **ONE JOB PER TRIGGER**
> Although a single `JobDetail` can support multiple triggers, a trigger can be assigned to only a single job.

The Quartz Calendar

Don't confuse the Quartz Calendar object with the `java.util.Calendar` in the Java API. They are two different components and are used for two different purposes. As you are probably aware, Java's Calendar object is used for general-purpose Date and Time utilities; much of the functionality that used to reside in Java's `Date` class now resides within the Calendar classes.

The Quartz Calendar, on the other hand, is used exclusively to block out sections of time so that triggers are prevented from firing during those blocked-out periods. For example, let's assume that you work for a financial institution such as a bank. It's very common for banks to have many "bank holidays." Suppose you don't need (or want) the jobs to run on those days. You can accomplish this in one of several ways:

- Let your jobs run anyway. (This might mess things up for the bank.)

- Manually stop your jobs during the holidays. (Someone would need to be there to do it.)

- Create multiple triggers that don't include these days. (This would be time-consuming to set up and maintain.)

- Set up a bank holiday calendar that excludes these days. (Very easy to do!)

Although you could use each of these solutions to solve the problem, the Quartz Calendar is specifically designed for this.

The `org.quartz.Calendar` Interface

Quartz defines the `org.quartz.Calendar` interface that all Quartz Calendars must implement. It contains several methods, but these are the two most important ones:

```
public long getNextIncludedTime(long timeStamp);
public boolean isTimeIncluded(long timeStamp);
```

GRANULARITY OF CALENDAR EXCLUDED TIMES

The parameter types for the Calendar interface are of type Long. This means that the Quartz Calendar is capable of excluding times down to the millisecond level. You will most likely never need to get that granular because most jobs exclude particular days or maybe hours. If you need to exclude at the millisecond level, however, this capability is there for you.

As a Quartz job creator and developer, you don't necessarily need to be that familiar with the Calendar interface. It's mainly for situations for which the existing Calendars (those that come with Quartz) are not sufficient. Out of the box, Quartz includes many Calendar implementations that should fill your needs. Table 4.1 lists the Calendars that come with Quartz ready to use.

Table 4.1   Quartz Includes Many Calendar Types That Your Applications Can Use

Calendar Name	Class	Usage
BaseCalendar	org.quartz.impl.calendar.BaseCalendar	Implements base functionality for more advanced Calendars. Implements the org.quartz.Calendar interface.
WeeklyCalendar	org.quartz.impl.calendar.WeeklyCalendar	Excludes one or more days of the week—for example, can be used to exclude weekends.

Calendar Name	Class	Usage
MonthlyCalendar	org.quartz.impl.calendar.MonthlyCalendar	Excludes days of the month—for example, can be used to exclude the last day of every month.
AnnualCalendar	org.quartz.impl.calendar.AnnualCalendar	Excludes one or more days during the year.
HolidayCalendar	org.quartz.impl.calendar.HolidayCalendar	Made especially to exclude holidays from the trigger.

Using Quartz Calendars

To use a Quartz Calendar, you simply need to instantiate one, add your excluded dates to it, and then register it with the Scheduler. Finally, associate the Calendar instance with each trigger instance that you want to use the Calendar with.

USING A CALENDAR FOR MULTIPLE JOBS

You can't schedule the Calendar for all jobs just by adding it to the Scheduler. You need to associate the Calendar instance with each trigger. Adding the Calendar instance to the Scheduler allows it to be stored only with the JobStore in use; you must attach the Calendar to the trigger instance.

Listing 4.10 shows an example of excluding bank holidays using the Quartz AnnualCalendar class.

Listing 4.10   Using the AnnualCalendar to Exclude Bank Holidays

```
public class Listing_4_10 {
    static Log logger = LogFactory.getLog(Listing_4_10.class);

    public static void main(String[] args) {
        Listing_4_10 example = new Listing_4_10();
        example.startScheduler();
    }

    public void startScheduler() {
        try {
            // Create and start the scheduler
            Scheduler scheduler =
                        StdSchedulerFactory.getDefaultScheduler();
```

Listing 4.10   Continued

```
            scheduler.start();

            scheduleJob(scheduler, PrintInfoJob.class);

            logger.info("Scheduler starting up...");
            scheduler.start();

        } catch (SchedulerException ex) {
            logger.error(ex);
        }
    }

    private void scheduleJob(Scheduler scheduler, Class jobClass) {
        try {
            // Create an instance of the Quartz AnnualCalendar
            AnnualCalendar cal = new AnnualCalendar();

            // exclude July 4th
            Calendar gCal = GregorianCalendar.getInstance();
            gCal.set(Calendar.MONTH, Calendar.JULY);
            gCal.set(Calendar.DATE, 4);

            cal.setDayExcluded(gCal, true);

            // Add to scheduler, replace existing, update triggers
            scheduler.
                        addCalendar("bankHolidays", cal, true, true);

            /*
                * Set up a trigger to start firing now, repeat forever
                * and have (60000 ms) between each firing.
             */
            Trigger trigger =
                        TriggerUtils.makeImmediateTrigger("myTrigger",
                -1,60000);

            // Trigger will use Calendar to exclude firing times
            trigger.setCalendarName("bankHolidays");

            JobDetail jobDetail =
                        new JobDetail(jobClass.getName(),
                    Scheduler.DEFAULT_GROUP, jobClass);

            // Associate the trigger with the job in the scheduler
            scheduler.scheduleJob(jobDetail, trigger);

        } catch (SchedulerException ex) {
            logger.error(ex);
        }
    }
}
```

When you run the example from Listing 4.10, unless it's July 4, you should see the job execute. As an exercise that's left for you to do, change the excluded date in the scheduleJob()

method to the current date that you're reading this. If you run
the code again, you should see that the current date has been
excluded and the next firing time will be tomorrow.

WHY DIDN'T WE USE HolidayCalendar?

You might be wondering why we didn't choose to use the HolidayCalendar in the previous
example. The HolidayCalendar class takes year into account. So if you wanted to exclude
July 4 for the next 3 years, you would need to add each one of those entries in as an
excluded date. AnnualCalendar simply excludes dates for every year and was much easier
to use in this case.

Creating Your Own Calendars

This last section demonstrates how easy it is to create your own
Calendar class. Suppose that you need a Calendar to exclude
certain minutes of the hour. For example, suppose you need to
exclude the first five minutes of every hour or the last 15 minutes of every hour. You can create a new Calendar to support
this functionality.

WE COULD PROBABLY USE A CronTrigger

We could probably come up with a cron expression to exclude these times, but that takes
the fun out of creating a new Calendar class.

Listing 4.11 shows the HourlyCalendar that we can use to
exclude sets of minutes from the hour.

Listing 4.11   The HourlyCalendar Can Exclude Certain Minutes from Every Hour

```
public class HourlyCalendar extends BaseCalendar {

    // Array of Integer from 0 to 59
    private List excludedMinutes = new ArrayList();

    public HourlyCalendar() {
        super();
    }
```

Listing 4.11 Continued

```java
    public HourlyCalendar(Calendar baseCalendar) {
        super(baseCalendar);
    }

    public List getMinutesExcluded() {
        return excludedMinutes;
    }

    public boolean isMinuteExcluded(int minute) {

        Iterator iter = excludedMinutes.iterator();
        while (iter.hasNext()) {
            Integer excludedMin = (Integer) iter.next();

            if (minute == excludedMin.intValue()) {
                return true;
            }

            continue;
        }
        return false;
    }

    public void setMinutesExcluded(List minutes) {
        if (minutes == null)
            return;

        excludedMinutes.addAll(minutes);
    }

    public void setMinuteExcluded(int minute) {
        if (isMinuteExcluded(minute))
            return;

        excludedMinutes.add(new Integer(minute));
    }

    public boolean isTimeIncluded(long timeStamp) {

        if (super.isTimeIncluded(timeStamp) == false) {
            return false;
        }

        java.util.Calendar cal = getJavaCalendar(timeStamp);
        int minute = cal.get(java.util.Calendar.MINUTE);

        return !(isMinuteExcluded(minute));
    }


    public long getNextIncludedTime(long timeStamp) {
        // Call base calendar implementation first
        long baseTime = super.getNextIncludedTime(timeStamp);
        if ((baseTime > 0) && (baseTime > timeStamp))
            timeStamp = baseTime;

        // Get timestamp for 00:00:00
        long newTimeStamp = buildHoliday(timeStamp);
```

Listing 4.11   Continued

```java
        java.util.Calendar cal = getJavaCalendar(newTimeStamp);
        int minute = cal.get(java.util.Calendar.MINUTE);

        if (isMinuteExcluded(minute) == false)
            return timeStamp; // return the
        // original value

        while (isMinuteExcluded(minute) == true) {
            cal.add(java.util.Calendar.MINUTE, 1);
        }

        return cal.getTime().getTime();
    }
}
```

If you use the HourlyCalendar to schedule a job, all you need to do is set the minutes of the hour that you want to exclude; the Calendar and the Scheduler do the rest. You can see the HourlyCalendar demonstrated in Listing 4.12.

Listing 4.12   The HourlyCalendar Executes Based on Certain Excluded Minutes of the Hour

```java
public class Listing_4_12 {
    static Log logger = LogFactory.getLog(Listing_4_12.class);

    public static void main(String[] args) {
        Listing_4_12 example = new Listing_4_12();
        example.startScheduler();
    }

    public void startScheduler() {
        try {
            // Create a default instance of the Scheduler
            Scheduler scheduler =
                    StdSchedulerFactory.getDefaultScheduler();

            // Using the NoOpJob, but could have been any
            scheduleJob(scheduler, PrintInfoJob.class);

            logger.info("Scheduler starting up...");
            scheduler.start();

        } catch (SchedulerException ex) {
            logger.error(ex);
        }
    }

    private void scheduleJob(Scheduler scheduler, Class jobClass) {
        try {
            // Create an instance of the Quartz AnnualCalendar
            HourlyCalendar cal = new HourlyCalendar();
```

Listing 4.12   Continued

```
          cal.setMinuteExcluded(47);
          cal.setMinuteExcluded(48);
          cal.setMinuteExcluded(49);
          cal.setMinuteExcluded(50);

          // Add Calendar to the Scheduler
          scheduler.
                  addCalendar("hourlyExample", cal, true, true);

          Trigger trigger =
                  TriggerUtils.makeImmediateTrigger("myTrigger",
                  -1, 10000);

          // Trigger will use Calendar to exclude firing times
          trigger.setCalendarName("hourlyExample");

          JobDetail jobDetail =
                  new JobDetail(jobClass.getName(),
                  Scheduler.DEFAULT_GROUP, jobClass);

          // Associate the trigger with the job in the scheduler
          scheduler.scheduleJob(jobDetail, trigger);

      } catch (SchedulerException ex) {
          logger.error(ex);
      }
    }
}
```

When you run Listing 4.12, you should see that the PrintInfoJob is not executed during the excluded minutes. Change the minutes that are excluded using the setMinuteExcluded() method and see for yourself how the new Calendar works.

## CHAPTER 5

CRON TRIGGERS AND MORE

We promised in the last chapter that we would spend more time on the Quartz `CronTrigger`, and we won't let you down. `SimpleTriggers` are fine for jobs that need to execute at a specified millisecond in time, but if your jobs require more complex execution schedules, you need the power and flexibility that `CronTriggers` offer.

Quick Lesson in Cron

The idea of cron comes from the UNIX world. In UNIX, cron is a daemon that runs in the background and is responsible for all timed events. Although Quartz shares nothing with UNIX cron other than the name and similar expression syntax, it's worth spending a couple of paragraphs to understand the history behind cron. Our goal here is not to confuse UNIX cron expressions and Quartz cron expressions, but you should understand the history behind the Quartz expressions and explore why they look like they do. There is obviously a great deal of intentional similarity.

MANY DIFFERENT VERSIONS OF UNIX CRON

You'll find different versions of cron, each with slightly different features. We're interested only in comparing against the Quartz CronTrigger, so we generalize the various UNIX versions of cron for our discussion.

The UNIX cron daemon wakes up every minute and examines the configuration files, which are called *crontabs*. (*Crontab* comes from the phrase CRON TABle, which is a list of jobs and other instructions for the cron daemon.) The daemon inspects the commands that are stored within the crontabs and determines whether any tasks need to be executed.

UNIX Cron Format

You can think of the UNIX crontab as a combination of triggers and jobs because they list both the execution schedule and the command (job) to be executed.

THE CRON EXPRESSION FORMAT

The crontab format contains six fields—five for the schedule and the sixth for the command to execute. (Quartz cron expression has seven fields.) These are the five schedule fields:

- Minute (00–59)
- Hour (00–23)

- Day (1-31)
- Month (1-12)
- Weekday (0-6 or sun-sat)

The UNIX cron format allows for a few special characters in the cron expression, such as the asterisk character (*), which matches all values. Here's an example of a UNIX crontab:

```
0 8 * * * echo "WAKE UP" 2>$1 /dev/console
```

This crontab entry prints the string "WAKE UP" to the UNIX device /dev/console every morning at 8 AM. Figure 5.1 shows it in action.

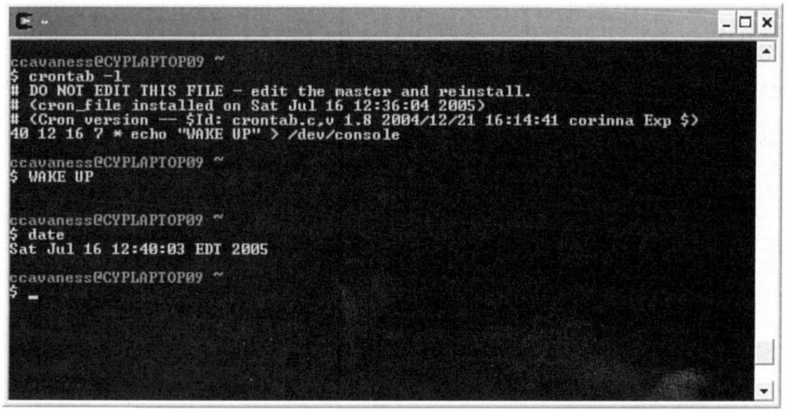

FIGURE 5.1   The UNIX Cron executing the 0 8 * * * echo "WAKE UP" 2>$1 /dev/console expression

Using the Quartz CronTrigger

In the real world, job schedules are normally much more complex than SimpleTriggers will support. CronTriggers can be used to specify very complicated schedules, which is good because those are usually the ones we find we need. Before we get into the details of what makes a CronTrigger tick, let's look at an example. Listing 5.1 shows an example of using a CronTrigger (along with a Quartz cron expression) to schedule the PrintInfoJob from previous examples. For the most part, this code is identical to the examples in the previous chapter. The only difference is that we are using a CronTrigger instead of a SimpleTrigger. Because of that, we have to supply it with a cron expression.

Listing 5.1   Simple Use of CronTrigger to Schedule a Job

```
public class Listing_5_1 {
    static Log logger = LogFactory.getLog(Listing_5_1.class);

    public static void main(String[] args) {
        Listing_5_1 example = new Listing_5_1();
        example.runScheduler();
    }

    public void runScheduler() {
        Scheduler scheduler = null;

        try {
            // Create a default instance of the Scheduler
            scheduler = StdSchedulerFactory.getDefaultScheduler();
            scheduler.start();
            logger.info("Scheduler was started at " + new Date());

            // Create the JobDetail
            JobDetail jobDetail =
                        new JobDetail("PrintInfoJob",
                    Scheduler.DEFAULT_GROUP,
                            PrintInfoJob.class);

            // Create a CronTrigger
            try {
                // CronTrigger that fires @7:30am Mon - Fri
                CronTrigger trigger = new
                            CronTrigger("CronTrigger", null,
                    "0 30 7 ? * MON-FRI");

                scheduler.scheduleJob(jobDetail, trigger);
            } catch (ParseException ex) {
                logger.error("Error parsing cron expr", ex);
            }

        } catch (SchedulerException ex) {
            logger.error(ex);
        }
    }
}
```

The example in Listing 5.1 uses the following cron expression:

```
0 30 7 ? * MON-FRI
```

When interpreted by the Scheduler, this causes the trigger to fire at 7:30 AM Monday through Friday. Let's look at the format of the cron expression for Quartz `CronTriggers`.

The Cron Expression Format

The format of the Quartz cron expression is very similar to the UNIX cron format, with a few very clear differences. One of the differences is that the Quartz format supports schedules down to the second, whereas the UNIX cron supports schedules only to the minute. Many of our firing schedules are based on second-level increments (for example, every 45 seconds), so this is a very nice difference.

With UNIX cron, the job (or command) that is to be executed is stored with the cron expression, in the sixth position. Quartz uses the cron expression to store the firing schedule. The `CronTrigger`, which references the cron expression, is associated with the job at schedule time.

Another difference between the UNIX cron expression format and Quartz is the number of supported fields in the expression. Where UNIX gives five (`minute`, `hour`, `day`, `month`, and `dayofweek`), Quartz provides seven. Table 5.1 lists the seven cron expression fields Quartz supports.

Table 5.1   Quartz Cron Expressions Support up to Seven Fields

Name	Required	Allowed Values	Special Characters
Seconds	Yes	0–59	, – * /
Minutes	Yes	0–59	, – * /
Hours	Yes	0–23	, – * /
Day of Month	Yes	1–31	, – * ? / L W C
Month	Yes	1–12 or JAN–DEC	, – * /
Day of Week	Yes	1–7 or SUN–SAT	, – * ? / L C #
Year	No	Blank or 1970–2099	, – * /

The names of months and days of the week are not case sensitive. FRI *is the same as* fri.

The fields are separated by a space, just as with UNIX cron. Arguably, the simplest expression we could write would look something like this:

```
* * * ? * *
```

This expression would fire the scheduled job every second, for every minute, for every hour of every day.

Understanding the Special Characters

As with UNIX cron, Quartz cron expressions support special characters that can be used to create more complicated execution schedules. However, Quartz supports many more than the standard UNIX cron expression.

THE * CHARACTER

Using the asterisk (*) in a field indicates that you want to include all legal values for that field. For example, using this character in the month field means to fire the trigger for every month.

Example expression:

```
0 * 17 * * ?
```

Meaning: Fire the trigger every minute, every day starting at 5 PM until 5:59 PM. It stops at 5:59 PM because the value 17 is in the hour field, and at 6 PM, the hour becomes 18 and doesn't agree with this trigger until the next day at 5 PM.

Use the * character when you want the trigger to fire for every valid value of the field.

THE ? CHARACTER

The question mark (?) character can be used only in the dayofmonth and dayofweek fields, but not at the same time. You can think of the ? character as "I don't care what value is in this field." This is different from the asterisk, which indicates every value for the field. The ? character says that no value was specified for this field.

The reasons a value can't be specified for both fields are tough to explain and even tougher to understand. Basically, if a value was specified for each, the meaning would become ambiguous: Consider if an expression had the value 11 in a field for the day of the month and a value of WED in the field for the day of the week. Should that trigger fire only on the 11th of the month if it falls on a Wednesday? Or should it fire on both the 11th and every Wednesday? The ambiguity is removed by not allowing a value in both fields at the same time.

Just remember that if you specify a value in one of the two fields, you must put a ? in the other.

Example expression:

`0 10,44 14 ? 3 WED`

Meaning: Fire at 2:10 PM and 2:44 PM every Wednesday in the month of March.

THE , CHARACTER

The comma (,) character is used to specify a list of additional values within a given field. For example, using the value 0,15,30,45 in the second field means to fire the trigger every 15 seconds.

Example expression:

`0 0,15,30,45 * * ?`

Meaning: Fire the trigger on every quarter-hour.

THE / CHARACTER

The slash (/) character is used to schedule increments. We just used the comma to increment every 15 minutes, but we could have also written it like 0/15.

Example expression:

`0/15 0/30 * * ?`

Meaning: Fire the trigger every 15 seconds on the hour and half-hour.

You can't increment beyond the fields range. For example, you can't specify 30/20 in the second field and expect the scheduler to fire correctly.

THE – CHARACTER

The hyphen (-) character is used to specify a range. For example, 3-8 in the hour field means "the hours 3, 4, 5, 6, 7, and 8." The fields will not wrap, so values such as 50-10 are not allowed.

Example expression:

0 45 3-8 ? * *

Meaning: Fire the trigger on 45 past the hours 3 AM through 8 AM.

THE L CHARACTER

The L character represents the *last* allowed value for the field. It is supported by the dayofmonth and dayofweek fields only. When used in the dayofmonth field, it represents the last day of the month for the value specified in the month field. For example, when the month field has JAN specified, using L in the dayofmonth field would cause the trigger to fire on January 31. If SEP was specified as the month, then L would mean to fire on September 30. In order words, it means to fire the trigger on the last day of whatever month is specified.

The expression 0 0 8 L * ? means to fire the trigger at 8:00 AM the last day of every month. The * character in the month field gives us the "every month" part.

When the L character is used in the dayofweek field, it indicates the last day of the week, which is Saturday (or, numerically, 7). So if you needed to fire the trigger on the last Saturday of every month at 11:59 PM, you could use the expression 0 59 23 ? * L.

When used in the dayofweek field, you can use a numerical value in conjunction with the L character to represent the last *X* day of the month. For example, the expression 0 0 12 ? * 2L says to fire the trigger on the last Monday of every month.

> ### DON'T USE RANGE OR LIST OPTIONS WITH THE L CHARACTER
>
> Although you can use a day of the week (1-7) value in conjunction with the L character, you're not allowed you to use a range of values or a list with it. This will produce unpredicted results.

THE W CHARACTER

The W character stands for weekday (Mon–Fri) and can be used only in the dayofmonth field. It is used to specify the weekday that is nearest to the given day. Most business processes are based on the work week, so the W character can be very important. For example, a value of 15W in the dayofmonth field means "the nearest weekday to the 15th of the month." If the 15th was on a Saturday, the trigger would fire on Friday the 14th because it's closer to the 15th than Monday, which would be the 17th in this example. The W character can be specified only when the day of the month is a single day, not a range or list of days.

THE # CHARACTER

The # character can be used only in the dayofweek field. It's used to specify the *n*th *XXX* day of the month. For example, if you specified the value 6#3 in the dayofweek field, it would mean the third Friday of the month (6 = Friday and #3 means the third one in the month). Another example of 2#1 means the first Monday of the month (2 = Monday and #1 means the first one of the month). Note that if you specify #5 and there is no 5 of the given day of the week in the month, no firing will occur that month.

Using Start and End Dates with CronTrigger

The cron expression is used to determine the dates and times that a trigger will fire and execute a job. When you create the CronTrigger instance, if you don't provide a begin time, the trigger assumes that it can begin firing as early as the current

date/time—depending on the cron expression, of course. For
example, if you used the expression

```
0 * 14-20 * * ?
```

the trigger would fire every minute from 2 PM to 7:59 PM,
every day. As soon as you ran the CronTrigger for this expression, if it was after 2 PM, it would start firing. It would do this
every day indefinitely.

On the other hand, if you wanted this schedule to not start
until the next day and to continue for only a couple days, you
could use the setStartTime() and setEndTime() methods on
the CronTrigger to "time box" the firings. Listing 5.2 illustrates an example that confines the CronTrigger to just a
couple days.

Listing 5.2   You Can Use startTime and endTime with a CronTrigger

```
public class Listing_5_2 {
    static Log logger = LogFactory.getLog(Listing_5_2.class);

    public static void main(String[] args) {
        Listing_5_2 example = new Listing_5_2();
        example.runScheduler();
    }

    public void runScheduler() {
        Scheduler scheduler = null;

        try {
            // Create a default instance of the Scheduler
            scheduler = StdSchedulerFactory.getDefaultScheduler();
            scheduler.start();
            logger.info("Scheduler was started at " + new Date());

            // Create the JobDetail
            JobDetail jobDetail = new JobDetail("PrintInfoJob",
                    Scheduler.DEFAULT_GROUP,
                            PrintInfoJob.class);

            // Create a CronTrigger
            try {
                // cron that fires every min from 2 - 8pm
                CronTrigger trigger =
                                new CronTrigger("MyTrigger", null,
                                    "0 * 14-20 * * ?");

                Calendar cal = Calendar.getInstance();
                // Set the date to 1 day from now
                cal.add(Calendar.DATE, 1);
```

Listing 5.2   Continued

```
                    trigger.setStartTime(cal.getTime());

                    // Move ahead 2 days to set the end time
                    cal.add(Calendar.DATE, 2);
                    trigger.setEndTime(cal.getTime());

                    scheduler.scheduleJob(jobDetail, trigger);
            } catch (ParseException ex) {
                logger.error("Couldn't parse cron expr", ex);
            }

        } catch (SchedulerException ex) {
            logger.error(ex);
        }
    }
}
```

The example in Listing 5.2 uses the `java.utl.Calendar` to select a begin time and end time period for the trigger. In the case of this example, the trigger will start firing the day after it's scheduled and will fire for only two days after it starts to fire.

Use the `startTime` and `endTime` properties of the `CronTrigger` just as you would for `SimpleTriggers`.

Using `TriggerUtils` with the `CronTrigger`

Chapter 4, "Scheduling Jobs," introduced the `TriggerUtils` class in the `org.quartz` package, which simplifies the creation of triggers of both types. When possible, you should attempt to use the methods within the `TriggerUtils` class to create your triggers.

For example, if you needed to execute a job every day at 5:30 PM, you could use the following code:

```
try {

    // A CronTrigger that fires @ 5:30PM
    CronTrigger trigger =
new CronTrigger("CronTrigger", null, "0 30 17 ? * *");

} catch (ParseException ex) {
logger.error("Couldn't parse cron expression", ex);
}
```

Or you could use the `TriggerUtils` like this:

```
// A CronTrigger that fires @ 5:30PM
Trigger trigger = TriggerUtils.makeDailyTrigger(17, 30);
trigger.setName("CronTrigger");
```

`TriggerUtils` makes it easier and more convenient to use triggers, without giving up too much of the flexibility.

Using `CronTriggers` in the `JobInitializationPlugin`

Although plug-ins are not discussed until Chapter 8, "Using Quartz Plug-Ins," it's worth jumping ahead to show how `CronTriggers` can be used within the `quartz_jobs.xml` file to specify job information. The `JobInitializationPlugin` can be used to load job information from an XML file.

Just as with `SimpleTriggers`, you can specify `CronTrigger` expressions in the XML file, and the Quartz Scheduler will use this information to schedule your jobs. This is extremely convenient if you want to declare your job information externally to your application code. Listing 5.3 shows the `quartz_jobs.xml` file that is used with the `JobInitializationPlugin` to load job information.

Listing 5.3   CronTriggers Can Be Specified in an XML File and Loaded with the
JobInitializationPlugin

```xml
<?xml version='1.0' encoding='utf-8'?>

<quartz>
  <job>
    <job-detail>
      <name>PrintInfoJob</name>
     <group>DEFAULT</group>
     <description>
       A job that prints out some basic information.
     </description>
     <job-class>
       org.cavaness.quartzbook.common.PrintInfoJob
     </job-class>
    </job-detail>

    <trigger>
```

Listing 5.3   Continued

```
    <cron>
     <name>printJobInfoTrigger</name>
     <group>DEFAULT</group>
     <job-name>PrintInfoJob</job-name>
     <job-group>DEFAULT</job-group>

     <!- Fire 7:30am Monday through Friday ->
     <cron-expression>0 30 7 ? * MON-FRI</cron-expression>
    </cron>
   </trigger>
  </job>
</quartz>
```

The cron expression shown in Listing 5.3 is the same one from Listing 5.1. When Quartz loads the XML file, it will schedule the PrintInfoJob (also listed in the XML file) to execute at 7:30 AM Monday through Friday. More is said about the JobInitializationPlugin in Chapter 8.

Cron Expressions Cookbook

The purpose of this cron expression cookbook is to provide solutions for very specific execution needs. Although it's not possible to show every expression, the ones listed here should provide you with enough examples to meet your business needs. We have separated the expressions into tables based on frequency.

Minute Cron Expressions

Table 5.2   Cron Expressions for Schedules That Involve a Minute Frequency

Usage	Expression
Fire every minute, starting at 5 PM and ending at 5:59 PM, every day	0 * 17 * * ?
Fire every 5 minutes, starting at 11 PM and ending at 11:55 PM, every day	0 0/5 23 * * ?
Fire every 5 minutes, starting at 3 PM and ending at 2:55 PM, and fire every 5 minutes starting at 6 PM and ending at 6:55 PM, every day	0 0/5 15,18 * * ?
Fire every minute, starting at 5 AM and ending at 5:05 AM, every day	0 0-5 5 * * ?

Daily Cron Expressions

Table 5.2   Cron Expressions for Schedules Based on a Daily Frequency

Usage	Expression
Every day at 3:00 AM	0 0 3 * * ?
Every day at 3:00 AM (alternate format)	0 0 3 ? * *
Every day at 12 PM (noon)	0 0 12 * * ?
Fire at 10:15 AM every day during the year 2005	0 15 10 * * ? 2005

Weekly and Monthly Cron Expressions

Table 5.3   Cron Expressions for Schedules That Are Based on a Weekly and/or Monthly Frequency

Usage	Expression
Fire at 10:15 AM every Monday, Tuesday, Wednesday, Thursday, and Friday	0 15 10 ? * MON-FRI
Fire at 10:15 AM on the 15th day of every month	0 15 10 15 * ?
Fire at 10:15 AM on the last day of every month	0 15 10 L * ?
Fire at 10:15 AM on the last Friday of every month	0 15 10 ? * 6L
Fire at 10:15 AM on every last Friday of every month during the years 2002, 2003, 2004, and 2005	0 15 10 ? * 6L 2002-2005
Fire at 10:15 AM on the third Friday of every month	0 15 10 ? * 6#3
Fire at 12 PM (noon) every 5 days every month, starting on the first day of the month	0 0 12 1/5 * ?
Fire every November 11 at 11:11 am	0 11 11 11 11 ?
Fire at 2:10 PM and at 2:44 PM every Wednesday in the month of March	0 10,44 14 ? 3 WED

Creating a Fire-Now Trigger

Sometimes you need to execute a job immediately. For example, imagine that you're building a GUI that allows users to execute jobs right away. As another example, you might have detected that a job didn't complete successfully, so you want to rerun the job immediately. In Quartz 1.5, several methods were added to

the `TriggerUtils` class to make that easier. Listing 5.4 shows
how to schedule a job to run only once, right away.

Listing 5.4   You Can Use the `TriggerUtils` to Execute an Immediate Job

```java
public class Listing_5_4 {
    static Log logger = LogFactory.getLog(Listing_5_4.class);

    public static void main(String[] args) {
        Listing_5_4 example = new Listing_5_4();
        example.runScheduler();
    }

    public void runScheduler() {
        Scheduler scheduler = null;

        try {
            // Create a default instance of the Scheduler
            scheduler = StdSchedulerFactory.getDefaultScheduler();
            scheduler.start();
            logger.info("Scheduler was started at " + new Date());

            // Create the JobDetail
            JobDetail jobDetail =
                        new JobDetail("PrintInfoJob",
                                Scheduler.DEFAULT_GROUP,
                                PrintInfoJob.class);

            // Create a trigger that fires once right away
            Trigger trigger =
                        TriggerUtils.makeImmediateTrigger(0, 0);

            trigger.setName("FireOnceNowTrigger");

            scheduler.scheduleJob(jobDetail, trigger);
        } catch (SchedulerException ex) {
            logger.error(ex);
        }
    }
}
```

In Listing 5.4, the `makeImmediateTrigger()` method of
`TriggerUtils` is used to execute an immediate job. The first
parameter is the number of times the trigger will fire. The second parameter is the interval between the executions. The
method signature is shown here for convenience:

```java
public static Trigger
    makeImmediateTrigger(int repeatCount,
    ➥long repeatInterval);
```

The `TriggerUtils` class offers many convenience methods for simplifying the use of triggers. Be sure to check this utility class first to see if it has what you need. You'll see more examples of the `TriggerUtils` class throughout the book.

## CHAPTER 6

JOBSTORES AND PERSISTENCE

Quartz uses `JobStores` to provide a storage mechanism for jobs, triggers, calendars, and Scheduler data. The Scheduler uses the configured `JobStore` to store and retrieve scheduling information and to determine its responsibilities for triggering jobs. All knowledge about which jobs to execute and on what schedule to execute them comes from the `JobStore`. This chapter looks at the various types of `JobStores` available in Quartz—how to use each one and which one makes sense for your requirements.

"Rome wasn't burned in a day."

—Douglas Adams, Hitchhiker's Guide to the Universe

Job Storage

In the previous chapters, we didn't spend any time discussing where the job and trigger information for the Scheduler was stored. You might have realized, however, that when you stopped the Scheduler, the knowledge of which jobs had run and which ones had not was lost. In fact, all the information about the running jobs was destroyed.

When the application was restarted, the trigger and job information was added back, and everything was fine again. Suppose, however, that a job was scheduled for execution at 5 PM and the Scheduler was stopped five minutes before that time, at 4:55 PM. What would happen if you restarted the Scheduler at 5:05 PM? Would the Scheduler remember that it was supposed to fire the job at 5 PM? The answer is that it depends on which type of JobStore you're using and how you have it configured.

Job Storage in Quartz

Quartz supports several different types of storage mechanisms for Scheduler information. Two types of Job storage are available in Quartz:

- Memory (nonpersistent) storage
- Persistent storage

By default, we've been using the memory storage mechanism in the examples from the past several chapters. Both types are designed to serve the same purpose: to store job information. How they each go about it, however, and what functionality they provide the Scheduler is very different.

The JobStore Interface

Quartz provides an interface for all types of job storage. The interface located in the org.quartz.spi package is called JobStore. All job storage mechanisms, regardless of where or how they store their information, must implement this interface.

The JobStore interface has too many methods to list here, but the API for the JobStore interface can be generalized into the following categories:

- Job-related API
- Trigger-related API
- Calendar-related API
- Scheduler-related API

Quartz users almost never access or see concrete classes that implement the `JobStore` interface; they are used internally by the Quartz Scheduler to retrieve job and trigger information during runtime. It is a worthwhile exercise, however, to familiarize yourself with each type so that you better understand the facilities these provide on your behalf and to choose the right one for your Quartz application.

Using Memory to Store Scheduler Information

Out of the box, Quartz is configured to store job and trigger information in memory. This explains why, for the examples in the past several chapters, every time we restarted the Quartz application, the Scheduler state, including job and trigger information, was lost. Each time the Java Virtual Machine (JVM) is halted, its memory is released back to the operating system, and any information about jobs and triggers is lost with it.

The memory job storage facility for Quartz is provided by a class called `org.quartz.simpl.RAMJobStore`, which, as we said, implements the `JobStore` interface. The `RAMJobStore` is the out-of-the-box solution for Quartz. By this, we mean that unless you change the configuration, this is the `JobStore` that will be used for any Quartz application. Using this `JobStore` over the others brings several advantages.

First, the `RAMJobStore` is the easiest `JobStore` to configure: It's already configured for you. When you download and install Quartz, it's configured to use the `RAMJobStore` as the storage mechanism. You can see this in the default `quartz.properties` file, shown in Listing 6.1.

Listing 6.1   Default `quartz.properties` File When No Other Is Configured

```
# Default Properties file for use by StdSchedulerFactory
# to create a Quartz Scheduler Instance, if a different
# properties file is not explicitly specified.

org.quartz.scheduler.instanceName = DefaultQuartzScheduler
org.quartz.scheduler.rmi.export = false
org.quartz.scheduler.rmi.proxy = false
org.quartz.scheduler.wrapJobExecutionInUserTransaction = false
```

Listing 6.1   Continued

```
org.quartz.threadPool.class = org.quartz.simpl.SimpleThreadPool
org.quartz.threadPool.threadCount = 10
org.quartz.threadPool.threadPriority = 5
org.quartz.threadPool.threadsInheritContextClassLoaderOfInitializingThread = true

org.quartz.jobStore.misfireThreshold = 60000

org.quartz.jobStore.class = org.quartz.simpl.RAMJobStore
```

Listing 6.1 shows the default `quartz.properties` file that is included with the Quartz binary. When you don't include a `quartz.properties` file of your own in your application, this is the properties file that gets used. You can see from the last line in the default `quartz.properties` file that the `RAMJobStore` is the default value for the configuration property named `org.quartz.jobstore.class`. Even if the `org.quartz.jobstore.class` property is not set in `quartz.properties`, the `RAMJobStore` is the default `JobStore` that is used. This is hardwired into the Scheduler factory initialization routine.

Another advantage to using the `RAMJobStore` is its speed. Because all the Scheduler information is stored in the computer's memory, accessing this data is as fast as it gets. There are no out-of-process calls, no database connections—just plain old simple memory access. It doesn't get any better.

Job Volatility with RAMJobStore

You might remember from Chapter 4, "Scheduling Jobs," that jobs can be configured with a volatility property. When the volatility property is set to `false`, the job will be persisted between application shutdowns. This is not true when the `RAMJobStore` is being used; that behavior is explicitly reserved for persistent `JobStores`.

Configuring the RAMJobStore

Configuring your Quartz application to use the `RAMJobStore` is extremely easy. If you are using a custom `quartz.properties` file, not the one that comes with the Quartz JAR file, add this line to your properties file:

```
org.quartz.jobStore.class = org.quartz.simpl.RAMJobStore
```

That's all you have to do to use the RAMJobStore. As we said, it doesn't get any easier.

Loading Jobs into the RAMJobStore

If the purpose of the RAMJobStore is to store Scheduler information, how does that information get loaded into memory in the first place? You can load job information in two ways. First, you can hardcode your jobs, triggers, calendars, and listeners into the code itself. As Chapters 3, "Hello, Quartz," and 4, "Scheduling Jobs," pointed out, however, this is always a dangerous thing to do because maintenance can become a nightmare. Any change, regardless of how trivial it is, requires a code change and recompile. Even if the change is a change to the firing times, code has to be modified and recompiled. Not a big deal, you say? That might be true for small, trivial applications, but this can become a real problem for larger numbers of jobs and triggers.

The second approach is to use the JobInitialization-Plugin, which is discussed in detail in Chapter 8, "Using Quartz Plug-Ins." This Quartz plug-in uses an XML file to load jobs, triggers, calendars, and everything else that you need to load. The advantage to this approach is that a change requires a simple change to the XML file—no code changes, no recompilation, just a text editor. Read Chapter 8 for more information on Quartz plug-ins.

Disadvantage to RAMJobStore

"The RAMJobStore can't be all positive, right?" you ask. Well, that's true. We mentioned several of the advantages of using a RAMJobStore. Now let's talk about the one big negative: Because a computer's memory is volatile, when your Quartz application is stopped, it releases the memory back to the operating system. Of course, along with everything else stored in that released memory is the scheduling information.

If your application requires Scheduler information to be maintained between application restarts, you need to take a look at persistent JobStores.

Using Persistent JobStores

In many ways, JobStores that use memory for storage and those that use some form of long-term persistence share similar traits. This shouldn't be that surprising because they both serve the same purpose.

As with RAMJobStore, persistent JobStores have both advantages and disadvantages. You should be careful to understand the pros and cons before choosing a persistent JobStore. This section explains the differences and the circumstances under which you would want to use a persistent JobStore.

Currently, Quartz provides two types of persistent JobStores, each one unique in its persistence mechanism.

PERSISTENT JobStores = JDBC + RELATIONAL DATABASE

Although several different persistence mechanisms can used to persist Scheduler information for Quartz, Quartz relies on a relational database-management system (RDMS) for persistent storage. If you want to use something other than a database for persistent storage, you must build it yourself by implementing the JobStore interface. Suppose that you wanted to use the file system for persistent storage. You could create a class that implements the JobStore interface. In this chapter, when we say "persistent," we are implicitly talking about using JDBC to persist Scheduler state into the database.

All the persistent JobStores that ship with Quartz extend the org.quartz.impl.jdbcjobstore.JobStoreSupport class.

The JobStoreSupport Class

The JobStoreSupport class is abstract and implements the JobStore interface, discussed earlier in the chapter. It provides base functionality for all JDBC-based JobStores. Figure 6.1 shows the type hierarchy for JobStores.

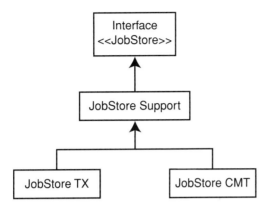

FIGURE 6.1 The JobStore type hierarchy

As Figure 6.1 illustrates, JobStoreSupport implements the JobStore interface and acts as a base class for the two concrete persistent JobStores that Quartz offers.

> **JobStoreSupport SHOULD HAVE BEEN NAMED JDBCJobStoreSupport**
>
> A better name for this class would have been JDBCJobStoreSupport because this class is specifically designed to work with JDBC-based storage solutions. However, the name doesn't detract from the functionality that it provides for persistent JobStores.

Because the JobStoreSupport class is abstract, Quartz offers two different types of concrete persistent JobStores, each one designed for a specific database environment and configuration:

- org.quartz.impl.jdbcjobstore.JobStoreTX
- org.quartz.impl.jdbcjobstore.JobStoreCMT

Both persistent JobStores are discussed shortly. For now, let's talk about the database that is required for both versions.

Using the Database for Job Storage

The persistent JobStores in Quartz are sometimes referred to as JDBC JobStores because of their unmistaken dependency on a JDBC driver to communicate with a relational database. The persistent JobStores use many of the features of JDBC, including support for transactions, locking, and isolation levels, just to name a few.

Because the persistent JobStores in Quartz are dependent on JDBC, you must ensure that your platform supports JDBC.

WHAT IF MY DATABASE DOESN'T SUPPORT JDBC?

If your database doesn't support JDBC, you most certainly have a problem. You're not completely out of luck, but you have a lot more work ahead of you. You would be better off switching to one of the supported database platforms. If your database doesn't support JDBC, you'll need to create a new implementation that implements the JobStore interface. You might want to check with users on the Quartz user forum to see if anyone has already done the work and is willing to share code—or at least an approach.

Databases Supported by Persistent JobStores

The persistent JobStores in Quartz are designed to be used with the following database platforms:

- Oracle
- MySQL
- MS SQL Server 2000
- HSQLDB
- PostgreSQL
- DB2
- Cloudscape/Derby
- Pointbase
- Informix
- Firebird
- Most other RDBMSs with a fully JDBC-compliant driver

Persistent Storage in a Stand-Alone Environment

The JobStoreTX class is designed to be used in a stand-alone environment. By "stand-alone," we mean an environment in which there is no transactional integration with an application container. This doesn't mean that you can't use the JobStoreTX within a container—just that it's not designed to have its transactions managed by the container. The difference is whether Quartz transactions should participate in the transaction of the container.

Persistent Storage in an Application Container

The JobStoreCMT class is designed to be used when you want the application container to manage the transactions for your JobStore and those transactions should participate within the transactional boundaries that are managed by the container. This should be obvious from the "Container Managed Transactions (CMT)" in the name.

Creating the Quartz Database Structure

JobStores based on JDBC require a database for the Scheduler information to be persisted. Quartz requires 12 database tables to be created. The table names and description are listed in Table 6.1.

Table 6.1   Quartz Requires the Following Tables for All JDBC-persistent JobStores

Table Name	Description
QRTZ_CALENDARS	Stores Quartz calendar information as blobs
QRTZ_CRON_TRIGGERS	Stores cron triggers, including cron expression and time zone information
QRTZ_FIRED_TRIGGERS	Stores status information relating to triggers that have fired and the relevant execution information about the related job.
QRTZ_PAUSED_TRIGGER_GRPS	Stores the trigger groups that have been paused

Table 6.1   Quartz Requires the Following Tables for All JDBC-persistent
JobStores *(continued)*

Table Name	Description
QRTZ_SCHEDULER_STATE	Stores a few pieces of information about the state of the Scheduler and other Scheduler instances (if used within a cluster)
QRTZ_LOCKS	Stores pessimistic lock information for the application (if pessimistic locking is used)
QRTZ_JOB_DETAILS	Stores detailed information for every configured Job
QRTZ_JOB_LISTENERS	Stores information about configured JobListeners
QRTZ_SIMPLE_TRIGGERS	Stores simple triggers, including repeat count, internal, and number of times triggered
QRTZ_BLOB_TRIGGERS	Triggers stores as blobs (this is used when Quartz users create their own custom trigger types—with JDBC, JobStore does not have specific knowledge about how to store instances)
QRTZ_TRIGGER_LISTENERS	Stores information about configured TriggerListeners
QRTZ_TRIGGERS	Stores information about configured triggers

In Table 6.1, all tables start with the prefix QRTZ_. This is the default, but you can change it by providing an alternate prefix in the quartz.properties file. Changing the prefix is necessary if you use multiple table sets for different Scheduler instances. This would be the case if you need multiple nonclustered schedulers but want to use a single database instance.

Installing the Quartz Database Tables

Quartz includes SQL scripts for all the supported database platforms. You can find the SQL scripts in the <quartz home>/docs/dbTables directory, where <quartz_home> is the directory where you unzipped the Quartz distribution.

About 18 different database platform scripts are available. This should cover just about any database that you can come up with. If yours is not included, you can use one of the existing ones and modify it for your database platform.

To install the required database tables, open the .sql file that is specifically designed for your database platform and run the commands using your preferred query tool. With MS SQL Server, for example, you need to run the commands in the file `tables_sqlServer.sql` using the Query Analyzer tool that comes with the database. With certain databases (including MS SQL Server), you need to create an empty database before running the commands. The SQL commands don't include creating the database. You should also pay careful attention to any notes at the top of the SQL file. Usually, you must follow a few instructions before executing the commands. For example, with the MS SQL Server SQL file, you need to modify this command at the top of the file with the name that you gave the empty database when you created it:

```
USE [enter_db_name_here]
```

The SQL files create the necessary table structures and also put some basic constraints and indexes on the tables. Later in this chapter, we talk about how you can improve performance by making some additional changes to the structure.

Using JobStoreTX

The first persistent `JobStore` that we discuss is called `JobStoreTX`. The "TX" in the name stands for "transaction." As we stated earlier, the `JobStoreTX` is designed to be used in an environment in which you want Quartz to manage the transactions. For example, if you are building a J2SE application and are not using an application server such as WebLogic or JBoss, `JobStoreTX` would be the right choice for a persistent `JobStore`.

In the last section, you saw how easy it is to configure the `RAMJobStore`. We mentioned that one of the advantages to the `RAMJobStore` is its simple configuration. We've already discussed what has to be done to the database to get it ready; we now discuss what's needed to configure the Quartz application for a JDBC `JobStore`.

Configuring the JobStoreTX

To tell the Quartz runtime environment that you want to use a JobStore other than the default RAMJobStore, you must configure several properties. It doesn't matter what order you do them in, but they all must be done before you run the application for the first time.

SETTING THE JobStore PROPERTY

To inform the Scheduler that JobStoreTX should be used, you must add the following line to the quartz.properties file:

```
org.quartz.jobStore.class =
➥org.quartz.impl.jdbcjobstore.JobStoreTX
```

Be sure to remove the RAMJobStore line (if present) when switching to the JobStoreTX.

CONFIGURING THE DRIVER DELEGATE

In the same way that the JDBC API relies on a JDBC driver designed specifically for a database platform, Quartz relies on a DriverDelegate to communicate with a given database. As the name implies, database calls from the Scheduler to the JobStore are delegated to a preconfigured DriverDelegate instance. The delegate is responsible for all communications with the JDBC driver and, thus, the database.

All DriverDelegate classes extend the org.quartz.impl.jdbcjobstore.StdDriverDelegate class. The StdDriverDelegate has base functionality that all delegates, regardless of platform, can use. However, there is enough difference between some of these database platforms that a specialized delegate needs to be created for some platforms. Table 6.2 lists the specialized delegates.

Table 6.2   You Must Configure One of the `DriverDelegates` **Classes for Your Platform**

Database Platform	Quartz Delegate Class
Cloudscape/Derby	`org.quartz.impl.jdbcjobstore.CloudscapeDelegate`
DB2 (version 6.*x*)	`org.quartz.impl.jdbcjobstore.DB2v6Delegate`
DB2 (version 7.*x*)	`org.quartz.impl.jdbcjobstore.DB2v7Delegate`
DB2 (version 8.*x*)	`org.quartz.impl.jdbcjobstore.DB2v8Delegate`
HSQLDB	`org.quartz.impl.jdbcjobstore.PostgreSQLDelegate`
MS SQL Server	`org.quartz.impl.jdbcjobstore.MSSQLDelegate`
Pointbase	`org.quartz.impl.jdbcjobstore.PointbaseDelegate`
PostgreSQL	`org.quartz.impl.jdbcjobstore.PostgreSQLDelegate`
(WebLogic JDBC Driver)	`org.quartz.impl.jdbcjobstore.WebLogicDelegate`
(WebLogic 8.1 with Oracle)	`org.quartz.impl.jdbcjobstore.oracle.weblogic.` `    WebLogicOracleDelegate`
Oracle	`org.quartz.impl.jdbcjobstore.oracle.OracleDelegate`

WHAT IF MY DATABASE PLATFORM IS NOT LISTED IN TABLE 6.2?

If your RDBMS isn't listed here, there is a good chance it will work with the standard JDBC delegate, `org.quartz.impl.jdbcjobstore.StdDriverDelegate`.

After you determine which delegate you need based on your database platform, you need to add the following to the `quartz.properties` file:

```
org.quartz.jobStore.driverDelegateClass=
➥<FQN of driver delegate class>
```

As an example, if you are using MS SQL Server as your database platform, you would need to add the following to the properties file:

```
org.quartz.jobStore.driverDelegateClass=
            org.quartz.impl.jdbcjobstore.MSSQLDelegate
```

CONFIGURING THE DATABASE TABLE PREFIX

Back when we first discussed the database tables for Quartz, we mentioned that all the tables had the prefix QRTZ_ added to them. Under certain circumstances, you might need to create multiple sets of Quartz database tables. In that situation, you would need to change the prefix for each set.

The prefixes for the table names are configured in the quartz.properties file using the property org.quartz.jobStore.tablePrefix. To change the prefix, just set the property to a different value:

```
org.quartz.jobStore.tablePrefix = SCHEDULER2_
```

Make sure the table names all start with this prefix.

DATABASE TABLE AND COLUMN NAMES

Just in case you were wondering, the names for the database tables (minus the prefixes) and the table column names are in the org.quartz.impl.jdbcjobstore.Constants interface. This interface is implemented by the JobStoreSupport class, and the constant values are used within the JobStoreTX or JobStoreCMT classes.

Table 6.3 shows the set of properties that can be used to tune the JobStoreTX.

Table 6.3   The Configuration Properties Available to Be Set for JobStoreTX

Property	Default
org.quartz.jobStore.driverDelegateClass	—
Description: Driver delegates understand the particular dialects of various database systems.	
org.quartz.jobStore.dataSource	—
Description: This is the name used in the DataSource configuration section of the quartz.properties file.	
org.quartz.jobStore.tablePrefix	QRTZ_
Description: This is the prefix given to the set of database tables for this Scheduler. Schedulers can use different tables from the same database if the prefixes are different.	

Property	Default

org.quartz.jobStore.useProperties   False
Description: The "use properties" flag instructs the persistent JobStore that all values in JobDataMaps will be Strings and, therefore, can be stored as name-value pairs instead of storing more complex objects in their serialized form in the BLOB column. This is can be handy because you avoid the class-versioning issues that can arise from serializing your non-String classes into a BLOB.

org.quartz.jobStore.misfireThreshold   60000
Description: The number of milliseconds the Scheduler will tolerate a trigger to pass its next-fire-time before being considered misfired. The default value (if you don't make an entry of this property in your configuration) is 60000 (60 seconds). This is not specific to JDBC-JobStore; it is also a parameter used by RAMJobStore.

org.quartz.jobStore.isClustered   False
Description: Set this to true to turn on clustering features. This property must be set to true if you are having multiple instances of Quartz use the same set of database tables.

org.quartz.jobStore.clusterCheckinInterval   15000
Description: Set the frequency (in milliseconds) at which this instance checks in with the other instances of the cluster. This affects the quickness of detecting failed instances. It is used only when isClustered is set to true.

org.quartz.jobStore.maxMisfiresToHandleAtATime   20
Description: This is the maximum number of misfired triggers the JobStore will handle in a given pass. Handling many (more than a couple dozen) at once can cause the database tables to be locked long enough to hamper the performance of firing other (not yet misfired) triggers.

org.quartz.jobStore.dontSetAutoCommitFalse   False
Description: Setting this parameter to true tells Quartz not to call setAutoCommit(false) on connections obtained from the DataSource(s). This can be helpful in a few situations, such as if you have a driver that complains if it is called when it is already off. This property defaults to false because most drivers require that setAutoCommit(false) be called.

org.quartz.jobStore.selectWithLockSQL   SELECT * FROM {0}LOCKS WHERE LOCK_NAME = ? FOR UPDATE
Description: This must be a SQL string that selects a row in the LOCKS table and places a lock on the row. If it is not set, the default is SELECT * FROM {0}LOCKS WHERE LOCK_NAME = ? FOR UPDATE, which works for most databases. The {0} is replaced during runtime with the TABLE_ PREFIX that you configured earlier.

org.quartz.jobStore.txIsolationLevelSerializable   False
Description: A value of true tells Quartz (when using JobStoreTX or CMT) to call setTransactionIsolation(Connection.TRANSACTION_SERIALIZABLE) on JDBC connections. This can be helpful to prevent lock timeouts with some databases under high load and long-lasting transactions.

Configuring a DataSource for JobStoreTX

When using persistent JobStores, Quartz requires a Datasource. A Datasource acts as a factory for database connections. In Java, all Datasources implement the java.sql.Datasource interface. Quartz doesn't provide the Datasource functionality all by itself; it delegates that responsibility. By default, Quartz can use another open source framework, called Commons DBCP, or it can use DataSources defined within an application server via JNDI lookup.

The DBCP is a Jakarta Commons project, found at http://jakarta.apache.org/commons/dbcp. The binary for this framework is included in the Quartz distribution, and you should add it to your Quartz application. You also need to add the Commons Pool library, which is included in the Quartz distribution and is used by DBCP.

When using a JobStoreTX, you must specify the Datasource properties within the quartz.properties file. This allows Quartz to create and manage the Datasource for you. Table 6.4 lists the Datasource properties that need to be configured when using a JobStoreTX.

Table 6.4   Available Properties for Configuring a Quartz Datasource

Property	Required
org.quartz.dataSource.NAME.driver **Description:** Fully qualified name of your JDBC Driver class.	Yes
org.quartz.dataSource.NAME.URL **Description:** The connection URL (host, port, and so on) for connection to your database.	Yes
org.quartz.dataSource.NAME.user **Description:** The username to use when connecting to your database.	No
org.quartz.dataSource.NAME.password **Description:** The password to use when connecting to your database.	No
org.quartz.dataSource.NAME.maxConnections **Description:** The maximum number of connections that the DataSource can create in its pool of connections.	No

Property	Required
`org.quartz.dataSource.NAME.validationQuery`	No

Description: An optional SQL query string that the `DataSource` can use to detect and replace failed/corrupt connections. For example, an Oracle user might choose `select table_name from user_tables`, which is a query that should never fail unless the connection is actually bad.

For each property listed in Table 6.4, you need to substitute a name of your choice for the `NAME` part of the property. It doesn't matter what it is as long as it's the same value for all properties of the `Datasource`. This name is used to uniquely identify the `Datasource`. If you need to configure multiple `Datasources` (which you will do when using a `JobStoreCMT`), each `Datasource` should have a unique `NAME` value.

Listing 6.2 shows an example of a configured `Datasource` for the `JobStoreTX` that should be added to the `quartz.properties` file.

Listing 6.2   An Example Quartz `Datasource` for Use in a Non-CMT Environment

```
org.quartz.dataSource.myDS.driver = net.sourceforge.jtds.jdbc.Driver
org.quartz.dataSource.myDS.URL = jdbc:jtds:sqlserver://localhost:1433/quartz
org.quartz.dataSource.myDS.user = admin
org.quartz.dataSource.myDS.password = myPassword
org.quartz.dataSource.myDS.maxConnections = 10
```

After adding a `Datasource` section to the `quartz.properties` file like the one from Listing 6.2, you still need to make it available to the Quartz `JobStoreTX` that has been configured. You do so by adding this property to the properties file:

```
org.quartz.jobStore.dataSource = <DS_NAME>
```

The value for <DS_NAME> should match the name assigned in the `Datasource` configuration. Using the `Datasource` example from Listing 6.2, you would add the following line to the `quartz.properties` file:

```
org.quartz.jobStore.dataSource = myDS
```

This value is then passed to the JobStoreSupport and becomes available to your JobStoreTX so that connections can be retrieved and passed to the DriverDelegate instance.

Running Quartz with JobStoreTX

When you have completed the previous configuration steps, your application is ready to be started. Just as in all the previous examples, you still need a startup class that creates a Scheduler instance from the factory and calls the start() method. A class like the one listed in Listing 6.3 will suffice.

Listing 6.3 Simple Startup Class Called from the Command Line to Start the Scheduler

```
public class SchedulerMain {
    static Log logger = LogFactory.getLog(SchedulerMain.class);

    public static void main(String[] args) {
        SchedulerMain app = new SchedulerMain();
        app.startScheduler();
    }

    public void startScheduler() {
        try {
            // Create an instance of the Scheduler
            Scheduler scheduler =
                    StdSchedulerFactory.getDefaultScheduler();

            logger.info("Scheduler starting up...");
            scheduler.start();

        } catch (SchedulerException ex) {
            logger.error(ex);
        }
    }
}
```

When you use the SchedulerMain class from Listing 6.3 to test the JobStoreTX configuration, you should get output similar to the following:

```
INFO [main] - Quartz Scheduler v.1.5.0 created.
INFO [main] - Using thread monitor-based data access locking (synchronization).
INFO [main] - Removed 0 Volatile Trigger(s).
INFO [main] - Removed 0 Volatile Job(s).
INFO [main] - JobStoreTX initialized.
INFO [main] - Quartz scheduler 'QuartzScheduler' initialized from default resource
file in Quartz package: 'quartz.properties'
```

```
INFO [main] - Quartz scheduler version: 1.5.0
INFO [main] - Scheduler starting up...
INFO [main] - Freed 0 triggers from 'acquired' / 'blocked' state.
INFO [main] - Recovering 0 jobs that were in-progress at the time of the last
shut-down.

INFO [main] - Recovery complete.
INFO [main] - Removed 0 'complete' triggers.
INFO [main] - Removed 0 stale fired job entries.
INFO [main] - Scheduler QuartzScheduler_$_NON_CLUSTERED started.
```

The log messages shown are using Log4j, so they might differ slightly from yours. A few things should be obvious from the output. First, no triggers or jobs were found in the database. This is a very important and sometimes confusing point. The database doesn't come loaded with any jobs or triggers: That's not possible because it wouldn't know which ones to load for you. This is something that you'll have to do yourself. You can get Scheduler information into the database in several ways.

Using Memory to Store Scheduler Information

Loading Jobs into the Database

Earlier in the section, "Using Memory to Store Scheduler Information," we talked about how to load job and trigger information into memory when using the RAMJobStore. So how are jobs and triggers loaded into the database? Several methods exist for getting job information into the database:

- Adding job information in your application
- Using the JobInitializationPlugin
- Using the Quartz Web application

We talked about the first two approaches back in the RAMJobStore section. When used with a JDBC JobStore, the approach is not much different, with a few exceptions. First, you need to understand that when using these two methods, the job information is in the database. Even if you stop the application, the information remains in the database. Even if you took the `JobInitializationPlugin` out of your application, the information would be in the database. In that sense, it is seeding the database with job information. Chapter 8 covers the `JobInitializationPlugin` and Quartz plug-ins in general.

The last approach is probably the most interesting one. We haven't yet talked about the Quartz Web application, but we do in Chapter 13, "Quartz and Web Applications." For now, you should know that the Quartz Web application is a browser-based GUI that is designed to manage the Quartz Scheduler. It was designed by Quartz users and presents a rather nice interface for adding jobs and triggers, starting and pausing the Scheduler, and delivering other functionality.

LOADING JOBS VIA A SQL TOOL

One last method can be used to load job information, but it's mentioned here only to discourage you from attempting it. This approach is to use native SQL and attempt to load and/or modify the information directly into the Quartz tables. Adding job information to the database using a native query tool works in some rare cases, but it's easy to corrupt the data and cause none of the jobs to function correctly. Avoid this approach at all costs.

Using the `JobStoreCMT`

Much of what we said and did in the last several sections for `JobStoreTX` holds true for the other version of the JDBC JobStore, `JobStoreCMT`. Again, this shouldn't be all that surprising because both are types of `JobStores` and are designed to use JDBC to interact with a relational database. Both also extend a common base class.

The `JobStoreCMT` is designed to participate within the transactional boundaries of a container. This means that the container creates a JTA transaction and makes it available to the `JobStore`. Quartz's interaction with the `JobStore` stays within that transaction. If there are any problems, Quartz can signal to the container that it wants the transaction to roll back by calling `setRollbackOnly()` on the transaction.

Configuring the JobStoreCMT

As with the JobStoreTX and the RAMJobStore before that, the
first step in using the JobStoreCMT is to inform the Scheduler
of your desire to use the JobStoreCMT. Similar to before, you
do this by setting the JobStore class property to the
quartz.properties file:

```
org.quartz.jobStore.class =
➥org.quartz.impl.jdbcjobstore.JobStoreCMT
```

Be sure to remove the RAMJobStore line if it's present in
the properties file.

CONFIGURING THE DriverDelegate CLASS

You also need to choose the DriverDelegate as you did for the
JobStoreTX. Quartz relies on a DriverDelegate to communicate with a given database. The delegate is responsible for all
communications with the JDBC driver and, thus, the database.

Look back at Table 6.2 for a list of DriverDelegates and
choose one based on your database platform and environment.
To add the MS SQL Server delegate to the quartz.properties
file, add the following line:

```
org.quartz.jobStore.driverDelegateClass=
➥org.quartz.impl.jdbcjobstore.MSSQLDelegate
```

You can use several properties to help tune the
JobStoreCMT. Table 6.5 shows the entire set.

Table 6.5   The Configuration Properties Available to Be Set for JobStoreCMT

Property	Default
org.quartz.jobStore.driverDelegateClass	—
Description: Driver delegates understand the particular dialects of various database systems.	
org.quartz.jobStore.dataSource	—
Description: This is the name used in the datasource configuration section of the quartz. properties file.	

Table 6.5 The Configuration Properties Available to Be Set for

JobStoreCMT *(continued)*

Property	Default

`org.quartz.jobStore.nonManagedTXDataSource` —

Description: JobStoreCMT requires a (second) datasource that contains connections that will not be part of container-managed transactions. The value of this property must be the name of one the DataSources defined in the configuration properties file. This datasource must contain non-CMT connections—in other words, connections for which it is legal for Quartz to directly call `commit()` and `rollback()` on.

`org.quartz.jobStore.tablePrefix` QRTZ_

Description: This is the prefix given to the set of database tables for this Scheduler. Schedulers can use different tables from the same database if the prefixes are different.

`org.quartz.jobStore.useProperties` False

Description: The "`use properties`" flag instructs the persistent JobStore that all values in JobDataMaps will be `Strings` and, therefore, can be stored as name-value pairs instead of storing more complex objects in their serialized form in the BLOB column. This is can be handy because you avoid the class-versioning issues that can arise from serializing your non-`String` classes into a BLOB.

`org.quartz.jobStore.misfireThreshold` 60000

Description: This is the number of milliseconds the Scheduler will tolerate a trigger to pass its next-fire-time before being considered misfired. The default value (if you don't make an entry of this property in your configuration) is 60000 (60 seconds).

`org.quartz.jobStore.isClustered` False

Description: Set this to `true` to turn on clustering features. This property must be set to `true` if you are having multiple instances of Quartz use the same set of database tables.

`org.quartz.jobStore.clusterCheckinInterval` 15000

Description: Set the frequency (in milliseconds) at which this instance checks in with the other instances of the cluster. This affects the quickness of detecting failed instances.

`org.quartz.jobStore.maxMisfiresToHandleAtATime` 20

Description: This is the maximum number of misfired triggers the JobStore will handle in a given pass. Handling many (more than a couple dozen) at once can cause the database tables to be locked long enough to hamper the performance of firing other (not yet misfired) triggers.

`org.quartz.jobStore.dontSetAutoCommitFalse` False

Description: Setting this parameter to `true` tells Quartz not to call `setAutoCommit(false)` on connections obtained from the DataSource(s). This can be helpful in a few situations, such as if you have a driver that complains if it is called when it is already off. This property defaults to `false` because most drivers require that `setAutoCommit(false)` be called.

Property	Default
	SELECT * FROM {0}LOCKS WHERE
`org.quartz.jobStore.selectWithLockSQL`	LOCK_NAME = ? FOR UPDATE

Description: This must be a SQL string that selects a row in the LOCKS table and places a lock on the row. If it is not set, the default is `SELECT * FROM {0}LOCKS WHERE LOCK_NAME = ? FOR UPDATE`, which works for most databases. The {0} is replaced during runtime with the `TABLE_PREFIX` that you configured earlier.

Property	Default
`org.quartz.jobStore.dontSetNonManagedTX`	False
`    ConnectionAutoCommitFalse`	

Description: This is the same as the property `org.quartz.jobStore.dontSetAutoCommitFalse`, except that it applies to the `nonManagedTXDataSource`.

Property	Default
`org.quartz.jobStore.txIsolationLevelSerializable`	False

Description: A value of `true` tells Quartz (when using JobStoreTX or CMT) to call `setTransactionIsolation(Connection.TRANSACTION_SERIALIZABLE)` on JDBC connections. Th s can be helpful to prevent lock timeouts with some databases under high load and long-lasting transactions.

Property	Default
`org.quartz.jobStore.txIsolationLevelReadCommitted`	False

Description: When set to `true`, this property tells Quartz to call `setTransactionIsolation(Connection.TRANSACTION_READ_UNCOMMITTED)` on the nonmanaged JDBC connections. This can be helpful to prevent lock timeouts with some databases (such as DB2) under high load and long-lasting transactions.

Configuring Datasources
for `JobStoreCMT`

As with `JobStoreTX`, we need to configure a `Datasource` so that we can use `JobStoreCMT`. However, `JobStoreCMT` requires two `Datasources` be configured instead of the one for `JobStoreTX`. One `Datasource` is set up as we did for the `JobStoreTX`: as a nonmanaged `Datasource`. Then we need to configure a second Datasource that is set up as a managed Datasource—one designed to be managed by the application server.

WHY DOES JobStoreCMT NEED TWO Datasources?

The original author of JobStoreCMT, Jeffrey Wescott, designed it to do its "own work" with a standard JDBC connection, whereas the work that it does on behalf of the client (such as the scheduling of the job) is performed using a JDBC connection that has its transaction under the control of the container. This design allows user interactions with Quartz to be part of their "larger" transaction, without JobStoreCMT having to use the application server's transaction manager (for example, via UserTransaction) to create and end transactions when it is doing its own internal work (such as the internal handling misfired triggers). It would be an improvement (from a configuration point of view) if JobStoreCMT did make use of UserTransaction because then only one datasource would be needed. However, when compared with the other feature requests and needed improvements, making this change has never become a top priority for the team, and JobStoreCMT continues to require two datasources.

Configuring the Nonmanaged Datasource

For the most part, we set up the nonmanaged DataSource in the same way that we did for JobStoreTX, except that we add one line to specify that this is the nonManagedTXDataSource:

```
# Add the property for the nonManagedTXDataSource
org.quartz.jobStore.nonManagedTXDataSource = myDS

org.quartz.dataSource.myDS.driver = net.sourceforge.jtds.jdbc.Driver
org.quartz.dataSource.myDS.URL = jdbc:jtds:sqlserver://localhost:1433/quartz
org.quartz.dataSource.myDS.user = admin
org.quartz.dataSource.myDS.password = myPassword
org.quartz.dataSource.myDS.maxConnections = 10
```

This sets up the nonmanaged Datasource and lets the JobStore know that the nonManagedTXDataSource is called "myDS."

Configuring the Managed Datasource

The second Datasource needs to be configured as a managed Datasource. This means that Quartz uses a Datasource that the container has already created to interact with the database while performing Scheduler functions. When Quartz grabs a connection from the Datasource, there should already be a JTA transaction in progress for Quartz to schedule jobs and triggers. For example, the code calling into Quartz could be within a method on a `SessionBean` that has its transaction descriptor set to `REQUIRED`. Another approach would be for the client program to start a transaction directly through the use of `javax.transaction.UserTransaction`.

As with the nonmanaged `Datasource`, the configuration for the container-managed `Datasource` goes in the `quartz.properties` file. The following example illustrates how to set up the managed `Datasource`:

```
org.quartz.dataSource.NAME.jndiURL=jdbc/quartzDS

org.quartz.dataSource.NAME.java.naming.factory.initial=
    weblogic.jndi.WLInitialContextFactory

    org.quartz.dataSource.NAME.java.naming.provider.url=t3://localhost:7001
    org.quartz.dataSource.NAME.java.naming.security.principal=weblogic
    org.quartz.dataSource.NAME.java.naming.security.credentials=weblogic
```

Table 6.6 lists the properties that are available for the managed `Datasource`.

Table 6.6   Properties for a `Datasource` Used with an Application Server

Property	Required
`org.quartz.dataSource.NAME.jndiURL` **Description:** The JNDI URL for a DataSource that is managed by your application server	Yes
`org.quartz.dataSource.NAME.java.naming.factory.initial` **Description:** The (optional) class name of the JNDI `InitialContextFactory` that you want to use	No
`org.quartz.dataSource.NAME.java.naming.provider.url` **Description:** The (optional) URL for connecting to the JNDI context	No
`org.quartz.dataSource.NAME.java.naming.security.principal` **Description:** The (optional) user principal for connecting to the JNDI context	No
`org.quartz.dataSource.NAME.java.naming.security.credentials` **Description:** The (optional) user credentials for connecting to the JNDI context	No

Using the properties from Table 6.6, here's an example of configuring the managed `Datasource` in `quartz.properties`.

```
org.quartz.dataSource.WL.jndiURL = OraDataSource
org.quartz.dataSource.WL.jndiAlwaysLookup = DB_JNDI_ALWAYS_LOOKUP
org.quartz.dataSource.WL.java.naming.factory.initial =
➥weblogic.jndi.WLInitialContextFactory
org.quartz.dataSource.WL.java.naming.provider.url = t3://localhost:7001
org.quartz.dataSource.WL.java.naming.security.principal = weblogic
org.quartz.dataSource.WL.java.naming.security.credentials = weblogic
```

Improving Performance with Persistent `JobStores`

Performance is one topic that receives the most attention when
there's the least amount of time to do anything about it. As
experienced developers, we know that it should be a consideration from the onset of the project.

When using Quartz with persistent `JobStores`, the biggest
area of concern has to be the interaction with the relational
database. Database I/O (just like file I/O) is usually not very fast.
You can improve performance by doing things such as tuning
the SQL, adding indexes, and manipulating tables and columns.
Because performance concerns were already taken into account
in the writing of Quartz, you don't want to dive right into doing
these things to Quartz without having an actual performance
problem, trying to solve it through a configuration setting, and
trying everything possible not to manipulate source code. The
good news is that Quartz is open source and you have complete
insight into what it's doing and how it's doing it. If you don't
like how it queries the database, it's your prerogative to fix it.
Before you take this route, however, be sure to check with the
users and developers on the Quartz forum to see if others have
had the problem and explore the recommended suggestions.

One very easy (and very effective) way to improve performance is to make sure the tables have indexes created on all the
appropriate columns. Some of the database-creation scripts that
ship with Quartz already have the commands for creating
indexes. If yours does not, you can simply refer to those defined

at the bottom of `tables_oracle.sql` and translate any syntax changes that are necessary for your RDBMs.

Whatever you do, if you make changes that improve performance, be sure to offer them back to the community and the Quartz project.

Creating New `JobStore`s

For most users, the `JobStore`s supplied out-of-the-box will be sufficient. When your application doesn't require state to be maintained between restarts, `RAMJobStore` should be your first choice. It's fast, easy to set up, and as painless as can be. On the other hand, if you do need to maintain Scheduler state between restarts and you are using a database or have access to a database, using one of the JDBC `JobStore`s is probably your best choice.

So what happens if you need a totally different type of `JobStore`? You're going to need to create a new type. This section discusses several approaches and offers ideas for how you can create a new `JobStore` when the provided solutions just don't fill the need.

Implementing the `JobStore` Interface

Regardless of whether they use a database, a file system, or even just memory, all `JobStore`s must implement the `JobStore` interface. New `JobStore`s that you create are no exception. Looking back through this chapter, you can see that `RAMJobStore` directly implements the `JobStore` interface, the JDBC `JobStore`s subclass `JobStoreSupport`, which itself implements the `JobStore` interface.

The `JobStore` interface has 40 methods that must be implemented by any `JobStore` implementation, yours included. How you implement those methods depends entirely on the type of `JobStore` that you are building. That doesn't mean that your `JobStore` will have only 40 methods; this is just the minimum that the interface requires. These 40 methods represent the public contract between a `JobStore` and the Scheduler.

Let's pick one of the methods and talk about it for a second. Let's pick the JobStore interface method:

```
public void schedulerStarted() throws SchedulerException ;
```

The Scheduler calls the JobStore's schedulerStarted() method to inform the JobStore that the Scheduler has been started. If you look at the implementation in RAMJobStore, you can see that nothing is done inside this method for this implementation:

```
public void schedulerStarted() throws SchedulerException {
    // nothing to do
}
```

However, if you look at the implementation for the two JDBC JobStores, you can see that some work has to be carried out when the Scheduler is first started:

```
public void schedulerStarted() throws SchedulerException {

    if (isClustered()) {
        clusterManagementThread = new ClusterManager(this);
        clusterManagementThread.initialize();
    }
    else {
        try {
            recoverJobs();
        } catch (SchedulerException se) {
            throw new SchedulerConfigException(
                    "Failure occurred during job recovery.", se);
        }
    }

    misfireHandler = new MisfireHandler(this);
    misfireHandler.initialize();
}
```

Each JobStore implementation will be unique, and the functionality that is carried out within the interface method will vary. If you are serious about creating your own JobStore, you should review the source code for RAMJobStore to fully understand the responsibilities a JobStore has. The RAMJobStore should be used as a guide for any custom JobStore you need.

## CHAPTER 7

IMPLEMENTING QUARTZ LISTENERS

Listeners provide a convenient and unobtrusive mechanism for getting notified when certain events of interest occur. Quartz provides three types of listeners: one for jobs, one for triggers, and one for the Scheduler itself. This chapter explains how to use each type to better manage your Quartz applications and be aware of what events are occurring.

Listeners as Extension Points

The phrase *extension point* is used in software development to indicate a place in a framework or application where the creators expect users to extend or customize the framework to meet their needs. (You will also hear the word *hook* used for the same meaning.)

Quartz listeners are a type of extension point in which you, as a Quartz user, can extend the framework and customize it to do new things. This customization takes place within the listener class implementations that we show you how to build in this chapter.

Listeners are not the only extension points in the framework. Along with plug-ins and a few other customization options, listeners provide a simple means of customizing the framework and making it do what you need it to do. Because the extension points for listeners are supported through a publicized interface, you don't have to worry about creating your own branch of the code that then is unsupportable.

Implementing a Listener

In the discussion that follows, the approach for implementing a listener is generally the same for all three types. The steps can be generalized into the following:

1. Create a Java class that implements the listener interface.
2. Implement all the methods of the listener interface with logic that is specific to your application.
3. Register the listener.

Creating the Listener Class

The listener is a Java interface and must be implemented by a concrete class. The class doesn't have to be a specialized class created just for this purpose; it can be any Java class that you want to receive the callback methods on. In keeping with good program design, you should be careful to keep tight cohesion but loose coupling. Seriously consider which class you decide to implement the listener with; this is important from an overall design perspective.

Implementing the Listener Methods

Because listeners are ordinary Java interfaces, every method must be implemented in your listener implementation class. If there are any methods in the listener interface that you are not interested in, you are allowed to have an empty body for the method; however, you still must provide a valid method implementation of it. For example, the following code snippet shows an empty method body for one of the SchedulerListener methods:

```
... rest of the SchedulerListener not shown

public void schedulerShutdown(){
  // Don't care about the shutdown event
}
```

Registering the Listener

To receive the callback methods, the Scheduler must be aware of the listener instance. Figure 7.1 illustrates the process of registering a listener with the Scheduler and receiving the callbacks.

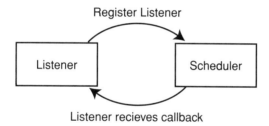

FIGURE 7.1   Listeners are registered with and receive callbacks from the Scheduler.

GLOBAL VS. NONGLOBAL LISTENERS

The JobListener and TriggerListener can be registered as either a global or nonglobal listener. A *global listener* is one that receives event notifications for all jobs/triggers. A *nonglobal listener* (or just a standard listener) receives event notifications for only those jobs or triggers that have registered listeners on them.

Whether you register your listener as a global or nonglobal listener depends on your specific application needs. We provide examples of both ways in the following sections. Another way

to look at global and nonglobal listeners comes from the creator
of the Quartz framework. James House describes global and
nonglobal listeners this way:

> Global listeners are active in the sense that they are eagerly
> seeking every possible event in order to perform their task
> upon it. Generally, the work done by global listeners [is] not
> specific to the particular job or trigger. Nonglobal listeners
> are generally passive in the sense that they do nothing until
> a trigger fires or job executes that has specifically named
> that listener. Hence, nonglobal listeners are more likely than
> global listeners to modify or add to the work performed by
> the job—somewhat like a decorator of the well-known deco-
> rator design pattern.

Listening for Job Events

The org.quartz.JobListener interface contains a set of methods that are invoked when certain key events occur in the life
cycle of a job. The methods available for JobListener are
shown in Listing 7.1.

Listing 7.1   Methods of the org.quartz.JobListener Interface

```
public interface JobListener {
    public String getName();
    public void jobToBeExecuted(JobExecutionContext context);
    public void jobExecutionVetoed(JobExecutionContext context);

    public void jobWasExecuted(JobExecutionContext context,
            JobExecutionException jobException);
}
```

The methods in the JobListener interface are fairly self-
explanatory. However, we should make a few points about them.

The getName() Method

The getName() method returns a String that represents the
name of the JobListener. For listeners that are registered as
global, the getName() method is primarily used for logging.
However, for JobListeners that are referenced by specific jobs,
the listener name registered with the JobDetail must match the

value returned from the getName() method on the listener instance. This will be more obvious after you see a few examples.

The jobToBeExecuted() Method

The Scheduler calls this method when the JobDetail is about to be executed.

The jobExecutionVetoed() Method

The Scheduler calls this method when the JobDetail was about to be executed but a TriggerListener vetoed the execution.

The jobWasExecuted() Method

The Scheduler calls this method after the JobDetail is executed.

Listing 7.2 shows a very simple JobListener implementation.

Listing 7.2   A Simplified JobListener Implementation

```
package org.cavaness.quartzbook.chapter7;

import org.apache.commons.logging.Log;
import org.apache.commons.logging.LogFactory;
import org.quartz.JobExecutionContext;
import org.quartz.JobExecutionException;
import org.quartz.JobListener;

public class SimpleJobListener implements JobListener {
    Log logger = LogFactory.getLog(SimpleJobListener.class);

    public String getName() {
        return getClass().getSimpleName();
    }

    public void jobToBeExecuted(JobExecutionContext context) {
        String jobName = context.getJobDetail().getName();
        logger.info(jobName + " is about to be executed");
    }

    public void jobExecutionVetoed(JobExecutionContext context) {
        String jobName = context.getJobDetail().getName();
        logger.info(jobName + " was vetoed and not executed()");
    }

    public void jobWasExecuted(JobExecutionContext context,
            JobExecutionException jobException) {

        String jobName = context.getJobDetail().getName();
        logger.info(jobName + " was executed");
    }
}
```

The JobListener in Listing 7.2 prints a log message, which, obviously, is a basic use of the Listener. The logic that you implement is entirely up to you and your application needs. You might want to send an e-mail when a job finishes successfully or schedule another job after one gets vetoed—you have the freedom to perform just about any action from within the callback method.

Earlier we stated that JobListeners (and TriggerListeners) can be either global or nonglobal. Notice that we didn't have to know in advanced whether the JobListener in Listing 7.2 was a global or nonglobal listener: We just implemented the interface and provided the listener methods. Listing 7.3 illustrates how to use the SimpleJobListener from Listing 7.2 and register it as global JobListener.

Listing 7.3   Using the SimpleJobListener **as a Global** JobListener

```
package org.cavaness.quartzbook.chapter7;

import java.util.Date;

import org.apache.commons.logging.Log;
import org.apache.commons.logging.LogFactory;
import org.cavaness.quartzbook.common.PrintInfoJob;
import org.quartz.JobDetail;
import org.quartz.JobListener;
import org.quartz.Scheduler;
import org.quartz.SchedulerException;
import org.quartz.Trigger;
import org.quartz.TriggerUtils;
import org.quartz.impl.StdSchedulerFactory;

public class Listing_7_3 {
    static Log logger = LogFactory.getLog(Listing_7_3.class);

    public static void main(String[] args) {
        Listing_7_3 example = new Listing_7_3();

        try {
            example.startScheduler();
        } catch (SchedulerException ex) {
            logger.error(ex);
        }
    }

    public void startScheduler() throws SchedulerException {

        // Create an instance of the factory
        Scheduler scheduler = null;

        // Create the scheduler and JobDetail
        scheduler = StdSchedulerFactory.getDefaultScheduler();
```

Listing 7.3   Continued

```
        JobDetail jobDetail = new JobDetail("PrintInfoJob",
                Scheduler.DEFAULT_GROUP, PrintInfoJob.class);

        /*
         * Set up a trigger to start firing now, with no end
         * date/time, repeat forever and have
         * 10 secs (10000 ms) between each firing.
         */
        Trigger trigger = TriggerUtils.makeSecondlyTrigger(10);
        trigger.setName("SimpleTrigger");
        trigger.setStartTime(new Date());

        // Register the JobDetail and Trigger
        scheduler.scheduleJob(jobDetail, trigger);

        // Create and register the global job listener
        JobListener jobListener =
            new SimpleJobListener("SimpleJobListener");

        scheduler.addGlobalJobListener(jobListener);

        // Start the scheduler
        scheduler.start();
        logger.info("Scheduler was started at " + new Date());
    }
}
```

The code in Listing 7.3 should be pretty straightforward by now. A JobDetail and trigger are created and registered with a Scheduler instance, just as we've done many times before.

A SimpleJobListener from Listing 7.2 is instantiated and registered with the Scheduler as a global JobListener by calling the addGlobalJobListener() method. Finally, the Scheduler is started.

Because we set up a single job (the PrintInfoJob), we get callbacks for only that JobDetail. However, if we had scheduled another job, we would also see callback log messages for the second job because the listener was configured as a global listener.

Registering Nonglobal JobListeners

You can also use the SimpleJobListener from Listing 7.2 as a nonglobal JobListener. To do this, you would only need to modify the code in the startScheduler() method from Listing 7.3. Listing 7.4 illustrates the small change that would need to be made.

Listing 7.4   Using the `SimpleJobListener` as a Nonglobal `JobListener`

```
package org.cavaness.quartzbook.chapter7;

import java.util.Date;

import org.apache.commons.logging.Log;
import org.apache.commons.logging.LogFactory;
import org.cavaness.quartzbook.common.PrintInfoJob;
import org.quartz.JobDetail;
import org.quartz.JobListener;
import org.quartz.Scheduler;
import org.quartz.SchedulerException;
import org.quartz.Trigger;
import org.quartz.TriggerUtils;
import org.quartz.impl.StdSchedulerFactory;

public class Listing_7_4 {
    static Log logger = LogFactory.getLog(Listing_7_4.class);

    public static void main(String[] args) {
        Listing_7_4 example = new Listing_7_4();

        try {
            example.startScheduler();
        } catch (SchedulerException ex) {
            logger.error(ex);
        }
    }

    public void startScheduler() throws SchedulerException {

        Scheduler scheduler = null;

        try {
            // Create the scheduler and JobDetail
            scheduler = StdSchedulerFactory.getDefaultScheduler();
            JobDetail jobDetail =
                    new JobDetail("PrintInfoJob",
                    Scheduler.DEFAULT_GROUP,
                    PrintInfoJob.class);

            /*
             * Set up a trigger to start firing now, with no end
             * date/time, repeat forever and have
             * 10 secs (10000 ms) between each firing.
             */
            Trigger trigger =
                TriggerUtils.makeSecondlyTrigger(10);

            trigger.setName("SimpleTrigger");
            trigger.setStartTime(new Date());

            // Create the job listener
            JobListener jobListener =
                new SimpleJobListener("SimpleJobListener");

            // Register Listener as a nonglobal listener
            scheduler.addJobListener(jobListener);
```

Listing 7.4 Continued

```
        // Listener set on JobDetail before scheduleJob()
            jobDetail.addJobListener(jobListener.getName());

        // Register the JobDetail and Trigger
        scheduler.scheduleJob(jobDetail, trigger);

        // Start the scheduler
        scheduler.start();
        logger.info("Scheduler started at " + new Date());

    } catch (SchedulerException ex) {
        logger.error(ex);
    }
    }
}
```

Listing 7.4 is very similar to the code from Listing 7.3. Because the JobListener is being registered as a nonglobal listener, you have to call the addJobListener() method on the Scheduler instead of the addGlobalJobListener() method. For a nonglobal JobListener, it should be added to the Scheduler before any JobDetail that references it is added using the schedulerJob() or addJob() methods.

Next, the name of the JobListener is set on the JobDetail. Notice that the JobListener instance is not set; just the name is. This is done by calling the addJobListener() method and passing in the name. The name passed into the addJobListener() method must match the name returned from the listener getName() method. If the Scheduler can't find a listener with that name, it throws a SchedulerException.

Finally, the Scheduler is started.

THE ORDER OF THE STEPS FOR NONGLOBAL JobListeners MATTERS

The steps for adding a nonglobal JobListener must be done in order. The JobListener must be added to the Scheduler first. Then the JobListener can be set on the JobDetail object. After that, you can safely add the JobDetail to the Scheduler using the scheduleJob() method.

Listening for Trigger Events

As with the `JobListener`, the `org.quartz.TriggerListener` interface contains a set of methods that the Scheduler calls. Unlike the `JobListener`, however, the `TriggerListener` interface contains life cycle methods for trigger instances. Listing 7.5 shows the methods of the `TriggerListener` interface.

Listing 7.5   The Methods of the `org.quartz.TriggerListener` Interface

```
public interface TriggerListener {
    public String getName();

    public void triggerFired(Trigger trigger,
        JobExecutionContext context);

    public boolean vetoJobExecution(Trigger trigger,
        JobExecutionContext context);

    public void triggerMisfired(Trigger trigger);

    public void triggerComplete(Trigger trigger,
        JobExecutionContext context,
        int triggerInstructionCode);

}
```

The getName() Method

As with the previous `JobListener`, the `getName()` method on the `TriggerListener` interface returns a `String` that represents the name of the listener. For nonglobal `TriggerListeners`, the name given in the `addTriggerListener()` method should match the value returned from the listener's `gettName()` method.

The triggerFired() Method

The Scheduler calls this method when the trigger associated with the listener has fired and the `execute()` method is about to be called on the job. In the case of a global `TriggerListener`, this method is called for all triggers.

The vetoJobExecution() Method

The Scheduler calls this method when the trigger has fired and the job is about to be executed. The TriggerListener is given a chance to veto the execution of the job. If this method returns true, the job will not be executed for this trigger firing.

The triggerMisfired() Method

The Scheduler calls this method when the trigger has misfired. As the JavaDocs for this method point out, you should be careful about performing long-lasting logic in this method: Doing so could cause a domino effect when there are many misfired triggers. You should keep the logic in this method to a minimum.

The triggerComplete() Method

The Scheduler calls this method when the trigger has fired and the job has finished executing. It doesn't mean that the trigger will not fire again—just that the current firing of the trigger (and subsequent job execution) has ended. The trigger might still have future firing times.

Listing 7.6 shows a very simple TriggerListener implementation.

Listing 7.6   A Simplified TriggerListener Implementation

```
package org.cavaness.quartzbook.chapter7;

import org.apache.commons.logging.Log;
import org.apache.commons.logging.LogFactory;
import org.quartz.JobExecutionContext;
import org.quartz.Trigger;
import org.quartz.TriggerListener;

public class SimpleTriggerListener implements TriggerListener {
    Log logger = LogFactory.getLog(SimpleTriggerListener.class);

    private String name;

    public SimpleTriggerListener(String name) {
        this.name = name;
    }

    public String getName() {
        return name;
    }
```

Listing 7.6 Continued

```
public void triggerFired(Trigger trigger,
    JobExecutionContext context) {

    String triggerName = trigger.getName();
    logger.info(triggerName + " was fired");
}

public boolean vetoJobExecution(Trigger trigger,
        JobExecutionContext context) {

    String triggerName = trigger.getName();
    logger.info(triggerName + " was not vetoed");
    return false;
}

public void triggerMisfired(Trigger trigger) {
    String triggerName = trigger.getName();
    logger.info(triggerName + " misfired");
}

public void triggerComplete(Trigger trigger,
    JobExecutionContext context,
    int triggerInstructionCode) {

    String triggerName = trigger.getName();
    logger.info(triggerName + " is complete");
}
}
```

Just as with the JobListener in Listing 7.2, the
TriggerListener in Listing 7.6 is rudimentary. It merely prints
a log message when the Scheduler invokes the method. The
code in Listing 7.7 tests the simple TriggerListener.

Listing 7.7 Using the SimpleTriggerListener as a Global TriggerListener

```
package org.cavaness.quartzbook.chapter7;

import java.util.Date;

import org.apache.commons.logging.Log;
import org.apache.commons.logging.LogFactory;
import org.cavaness.quartzbook.common.PrintInfoJob;
import org.quartz.JobDetail;
import org.quartz.Scheduler;
import org.quartz.SchedulerException;
import org.quartz.Trigger;
import org.quartz.TriggerListener;
import org.quartz.TriggerUtils;
import org.quartz.impl.StdSchedulerFactory;

public class Listing_7_7 {
    static Log logger = LogFactory.getLog(Listing_7_7.class);

    public static void main(String[] args) {
        Listing_7_7 example = new Listing_7_7();
```

Listing 7.7   Continued

```
        try {
            example.startScheduler();
        } catch (SchedulerException ex) {
            logger.error(ex);
        }
    }

    public void startScheduler() throws SchedulerException {

        // Create an instance of the factory
        Scheduler scheduler = null;

        // Create the scheduler and JobDetail
        scheduler = StdSchedulerFactory.getDefaultScheduler();
        JobDetail jobDetail = new JobDetail("PrintInfoJob",
                Scheduler.DEFAULT_GROUP, PrintInfoJob.class);

        // Create and register the global job listener
        TriggerListener triggerListener =
            new SimpleTriggerListener("SimpleTriggerListener");

        scheduler.addGlobalTriggerListener(triggerListener);

        /*
         * Set up a trigger to start firing now, with no end
         * date/time, repeat forever and have 10 secs
         * (10000 ms) between each firing.
         */
        Trigger trigger = TriggerUtils.makeSecondlyTrigger(10);
        trigger.setName("SimpleTrigger");
        trigger.setStartTime(new Date());

        // Register the JobDetail and Trigger
        scheduler.scheduleJob(jobDetail, trigger);

        // Start the scheduler
        scheduler.start();
        logger.info("Scheduler was started at " + new Date());
    }
}
```

Listing 7.7 shows how to register the
SimpleTriggerListener as a global TriggerListener. It
looks almost identical to the code from Listing 7.3 that registered a global JobListener. You just need to call the
addGlobalTriggerListener() method and pass it the
TriggerListener instance.

Registering a Nonglobal TriggerListener

To register a nonglobal TriggerListener, you need to call the
addTriggerListener() method and pass the TriggerListener
instance. Then call the addTriggerListener() method on the

trigger instance and pass the name of the TriggerListener. This is shown in Listing 7.8.

Listing 7.8 Using a Nonglobal TriggerListener

```
package org.cavaness.quartzbook.chapter7;

import java.util.Date;

import org.apache.commons.logging.Log;
import org.apache.commons.logging.LogFactory;
import org.cavaness.quartzbook.common.PrintInfoJob;
import org.quartz.JobDetail;
import org.quartz.Scheduler;
import org.quartz.SchedulerException;
import org.quartz.Trigger;
import org.quartz.TriggerListener;
import org.quartz.TriggerUtils;
import org.quartz.impl.StdSchedulerFactory;

public class Listing_7_8 {
    static Log logger = LogFactory.getLog(Listing_7_8.class);

    public static void main(String[] args) {
        Listing_7_8 example = new Listing_7_8();

        try {
            example.startScheduler();
        } catch (SchedulerException ex) {
            logger.error(ex);
        }
    }

    public void startScheduler() throws SchedulerException {

        // Create an instance of the factory
        Scheduler scheduler = null;

        // Create the scheduler and JobDetail
        scheduler = StdSchedulerFactory.getDefaultScheduler();
        JobDetail jobDetail = new JobDetail("PrintInfoJob",
                Scheduler.DEFAULT_GROUP, PrintInfoJob.class);

        // Create and register the nonglobal job listener
        TriggerListener triggerListener =
            new SimpleTriggerListener("SimpleTriggerListener");

        scheduler.addTriggerListener( triggerListener );

        /*
         * Set up a trigger to start firing now, with no end
         * date/time, repeat forever and have 10 secs
         * (10000 ms) between each firing.
         */
        Trigger trigger = TriggerUtils.makeSecondlyTrigger(10);
        trigger.setName("SimpleTrigger");
        trigger.setStartTime(new Date());

        // Set the listener name for the trigger
```

Listing 7.8   Continued

```
        trigger.addTriggerListener( triggerListener.getName() );

        // Register the JobDetail and Trigger
        scheduler.scheduleJob(jobDetail, trigger);

        // Start the scheduler
        scheduler.start();
        logger.info("Scheduler was started at " + new Date());
    }
}
```

The same warning that we mentioned earlier for nonglobal JobListeners applies here: You should add the TriggerListener to the Scheduler before setting it on the trigger instance and storing the trigger.

Listening for Scheduler Events

The org.quartz.SchedulerListener interface contains a set of callback methods that the Scheduler invokes when key events take place during the life cycle of a Scheduler. Listing 7.9 shows the methods that are included in the SchedulerListener interface.

Listing 7.9   The Methods in the org.quartz.SchedulerListener Interface

```
public interface SchedulerListener {
    public void jobScheduled(Trigger trigger);
    public void jobUnscheduled(String triggerName, String triggerGroup);
    public void triggerFinalized(Trigger trigger);
    public void triggersPaused(String triggerName, String triggerGroup);
    public void triggersResumed(String triggerName,String triggerGroup);
    public void jobsPaused(String jobName, String jobGroup);
    public void jobsResumed(String jobName, String jobGroup);
    public void schedulerError(String msg, SchedulerException cause);
    public void schedulerShutdown();
}
```

As you can see from the methods listed in Listing 7.9, the SchedulerListener is notified when events occur at the Scheduler level, whether it's the addition or removal of a job in the Scheduler or if the Scheduler encounters a serious error. These events are more about the management of the Scheduler than a particular job or trigger.

The jobScheduled() and jobUnscheduled() Methods

The Scheduler calls these methods when a new JobDetail is scheduled or unscheduled, respectively.

The triggerFinalized() Method

The Scheduler calls this method when a trigger has reached the state that it will never fire again. Unless the job has been set up as durable, it will be removed from the Scheduler.

The triggersPaused() Method

The Scheduler calls this method when a trigger or group of triggers has been paused. If it's a trigger group, the triggerName parameter will be null.

The triggersResumed() Method

The Scheduler calls this method when a trigger or group of triggers has been unpaused (or resumed). If it's a trigger group, the triggerName parameter will be null.

The jobsPaused() Method

The Scheduler calls this method when a JobDetail or a group of JobDetails has been paused.

The jobsResumed() Method

The Scheduler calls this method when a job or a group of jobs has been unpaused (or resumed). If it's a job group, the jobName parameter will be null.

The schedulerError() Method

The Scheduler calls this method when a serious error has occurred during the normal runtime of the Scheduler. The type of error can vary, but a few examples are listed here:

- Problems instantiating a job class
- Problems trying to find the next trigger
- Repeated problems with the JobStore
- DataStore connection problems

You can use the getErrorCode() or getUnderlyingException() methods of the SchedulerException to get more information about the specific error.

The schedulerShutdown() Method

The Scheduler calls this method to inform the SchedulerListener that the Scheduler is shutting down.

Listing 7.10 shows a simple SchedulerListener implementation.

Listing 7.10   A Simplified **SchedulerListener** Implementation

```
package org.cavaness.quartzbook.chapter7;

import org.apache.commons.logging.Log;
import org.apache.commons.logging.LogFactory;
import org.quartz.SchedulerException;
import org.quartz.SchedulerListener;
import org.quartz.Trigger;

public class SimpleSchedulerListener implements SchedulerListener {
    Log logger = LogFactory.getLog(SimpleSchedulerListener.class);

    public void jobScheduled(Trigger trigger) {
        String jobName = trigger.getJobName();
        logger.info(jobName + " has been scheduled");
    }

    public void jobUnscheduled(String triggerName,
        String triggerGroup) {

        if (triggerName == null) {
            // triggerGroup is being unscheduled
            logger.info(triggerGroup + " is being unscheduled");
        } else {
            logger.info(triggerName + " is being unscheduled");
```

Listing 7.10   Continued

```
        }
    }

    public void triggerFinalized(Trigger trigger) {
        String jobName = trigger.getJobName();
        logger.info("Trigger is finished for " + jobName);
    }

    public void triggersPaused(String triggerName,
        String triggerGroup) {

        if (triggerName == null) {
            // triggerGroup is being unscheduled
            logger.info(triggerGroup + " is being paused");
        } else {
            logger.info(triggerName + " is being paused");
        }
    }

    public void triggersResumed(String triggerName,
        String triggerGroup) {

        if (triggerName == null) {
            // triggerGroup is being unscheduled
            logger.info(triggerGroup + " is now resuming");
        } else {
            logger.info(triggerName + " is now resuming");
        }
    }

    public void jobsPaused(String jobName, String jobGroup) {
        if (jobName == null) {
            // triggerGroup is being unscheduled
            logger.info(jobGroup + " is pausing");
        } else {
            logger.info(jobName + " is pausing");
        }
    }

    public void jobsResumed(String jobName, String jobGroup) {
        if (jobName == null) {
            // triggerGroup is being unscheduled
            logger.info(jobGroup + " is now resuming");
        } else {
            logger.info(jobName + " is now resuming");
        }
    }

    public void schedulerError(String msg, SchedulerException cause) {
        logger.error(msg, cause.getUnderlyingException());
    }

    public void schedulerShutdown() {
        logger.info("Scheduler is being shutdown");
    }
}
```

As with the previous examples, the
SimpleSchedulerListener in Listing 7.10 provides simple
implementations for the listener methods. Listing 7.11 uses
the SimpleSchedulerListener class.

Listing 7.11   Using the **SimpleSchedulerListener**

```java
package org.cavaness.quartzbook.chapter7;

import java.util.Date;

import org.apache.commons.logging.Log;
import org.apache.commons.logging.LogFactory;
import org.cavaness.quartzbook.common.PrintInfoJob;
import org.quartz.JobDetail;
import org.quartz.Scheduler;
import org.quartz.SchedulerException;
import org.quartz.SchedulerListener;
import org.quartz.Trigger;
import org.quartz.TriggerUtils;
import org.quartz.impl.StdSchedulerFactory;

public class Listing_7_11 {
    static Log logger = LogFactory.getLog(Listing_7_11.class);

    public static void main(String[] args) {
        Listing_7_11 example = new Listing_7_11();
        try {
            example.startScheduler();
        } catch (SchedulerException ex) {
            logger.error(ex);
        }
    }

    public void startScheduler() throws SchedulerException {

        // Create an instance of the factory
        Scheduler scheduler = null;

        // Create the scheduler and JobDetail
        scheduler = StdSchedulerFactory.getDefaultScheduler();

        // Create and register the scheduler listener
        SchedulerListener schedulerListener =
            new SimpleSchedulerListener();

        scheduler.addSchedulerListener(schedulerListener);

        // Start the scheduler
        scheduler.start();
        logger.info("Scheduler was started at " + new Date());

        // Create the JobDetail
        JobDetail jobDetail = new JobDetail("PrintInfoJob",
                Scheduler.DEFAULT_GROUP, PrintInfoJob.class);
```

Listing 7.11   Using the `SimpleSchedulerListener`

```
        /*
         * Set up a trigger to start firing now, with no end
         * date/time, repeat forever and have 5 secs
         * between each firing.
         */
        Trigger trigger = TriggerUtils.makeSecondlyTrigger(5);
        trigger.setName("SimpleTrigger");
        trigger.setStartTime(new Date());

        // Register the JobDetail and Trigger
        scheduler.scheduleJob(jobDetail, trigger);

    }
}
```

We changed some things in Listing 7.11 from the previous examples, to actually cause more of the `SchedulerListener` methods to be called. In Listing 7.11, the Scheduler is created and started before the job is registered. This is so the `jobScheduled()` method gets called when the job is scheduled. We also changed the trigger to repeat two times instead of running indefinitely. This forces the `triggerFinalized()` method to be called because there were no more firing times for the trigger. Other than these contrived conditions, using the `SchedulerListener` is the same as using the job or trigger listeners.

Using the `FileScanListener`

The Quartz framework contains another listener that we haven't mentioned yet. This one is unlike the other listeners, in that it's designed for a specific purpose: to be used with a utility job that comes with the framework.

The Listener, which is the `org.quartz.jobs.` `FileScanListener` interface, is explicitly designed to be used with the `FileScanJob`, which is also located in the `org.` `quartz.jobs` package. The `FileScanJob` checks the `lastModifiedDate` on a specific file. When someone changes the file, the job invokes the `fileUpdated()` method on the `FileScanListener`.

As with the other types of Quartz listeners, you must create a concrete class that implements the `FileScanListener` interface. Only one method must be implemented:

```
public void fileUpdated(String fileName);
```

Listing 7.12 shows our extremely simple `FileScanListener`
implementation.

Listing 7.12   A Simple `FileScanListener` Implementation

```
package org.cavaness.quartzbook.chapter7;

import java.io.File;
import java.sql.Timestamp;

import org.apache.commons.logging.Log;
import org.apache.commons.logging.LogFactory;

public class SimpleFileScanListener implements org.quartz.jobs.FileScanListener {
    private static Log logger = LogFactory.getLog(SimpleFileScanListener.class);

    public void fileUpdated(String fileName) {
        File file = new File(fileName);
        Timestamp modified = new Timestamp(file.lastModified());

        logger.info( fileName + " was changed at " + modified );
    }
}
```

Obviously, you would want to do something more interesting than just writing out a log message, but you get the point
with the simple example in Listing 7.12. We also need to schedule the `FileScanJob` that uses the new type of listener. Listing
7.13 shows how to schedule the `FileScanJob`.

Listing 7.13   Scheduling the `FileScanJob`

```
package org.cavaness.quartzbook.chapter7;

import java.util.Date;

import org.apache.commons.logging.Log;
import org.apache.commons.logging.LogFactory;
import org.quartz.JobDataMap;
import org.quartz.JobDetail;
import org.quartz.Scheduler;
import org.quartz.SchedulerException;
import org.quartz.Trigger;
import org.quartz.TriggerUtils;
import org.quartz.impl.StdSchedulerFactory;
import org.quartz.jobs.FileScanJob;

public class Listing_7_13 {
    private static Log logger = LogFactory.getLog(Listing_7_13.class);

    public static void main(String[] args) {
        Listing_7_13 example = new Listing_7_13();
```

Listing 7.13   Continued

```
        try {
            Scheduler scheduler = example.createScheduler();
            example.scheduleJob(scheduler);
            scheduler.start();

        } catch (SchedulerException ex) {
            logger.error(ex);
        }
    }

    protected Scheduler createScheduler() throws
        SchedulerException {

        return StdSchedulerFactory.getDefaultScheduler();
    }

    protected void scheduleJob(Scheduler scheduler) throws
        SchedulerException {

        // Store the FileScanListener instance
        scheduler.getContext().put("SimpleFileScanListener",
                new SimpleFileScanListener());

        // Create a JobDetail for the FileScanJob
        JobDetail jobDetail = new JobDetail("FileScanJob", null,
                FileScanJob.class);

        // The FileScanJob needs some parameters
        JobDataMap jobDataMap = new JobDataMap();
        jobDataMap.put(FileScanJob.FILE_NAME,
                "C:\\quartz-book\\input1\\test.txt");
        jobDataMap.put(FileScanJob.FILE_SCAN_LISTENER_NAME,
                "SimpleFileScanListener");
        jobDetail.setJobDataMap(jobDataMap);

        // Create a Trigger and register the Job
        Trigger trigger = TriggerUtils.makeSecondlyTrigger(30);
        trigger.setName("SimpleTrigger");
        trigger.setStartTime(new Date());

        scheduler.scheduleJob(jobDetail, trigger);
    }
}
```

The program in Listing 7.13 is like almost every other Quartz application that needs to schedule a job. The FileScanJob requires two parameters: the FILE_NAME of the file to watch and the name of the FileScanListener (FILE_SCAN_LISTENER_NAME). The values for these two parameters are stored in the JobDataMap so the FileScanJob can access them.

The only "gotcha" that you should watch out for is to make sure that you add an instance of the FileScanListener to the

SchedulerContext. This is done in Listing 7.13 and shown in the following code fragment:

```
scheduler.getContext().put("SimpleFileScanListener",
    new SimpleFileScanListener());
```

This is necessary because the FileScanJob gets a reference to the SchedulerContext and looks for a FileScanListener using the name that was set in the JobDataMap:

```
jobDataMap.put(FileScanJob.FILE_SCAN_LISTENER_NAME,
    "SimpleFileScanListener");
```

If you are confused, don't worry: Look at the source code for the org.quartz.jobs.FileScanJob class. That's one of the best things about open source software.

Implementing Listeners in the `quartz_jobs.xml` File

All the examples in this chapter have shown how to set up listeners using a programmatic approach. This chapter wouldn't be complete if we didn't provide at least an example of configuring a listener using a declarative approach with the quartz_jobs.xml file.

Starting with Quartz 1.5, you are able to specify listeners in the job-definition file, otherwise known as the quartz_jobs.xml file. Listing 7.14 shows an example of using a global listener.

Listing 7.14   Quartz Listeners Can Be Implemented with the quartz_jobs.xml File

```xml
<?xml version='1.0' encoding='utf-8'?>

<quartz>
  <job-listener
    class-name="org.cavaness.quartzbook.chapter7.SimpleJobListener"
    name="SimpleJobListener">
</job-listener>

<job>
  <job-detail>
    <name>PrintInfoJob</name>
    <group>DEFAULT</group>
```

Listing 7.14   Continued

```
    <job-listener-ref>SimpleJobListener</job-listener-ref>
    <job-class>
      org.cavaness.quartzbook.common.PrintInfoJob
    </job-class>
  </job-detail>

  <trigger>
    <simple>
      <name>printJobTrigger</name>
      <group>DEFAULT</group>
      <job-name> PrintInfoJob</job-name>
      <job-group>DEFAULT</job-group>
      <start-time>2005-09-13 6:10:00 PM</start-time>
       <!- repeat indefinitely every 10 seconds ->
      <repeat-count>-1</repeat-count>
      <repeat-interval>10000</repeat-interval>
    </simple>
  </trigger>
 </job>
</quartz>
```

You see in Listing 7.14 the additional `<job-listener>` element with the two required attributes:

```
<job-listener
  class-name="org.cavaness.quartzbook.chapter7.SimpleJobListener"
  name="SimpleJobListener">
```

The `class-name` property identifies the fully qualified name of the listener class. The `name` attribute assigns a logical name to the listener used in the `<job-detail>` element.

The next step is to define a `<job-listener-ref>` element in the `<job-detail>` element in the same file for each job that you want the listener on. The value of the element must match the `name` property of one of the defined `<job-listener>` elements in the file.

After you have done that, make sure you've configured the Scheduler to use the `JobInitializationPlugin` by setting the properties in the `quartz.properties` file. Quartz plug-ins are discussed in detail in the next chapter. For now, just add the following lines to your `quartz.properties` file:

```
org.quartz.plugin.jobInitializer.class =
      org.quartz.plugins.xml.JobInitializationPlugin

org.quartz.plugin.jobInitializer.overWriteExistingJobs = true
org.quartz.plugin.jobInitializer.failOnFileNotFound = true
org.quartz.plugin.jobInitializer.validating=false
```

Then name your XML file `quartz_jobs.xml` and put the file in your classpath.

> ### Some "Gotchas" to Watch Out For
>
> It's worth mentioning a couple problems that you will likely run into when trying to set up listeners with the XML file. In Quartz 1.5, at least, the `setName()` method for the listeners was not included in the interface. The `getName()` method is present, but not the corresponding `setName()`. This doesn't seem to cause a problem when using listeners programmatically, but it will with the declarative approach. You simply need to create a `setName()` method for your listener.
>
> The other tip is to make sure you have a `no-arg` constructor for your listener. Under certain conditions, the Quartz framework won't complain, but when using this declarative approach, you will get an error. It's better just to declare the `no-arg` constructor and always be safe.

Thread Use in Listeners

As you look at the methods in the listener interfaces, you might wonder what role threads play in the invocation of the listener methods. There is indeed a sequence to the listener method calls, as you can imagine by looking at the names. During the life cycle of a job execution, the order of calls to the listener is generally fixed. Figure 7.2 illustrates the order in which the listener methods are called and how the worker threads are involved.

The sequence of listener method calls is fixed. As Figure 7.2 shows, the same thread that calls the job's `execute()` method is used to call the `JobListener` and `TriggerListener` methods before and after the execution. This is important to know if you are using any sort of third-party thread-management tools or have decided to implement your own thread-pool management. It can also have a negative impact on performance if you implement long-running logic in the listener methods. Because the thread that invokes the listener methods is the same worker thread executing jobs, you should not implement listener methods that are complicated and that take a long time to complete. Keep their execution times to a minimum.

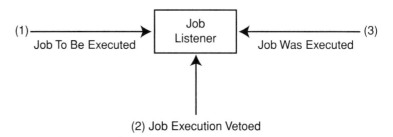

The Listener methods are called in Sequence.

FIGURE 7.2   Listener methods are called in a particular
sequence.

Uses of the Quartz Listeners

Armed with all this information, what can you do with these
listeners? Actually, you can do quite a bit. First, it's worth noting that, internally, Quartz uses these listeners to help manage
the Scheduler and your jobs and triggers. The framework also
includes a couple plug-ins that implement the listener interfaces
that log all job and trigger history: `org.quartz.plugins.`
`history.LoggingJobHistoryPlugin` and `org.quartz.`
`plugins.history.LoggingTriggerHistoryPlugin`, respectively. We talk about Quartz plug-ins in the next chapter.

Here are a few uses for listeners:

- Catching misfires and rescheduling
- Sending an e-mail after successful completion of a job
- Vetoing job execution based on certain flags set up in
  the database

- Scheduling other jobs based on successful or failed completion of a job
- Recording the actual time a job runs

These are only a few ideas. Quartz listeners provide a way for you to be notified programmatically when specific events take place during the runtime of your Quartz application. What you choose to do with that knowledge, if anything, is entirely up to you.

## CHAPTER 8

USING QUARTZ PLUG-INS

The Quartz framework offers several ways to extend the capabilities of the platform. By using various "hooks" (commonly referred to as extension points), Quartz becomes very easy to extend and customize to suit your needs. One of the easiest methods for extending the framework is to use Quartz plug-ins. This chapter looks at how to use the plug-in mechanism to make Quartz go where no Quartz user has gone before.

What Is a Plug-In?

If you have used other open source frameworks such as Apache Struts, you're already familiar with concept of plug-ins and their use. Quite simply, a Quartz plug-in is a Java class that implements the `org.quartz.spi.SchedulerPlugin` interface and is registered as a plug-in with the Scheduler. The plug-in interface contains three methods and is shown in Listing 8.1.

Listing 8.1   A Quartz Plug-In Must Implement the SchedulerPlugin Interface

```
public interface SchedulerPlugin {

    public void initialize(String name, Scheduler scheduler)
            throws SchedulerException;

    public void start();
    public void shutdown();

}
```

The methods of the SchedulerPlugin are called during the initialization and startup of a Scheduler. The Scheduler calls these methods on every plug-in that is registered. The following sections describe when each method of the plug-in is called.

The initialize() Method

The initialize() method is called during the creation of the Scheduler. When the getScheduler() method is called on the StdSchedulerFactory, the factory calls the initialize() method on all the registered plug-ins.

PLUG-INS DON'T WORK WITH THE DirectSchedulerFactory

Plug-ins are designed to be used only with the StdSchedulerFactory. It's a limitation within the framework. If you want to use plug-ins, then you'll need to use the StdSchedulerFactory to retrieve your Scheduler instance.

Each plug-in is registered with a unique name. This given name and Scheduler instance is included in the call to the initialize() method. You should take whatever action is necessary to initialize your plug-in. For example, your plug-in might need to read and parse data from a file or database.

SCHEDULER IS NOT FULLY SET UP AT initialize() TIME

The Scheduler has not been fully initialized when this method is called, so interaction with the Scheduler should be kept to a minimum. For example, you should not attempt to schedule any jobs during the initialize() method.

If there is a problem initializing your plug-in, you should throw an `org.quartz.SchedulerConfigException`, which is a subclass of `SchedulerException`. This prevents the plug-in from being loaded and stops any further interaction with the Scheduler.

The `start()` Method

The Scheduler instance calls the `start()` method to let the plug-in know that it can perform any startup actions it needs. For example, if you have jobs to schedule, this is the time to schedule them.

The `shutdown()` Method

The `shutdown()` method is called to inform the plug-in that the Scheduler is shutting down. This is an opportunity for the plug-in to clean up any open resources that are open. For example, database connections or open files should be closed.

SCHEDULER INSTANCE NOT PASSED IN `start()` OR `shutdown()`

Notice that the Scheduler instance is not passed as an argument to the `start()` or `shutdown()` methods. If your plug-in needs access to the Scheduler during `start()` or `shutdown()`, you need to store the Scheduler in an instance variable in the plug-in.

Creating a Quartz Plug-In

Creating a new plug-in is very simple. All you have to do is create a Java class (or reuse an existing one) that implements the `org.quartz.spi.SchedulerPlugin` interface. The Scheduler will create an instance of the plug-in during startup. The plug-in must have a no-argument constructor and obviously not be abstract.

The `JobInitializationPlugin`

The Quartz framework includes a plug-in for loading job and trigger information from an XML file. The plug-in is `org.quartz.plugins.xml.JobInitializationPlugin` and was discussed briefly back in Chapter 3, "Hello, Quartz." When you use this plug-in, the Quartz framework searches for a file called `quartz_jobs.xml` and attempts to load job and trigger information from this file.

CHANGING THE XML FILE THAT THE `JobInitializationPlugin` LOADS FROM
The plug-in enables you to change the name of the jobs file that it looks for to load job and trigger information. You change it by setting a different filename in the `quartz.properties` file. We talk more about setting parameters for plug-ins later in this chapter.

As Chapter 3 explained, this plug-in is very convenient when your application requirements don't involve loading job information from a database. It's also very useful during development and testing because you can quickly configure which jobs and triggers are to be fired. That is, arguably, it's easier to modify an XML file than a set of database tables.

A nice extension to this idea of loading job and trigger information from an XML file would be to have a directory where you can store job XML files, and, by using a plug-in, the Scheduler would load whatever job files were present. This would enable you to conveniently add or remove jobs at Scheduler startup by simply adding or removing them from the specified directory. In the rest of this chapter, we show you how to build this plug-in.

Creating the `JobLoaderPlugin`

We call this new plug-in the `JobLoaderPlugin`. Listing 8.2 shows the `JobLoaderPlugin` class.

Listing 8.2   A Quartz `SchedulerPlugin` **that Loads Multiple Job Files from a Directory**

```java
package org.cavaness.quartzbook.chapter8;

import java.io.File;

import org.apache.commons.logging.Log;
import org.apache.commons.logging.LogFactory;
import org.quartz.Scheduler;
import org.quartz.SchedulerConfigException;
import org.quartz.SchedulerException;
import org.quartz.spi.SchedulerPlugin;
import org.quartz.xml.JobSchedulingDataProcessor;

public class JobLoaderPlugin implements SchedulerPlugin {

    private static Log logger =
        LogFactory.getLog(JobLoaderPlugin.class);

    // The directory to load jobs from
    private String jobsDirectory;

    // An array of File objects
    private File[] jobFiles = null;

    private String pluginName;

    private Scheduler scheduler;

    private boolean validateXML = true;

    private boolean validateSchema = true;

    public JobLoaderPlugin() {
    }

    public File[] getJobFiles() {
        return jobFiles;
    }

    public void setJobFiles(File[] jobFiles) {
        this.jobFiles = jobFiles;
    }

    public boolean isValidateSchema() {
        return validateSchema;
    }

    public void setValidateSchema(boolean validatingSchema) {
        this.validateSchema = validatingSchema;
    }

    public void initialize(String name, final Scheduler scheduler)
            throws SchedulerException {

        this.pluginName = name;
        this.scheduler = scheduler;

        logger.debug("Registering Plugin " + pluginName);
        // Load the job definitions from the specified directory
```

Listing 8.2   Continued

```
        loadJobs();

    }

    private void loadJobs() throws SchedulerException {

        File dir = null;

        // Check directory
        if (getJobsDirectory() == null
                || !(dir =
                new File(getJobsDirectory())).exists()) {
            throw new SchedulerConfigException(
                    "The jobs directory was missing "
                            + jobsDirectory);
        }

        logger.info("Loading jobs from " + dir.getName());

        // Only XML files, filtering out any directories
        this.jobFiles = dir.listFiles(new XMLFileOnlyFilter());
    }

    public void start() {
        processJobs();
    }

    public void shutdown() {
        // nothing to clean up
    }

    public void processJobs() {
        // There should be at least one job
        if (getJobFiles() == null || getJobFiles().length == 0) {
            return;
        }

        JobSchedulingDataProcessor processor =
            new JobSchedulingDataProcessor(
                true, isValidateXML(), isValidateSchema());

        int size = getJobFiles().length;
        for (int i = 0; i < size; i++) {
            File jobFile = getJobFiles()[i];

            String fileName = jobFile.getAbsolutePath();
            logger.debug("Loading job file: " + fileName);

            try {

                processor.processFileAndScheduleJobs(
                    fileName, scheduler, true);

            } catch (Exception ex) {
                logger.error("Error loading jobs: " + fileName);
                logger.error(ex);
            }
```

Listing 8.2   Continued

```
            }
    }

    public String getJobsDirectory() {
        return jobsDirectory;
    }

    public void setJobsDirectory(String jobsDirectory) {
        this.jobsDirectory = jobsDirectory;
    }

    public String getPluginName() {
        return pluginName;
    }

    public void setPluginName(String pluginName) {
        this.pluginName = pluginName;
    }

    public boolean isValidateXML() {
        return validateXML;
    }

    public void setValidateXML(boolean validateXML) {
        this.validateXML = validateXML;
    }
}
```

The real work of the JobLoaderPlugin in Listing 8.2 is done in just two methods: initialize() and start(). Both are required by the SchedulerPlugin interface. The rest of the methods are just setXXX and getXXX methods to fulfill the JavaBean contract because private properties have been declared.

THE JobLoaderPlugin initialize() METHOD

As you can see, the initialize() method, which is called by the Scheduler, calls the private loadJobs() method. The loadJobs() method uses the jobsDirectory that was passed in from the quartz.properties file to retrieve all XML files stored in that directory. The plug-in doesn't try to schedule the jobs yet because the Scheduler isn't fully instantiated when the plug-in's initialize() method is called. The JobLoaderPlugin simply holds on to an array of File objects, waiting for the start() method to be called. We also hold on to the instance of the Scheduler so that we have access to it when the start() method is called.

THE `JobLoaderPlugin` `start()` METHOD

When the Scheduler calls the `start()` method in the `JobLoaderPlugin`, the `start()` method calls `processJobs()`. The `processJobs()` method loops through the array of job files and loads each one into the Scheduler instance.

The processing of the job file is done by an instance of an `org.quartz.xml JobSchedulingDataProcessor`. The `processFileAndScheduleJobs()` method is called and passed the filename, the Scheduler instance, and a Boolean that tells whether existing jobs should be overwritten.

When the `processJobs()` method is complete, all job files from the specified `jobsDirectory` should have been loaded and scheduled.

Registering Your Plug-Ins

When a `SchedulerFactory` is first initialized, it searches the `quartz.properties` file for any Quartz plug-ins that you configured. It creates a new instance of the plug-in using the `newInstance()` method on `java.lang.Class`. Your plug-in must have a no-argument constructor, as the `JobLoaderPlugin` did in Listing 8.2.

To register your plug-in in the `quartz.properties` file, create a property in the `quartz.properties` file using the following format:

```
org.quartz.plugin.<pluginName>.class=
    <fully_qualified_class_name_of_plugin>
```

Quartz looks for all entries in the properties file that have the key:

```
org.quartz.plugin.<pluginName>.class
```

Then it attempts to create an instance of the class that is on the right side of the equals sign and assumes that it's a plug-in. You name the plug-in by providing a unique name in the `<pluginName>` field.

Listing 8.3 shows a `quartz.properties` file for use with the
`JobLoaderPlugin`.

Listing 8.3   Register the `JobLoaderPlugin` in the `quartz.properties` File

```
#==================================================================
# Configure Main Scheduler Properties
#==================================================================

org.quartz.scheduler.instanceName = QuartzScheduler
org.quartz.scheduler.instanceId = AUTO

#==================================================================
# Configure ThreadPool
#==================================================================

org.quartz.threadPool.class = org.quartz.simpl.SimpleThreadPool
org.quartz.threadPool.threadCount =  5
org.quartz.threadPool.threadPriority = 5

#==================================================================
# Configure JobStore
#==================================================================

org.quartz.jobStore.misfireThreshold = 60000
org.quartz.jobStore.class = org.quartz.simpl.RAMJobStore

#==================================================================
# Configure Plugins
#==================================================================
org.quartz.plugin.jobLoader.class =
org.cavaness.quartzbook.chapter8.JobLoaderPlugin

org.quartz.plugin.jobLoader.jobsDirectory =
c:\\quartz-book\\sample\\chapter8
```

You should have seen most of the settings in the
`quartz.properties` file from Listing 8.3. The last section is
where the `JobLoaderPlugin` is registered.

Specifying the Plug-In in `quartz.properties`

During initialization and startup, the Quartz Scheduler loads the
properties from the `quartz.properties` file. You must follow a
particular format when specifying plug-ins in the
`quartz.properties` file. The format is shown here:

```
<plugin prefix>.<pluginName><.class>=<fully qualified Plugin class name>
```

- The `<plugin prefix>` is always `org.quartz.plugin`.
- The `<pluginName>` is a unique name that you assign.
- To specify the plug-in class, use the suffix `.class`.
- The right side is the fully qualified class name of the plug-in.

Looking back at Listing 8.3, you can see that our `JobLoaderPlugin` has this format:

```
org.quartz.plugin.jobLoader.class=
    org.cavaness.quartzbook.chapter8.JobLoaderPlugin
```

The name given to the plug-in is `jobLoader` and is arbitrary. We could have used any name, as long as it was unique from any other registered plug-in. On the right side of the equals sign, you must specify the fully qualified name of the plug-in class. This class must be in the classpath or available to the classloader.

Passing Parameters to the Plug-In

Most plug-ins require configuration values and, keeping with good programming practices, we don't want to have to hard-code these values into the plug-in class. Quartz provides a mechanism to pass parameter values to your plug-in class by providing these parameter values in the `quartz.properties` file.

The Scheduler finds all other properties that match a format of this:

```
<plugin prefix>.<plugin name>.<property name>=<someValue>
```

It treats them as JavaBean properties on the plug-in class. From Listing 8.3, this means that this property is turned into a `setJobsDirectory()` method call with the string value of `c:\\quartz-book\\sample\\chapter8` as a parameter for the method:

```
org.quartz.plugin.jobLoader.jobsDirectory=
    c:\\quartz-book\\sample\\chapter8
```

You can have as many properties as you need to configure your plug-in.

PLUG-IN PROPERTIES MUST HAVE set() METHODS

You must provide a setXXX() method for each property you intend to pass to the plug-in class. Quartz throws a SchedulerException and halts the Scheduler if it can't find a public setXXX() method for the property. Based on the JavaBean specification, you should provide both get() and set() methods for the properties.

The Quartz framework converts the property values to the type specified in the plug-in, assuming that it's a primitive type. For example, you can specify properties of type int and expect Quartz to convert the String from the quartz.properties file to an int. The framework, however, will not convert 1 to an integer class.

QUARTZ USES INTROSPECTION TO SET VALUES

Quartz uses introspection and reflection to convert the parameter values in the quartz.properties file to their correct type in the plug-in class. You might have guessed that it uses the Common BeanUtils from Jakarata, but this isn't the case yet.

Creating the Job File for the JobLoaderPlugin

The JobLoaderPlugin looks for all XML files in the specified directory and assumes that each file is a valid Quartz jobs file. By "valid," we mean that the XML file adheres to the latest job-scheduling XSD file, which at the time of this writing is job_scheduling_data_1_5.xsd.

To make the JobLoaderPlugin more useful, we put each job, along with its job detail and trigger information, in a single XML file. This enables us to add and remove complete jobs just by putting the file into the directory or taking it out. This is very helpful in a development environment when you want to test only certain jobs. A single job XML file is shown in Listing 8.4.

Listing 8.4   A Job XML File Read by the `JobLoaderPlugin`

```xml
<?xml version='1.0' encoding='utf-8'?>


<quartz xmlns="http://www.opensymphony.com/quartz/JobSchedulingData"
  xmlns:xsi="http://www.w3.org/2001/XMLSchema-instance"
  xsi:schemaLocation="http://www.opensymphony.com/quartz/JobSchedulingData
  http://www.opensymphony.com/quartz/xml/job_scheduling_data_1_5.xsd"
  version="1.5">

  <job>
    <job-detail>
      <name>PrintInfoJob1</name>
      <group>DEFAULT</group>
      <job-class>
        org.cavaness.quartzbook.chapter3.ScanDirectoryJob
      </job-class>
      <volatility>false</volatility>
      <durability>false</durability>
      <recover>false</recover>

      <job-data-map allows-transient-data="true">
        <entry>
          <key>SCAN_DIR</key>
          <value>c:\quartz-book\input1</value>
        </entry>
      </job-data-map>
    </job-detail>

    <trigger>
      <simple>
        <name>trigger1</name>
        <group>DEFAULT</group>
        <job-name>PrintInfoJob1</job-name>
        <job-group>DEFAULT</job-group>
        <start-time>2005-07-30T16:04:00</start-time>

        <!-- repeat indefinitely every 10 seconds -->
        <repeat-count>-1</repeat-count>
        <repeat-interval>10000</repeat-interval>
      </simple>
    </trigger>
  </job>


</quartz>
```

The job file is Listing 8.4 contains all the information necessary for the `JobLoaderPlugin` to schedule the job. This file also contains an entry for the `JobDataMap`, which is available to the job class at runtime. The example in Listing 8.4 uses a configured `SimpleTrigger` to schedule an infinitely repeating trigger that fires every 10 seconds. To further test the plug-in, we

created a second job file, which differs from the first in some
small way. Listing 8.5 shows the second job file.

Listing 8.5   A Second Job XML File Loaded by the `JobLoaderPlugin`

```xml
<?xml version='1.0' encoding='utf-8'?>

<quartz xmlns="http://www.opensymphony.com/quartz/JobSchedulingData"
  xmlns:xsi="http://www.w3.org/2001/XMLSchema-instance"
  xsi:schemaLocation="http://www.opensymphony.com/quartz/JobSchedulingData
  http://www.opensymphony.com/quartz/xml/job_scheduling_data_1_5.xsd"
  version="1.5">

  <job>
    <job-detail>
      <name>PrintInfoJob2</name>
      <group>DEFAULT</group>
      <job-class>
        org:cavaness.quartzbook.chapter3.ScanDirectoryJob</job-class>
      <volatility>false</volatility>
      <durability>false</durability>
      <recover>false</recover>

      <job-data-map allows-transient-data="true">
        <entry>
         <key>SCAN_DIR</key>
          <value>c:\quartz-book\input2</value>
        </entry>
      </job-data-map>

    </job-detail>

     <trigger>
      <simple>
        <name>trigger2</name>
        <group>DEFAULT</group>
        <job-name>PrintInfoJob2</job-name>
        <job-group>DEFAULT</job-group>
        <start-time>2005-07-30T16:04:00</start-time>
        <!-- repeat indefinitely every 10 seconds -->
        <repeat-count>-1</repeat-count>
        <repeat-interval>60000</repeat-interval>
      </simple>
    </trigger>
  </job>

</quartz>
```

The second job file in Listing 8.5 differs only slightly from
the one in Listing 8.4. We've changed the directory for the job,
which is scanned and changed the trigger schedule. The point
here is that you can have multiple jobs in the jobs directory,
and the `JobLoaderPlugin` will load them all and schedule them
individually with the Scheduler.

Using Multiple Plug-Ins

You can register as many plug-ins in the `quartz.properties` file as you like. However, the order of loading and initialization can't be guaranteed because Quartz loads all the properties into a map and then loops through the plug-ins in the order that they are retrieved from the map.

To get around this limitation, you can create a Quartz plug-in that acts as a parent plug-in and loads multiple other plug-ins in a given order. Listing 8.6 shows what the `ParentPlugin` looks like.

Listing 8.6 The `ParentPlugin` Can Load Child Plug-Ins in a Specified Order

```
package org.cavaness.quartzbook.chapter8;

import java.util.ArrayList;
import java.util.List;
import java.util.StringTokenizer;

import org.apache.commons.logging.Log;
import org.apache.commons.logging.LogFactory;
import org.quartz.Scheduler;
import org.quartz.SchedulerConfigException;
import org.quartz.SchedulerException;
import org.quartz.spi.SchedulerPlugin;

public class ParentPlugin implements SchedulerPlugin {
    private static Log logger = LogFactory.getLog(ParentPlugin.class);

    // A list of child plug-ins
    private List childPlugins = new ArrayList();

    private String childPluginNames;

    private String pluginName;

    private Scheduler scheduler;

    /**
     * Default no-arg Constructor
     *
     */
    public ParentPlugin() {
    }

    /**
     * Pass the initialize call on to the child plug-ins.
     *
     * @throws SchedulerConfigException
     *             if there is an error initializing.
     */
```

Listing 8.6   Continued

```java
    public void initialize(String name, final Scheduler scheduler)
            throws SchedulerException {

        this.pluginName = name;
        this.scheduler = scheduler;

        logger.info("Searching for child plugins to load");

        // The child plug-ins are comma-separated
        StringTokenizer tokenizer =
            new StringTokenizer(childPluginNames, ",");

        while (tokenizer.hasMoreElements()) {
            String pluginClassname = tokenizer.nextToken();

            try {
                Class pluginClass =
                    Class.forName(pluginClassname);

                Object obj = pluginClass.newInstance();

                // Make sure the specified class is a plug-in
                if (obj instanceof SchedulerPlugin) {
                    // Initialize the Plugin
                    SchedulerPlugin childPlugin =
                        (SchedulerPlugin) obj;

                        logger.info("Init child Plugin " +
                            pluginClassname);

                    childPlugin.initialize(pluginClassname,
                        scheduler);

                    // Store the child plug-in in the list
                    childPlugins.add(childPlugin);
                } else {
                    // Skip loading class
                    logger.error("Class is not a plugin " +
                        pluginClass);
                }

            } catch (Exception ex) {
                // On error, log and go to next child plug-in
                logger.error("Error loading plugin " +
                    pluginClassname, ex);
            }
        }
    }

    public void start() {
        // Start each child plug-in
        int size = childPlugins.size();
        for (int i = 0; i < size; i++) {
            SchedulerPlugin childPlugin =
                ((SchedulerPlugin) childPlugins.get(i));

            logger.info("Starting Child Plugin " + childPlugin);
            childPlugin.start();
```

Listing 8.6   Continued

```
        }
    }

    public void shutdown() {
        // Stop each child plug-in
        int size = childPlugins.size();
        for (int i = 0; i < size; i++) {
            SchedulerPlugin childPlugin =
                ((SchedulerPlugin) childPlugins.get(i));

            logger.info("Stopping Plugin " + childPlugin);
            childPlugin.shutdown();
        }
    }

    public String getPluginName() {
        return pluginName;
    }

    public void setPluginName(String pluginName) {
        this.pluginName = pluginName;
    }

    public String getChildPluginNames() {
        return childPluginNames;
    }

    public void setChildPluginNames(String childPluginNames) {
        this.childPluginNames = childPluginNames;
    }
}
```

The plug-in in Listing 8.6 doesn't do anything, as far as a plug-in goes, but it acts as a loader of the child plug-ins. A child plug-in is any valid Quartz plug-in. It can be one of your own or one of those included with the framework.

Configuring the `ParentPlugin` in the `quartz.properties` File

To configure the `ParentPlugin` in the `quartz.properties` file, just add the parent as you would any other plug-in. That is, add the following line:

```
org.quartz.plugin.parentPlugin.class =
    org.cavaness.quartzbook.chapter8.ParentPlugin
```

Then, to add the child plug-ins and the order you want them loaded, just specify a comma-separated list of plug-ins:

```
org.quartz.plugin.parentPlugin.childPluginNames=org.quartz.
➥plugins.history.LoggingJobHistoryPlugin,org.quartz.
➥plugins.history.LoggingTriggerHistoryPlugin
```

As Listing 8.6 shows, the `ParentPlugin` tokenizes the comma-separated string and loads the plug-ins in the order they were in the list. This might seem like a lot of complexity, but it gets the job done. A future version of the Quartz framework might support a load order mechanism for plug-ins, but for now, the `ParentPlugin` works fine.

Quartz Utility Plug-Ins

The Quartz framework includes several plug-ins that you can use in your application. This section briefly describes them and their purpose.

JobInitializationPlugin

We've already talked several times about this plug-in. It loads job and trigger information from an XML file (by default, `quartz_jobs.xml`). You can configure the name of the file by setting the filename parameter in the `quartz.properties` file for the plug-in. If you don't require a database to store your jobs or if you need the capability to quickly test specific jobs, this plug-in is very helpful.

JobInitializationPluginMulitple

The `JobInitializationPluginMultiple` is similar to the `JobInitializationPlugin`, as evident by its similar name. The difference is that it supports loading from multiple XML files instead of just one. In some ways, it's similar to the `JobLoaderPlugin` in Listing 8.2, except that the plug-in in Listing 8.2 looks at a directory instead of a set of files.

The files for the `JobInitializationPluginMultiple` are comma separated and specified in the `quartz.properties` file. A nice feature for this plug-in is that it can periodically scan the files for changes and then reload the job information when they change. It adds this behavior by implementing the `org.quartz.jobs.FileScanListener`. The scan interval (defined in seconds) can be specified in the properties file.

LoggingJobHistoryPlugin

The `org.quartz.plugins.history.` `LoggingJobHistoryPlugin` is used to log job history via the commons-logging framework. This includes job executions as well as any job vetoes. The plug-in allows for the log messages to be configurable but provides a default message format. The format can specify which fields from the job are included in the message. You can provide separate message formats for the following events:

- `jobFailedMessage`—Logged when a job fails execution
- `jobSuccessMessage`—Logged when a job completes execution
- `jobToBeFiredMessage`—Logged when a job is about to be executed
- `jobWasVetoedMessage`—Logged when a job gets vetoed

For example, if you wanted to override the default message for when a job is about to be executed and all you cared to see in the log message was the job name and time of execution, you could add this to the `quartz.properties` file:

```
org.quartz.plugin.jobHistory.class=org.quartz.plugins.
➥history.LoggingJobHistoryPlugin

org.quartz.plugin.jobHistory.jobToBeFiredMessage=Job {0} is
➥about to be fired at: {2, date, HH:mm:ss MM/dd/yyyy}
```

You can include several data elements about the job in the log message. Table 8.1 lists the elements and their data types.

Table 8.1   The Elements That Can Be Used in the Job Message Format

Element #	Data Type	Description
0	String	The name of the job
1	String	The name of the group for the job
2	Date	The current date
3	String	The name of the trigger
4	String	The name of the group for the trigger
5	Date	The scheduled firing time
6	Date	The next Scheduler firing time
7	Integer	The refire count from the JobExecutionContext

Each event can be separately configured in the quartz.properties file. The only downside to using this plug-in is that if you have many jobs, the log files can fill up quite fast, and it almost becomes too much information.

LoggingTriggerHistoryPlugin

This plug-in is equivalent to the job history plug-in but is used for trigger history information instead. You can provide log message formats for the following trigger events:

- triggerCompleteMessage—Logged when the trigger has finished all firings and will not fire again
- triggerFiredMessage—Logged when a trigger fires
- triggerMisfiredMessage—Logged after a trigger misfires

As with the LoggingJobHistoryPlugin, you can override the default message format in the properties file.

You can include several data elements about the job in the log message. Table 8.1 lists the elements and their data types. Table 8.2 lists the elements that can be used in the trigger history log message.

Table 8.2   The Elements that Can Be Used in the Trigger Message Format

Element #	Data Type	Description
0	String	The name of the trigger
1	String	The name of the group for the trigger
2	Date	The scheduled firing time
3	Date	The next firing time for the trigger
4	Date	The actual firing time of the trigger
5	String	The name of the job
6	String	The name of the group for the job
7	Integer	The refire count from the `JobExecutionContext`

Like the `LoggingJobHistoryPlugin`, this plug-in can log a lot of messages, especially if you have several triggers firing often.

ShutdownHookPlugin

This plug-in catches the shutdown event of the JVM and forces the Scheduler to shut down. You might be saying, "Why do I need to tell the Scheduler to shut down if the JVM is already shutting down?" The reason is mainly so the Scheduler can perform a "clean" shutdown.

When the `initialize()` method is called on the plug-in, it adds a new `java.lang.Thread` to the JVM. When the JVM gets a shutdown event, it is caused by one of two events:

- The program exits normally when the last nondaemon thread exits or when the `System.exit()` method is invoked.

- The JVM is terminated in response to user input, such as the user pressing Ctrl+C, or a system-wide event, such as a user logoff or system shutdown.

When the JVM gets the shutdown notification, it performs a callback to the shutdown thread and gives the thread a chance to run. In the case of the `ShutdownHookPlugin`, the `run()` method calls the Scheduler and tells it to shut down. Be default,

the shutdown() call to the Scheduler includes a Boolean value
of true, which tells the Scheduler to perform a "clean" shutdown. This means that the Scheduler will wait for all executing
triggers before stopping.

You can tell the plug-in to not perform a clean shutdown
by including that as a plug-in parameter in the quartz.
properties file.

## CHAPTER 9

USING QUARTZ REMOTELY

When running Quartz as a stand-alone application, access to the Scheduler is limited outside the JVM. As with any other J2SE application, there's no way to access objects within the JVM without using some alternative mechanism.

Fortunately, several techniques (or mechanisms) enable you to do this. The Quartz framework nicely supports one of those mechanisms, Remote Method Invocation (RMI). This chapter focuses on deploying Quartz as an RMI server so that you can access the Scheduler from outside the JVM. Several benefits arise from being able to do this, all of which are discussed in this chapter.

Why RMI with Quartz?

Imagine that you need to build a job Scheduler that receives dynamic job scheduling from various client applications. In this case, a single self-contained Quartz Scheduler will not work because these client applications need a way to talk to the Scheduler from within their own address space or JVM. In this case, using something such as RMI is the only way to solve this problem.

With RMI, objects that run in one address space (or JVM) are free to call objects running in other JVMs. This expands the Quartz toolkit and makes the framework more beneficial.

Brief Overview of Java RMI

In case RMI is new to you, it's worthwhile to get a brief overview of the technology before moving into the details of using RMI with Quartz. If you're completely comfortable with RMI—and, specifically, Java RMI—feel free to skip this material.

RMI is a mechanism that enables an object in one address space to communicate with objects in a different address space. These two address spaces can exist on the same machine or on entirely different ones. In general, you can think of RMI as an object-oriented Remote Procedure Call (RPC) mechanism.

RMI is not specific to Java, but Java does have its own version: Java RMI, which is released and supported by Sun (http://java.sun.com/products/jdk/rmi) as part of its Java SDK. Java RMI allows objects running in one JVM to communicate with and invoke methods on objects running in a second. These two JVMs can be running on the same machine or, more interestingly, on different ones. They might even be running on different platforms. For example, one JVM might be running on a Windows box, while the second runs on Linux. With Java RMI, it really doesn't matter. Figure 9.1 illustrates this scenario.

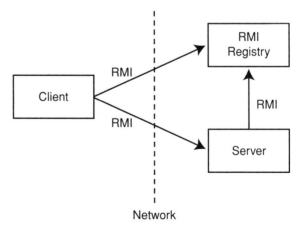

FIGURE 9.1 Java RMI enables developers to create distributed applications.

RMI is based on the principle of separation of responsibility. Interface definition is separated from the implementation. This coincides nicely with the goal of RMI: to allow a client, which is primarily concerned with the interface definition, to be separated (possibly physically) from the implementation of that interface definition. In order words, the client has an interface on which it can invoke the service call, while the implementation of that service lives on another machine. Figure 9.2 illustrates this separation within the Java programming language.

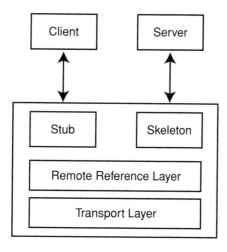

FIGURE 9.2
Java supports separating the service interface from the implementation.

When the RMI client invokes a method on the object, it is really invoking a method on a proxy object located in the client JVM. This proxy object knows how to communicate with the object located on the server. All communication, including values being passed to the server object and returned from it, occurs through the proxy object. This is shown in Figure 9.3.

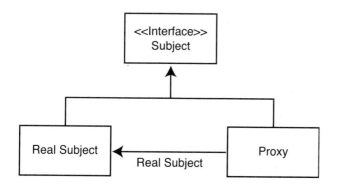

FIGURE 9.3
All communication from the client to the server goes through the proxy object.

Components of a Java RMI Application

Every Java RMI application consists of three components:

- The RMI server program
- The RMI client program
- The RMI Object Registry

THE RMI SERVER

The RMI server is responsible for creating the server object (which the client invokes methods on) and making the object available to remote clients. The RMI server runs in a standard JVM. The server objects are also regular Java objects and can be invoked locally as well as remotely.

THE RMI CLIENT

The RMI client is a Java program that (typically) runs in a separate JVM from the server; it might be on the same physical machine as the RMI or distributed on a separate machine. The client gets a reference to the server object by looking it up in the RMI Registry.

THE RMI OBJECT REGISTRY

The RMI Object Registry is used by both the RMI client and server. When the server wants to make an object available to remote clients, it registers the object (along with a unique name) with the Registry. After a server object has been registered, RMI clients and methods invoked on the object can look it up.

Requirements of RMI

RMI is a nice feature of the Java library. The capability to a call a method on an object from one JVM on a second JVM located on a machine in another part of the world is really powerful. But for RMI to work, several things must be in total alignment. Java is a very dynamic programming language. It supports the capability to (at runtime) download new class files that are not defined within the JVM's classpath. Along with this flexibility comes danger. You can imagine the bad things that could happen if your application were to download someone else's classes without you having knowledge of what's inside.

Using the `RMISecurityManager`

When using RMI, code that doesn't yet exist in the client can be dynamically downloaded from the server program. By default, the RMI application does not install a `SecurityManager`. This can be dangerous if an unsuspecting client downloads malicious code. To help secure the application, the RMI server application should install a special `SecurityManager` called `RMISecurityManager`.

The `RMISecurityManager` uses a Java security policy file to determine what permissions are granted to the RMI application. By default, Java looks for a policy file in the `java.home/lib/security` directory. A sample policy file entry is shown here:

```
grant {
  permission java.security.AllPermission;
};
```

This policy file entry grants full access to everyone. You should start with this setting to get everything working and then tighten your security policy.

Creating a Quartz RMI Server

You must follow a few steps to configure Quartz to use RMI. Some of these steps must be done on the Quartz RMI server, and a few are done on the Quartz client that connects to the server. We go through the server configuration steps first.

Configuring the Quartz RMI Server

The first step is to modify the `quartz.properties` file that will be deployed with the Quartz RMI server. When using RMI within Quartz, you must add several new properties. Table 9.1 includes the complete list of RMI properties.

Table 9.1 The Properties That Are Necessary for the RMI Server

Property	Default
`org.quartz.scheduler.rmi.export` **Notes:** This flag must be set to `true` if you want the Quartz Scheduler to be available as a RMI object.	`false`
`org.quartz.scheduler.rmi.registryHost` **Notes:** This is the host at which the RMI Registry is running.	`localhost`
`org.quartz.scheduler.rmi.registryPort` **Notes:** This is the port on which the RMI Registry is listening (usually 1099).	`1099`
`org.quartz.scheduler.rmi.createRegistry` **Notes:** This determines whether Quartz creates the RMI Registry. Use `false` or `never` if you don't want Quartz to create a Registry. Use `true` or `as_needed` if you want Quartz to first attempt to use an existing Registry and then fall back to creating one. Use `always` if you want Quartz to create a Registry and then fall back to using an existing one. If a Registry is created, it will be bound to a port number in the given `registryPort` and `registryHost`.	`never`
`org.quartz.scheduler.rmi.serverPort` **Notes:** This is the port on which the Quartz Scheduler service will bind and listen for connections. By default, the RMI service randomly selects a port as the Scheduler is bound to the RMI Registry.	`-1`

All the properties in Table 9.1 need to be added to the `quartz.properties` file for the Quartz RMI server. Although there are defaults for these properties, it's best to specify the values explicitly to prevent any confusion. Listing 9.1 shows an example properties file that is used with the Quartz RMI server.

Listing 9.1 An Example `quartz.properties` file for Use with the Quartz RMI Server

```
#================================================================
# Configure Main Scheduler Properties
#================================================================
org.quartz.scheduler.instanceName = RMIScheduler


#================================================================
# Configure RMI Properties
#================================================================
org.quartz.scheduler.rmi.export = true
org.quartz.scheduler.rmi.registryHost = localhost
org.quartz.scheduler.rmi.registryPort = 1099
```

Listing 9.1   Continued

```
org.quartz.scheduler.rmi.serverPort = 0
org.quartz.scheduler.rmi.createRegistry = true

#================================================================
# Configure ThreadPool
#================================================================
org.quartz.threadPool.class = org.quartz.simpl.SimpleThreadPool
org.quartz.threadPool.threadCount = 10
org.quartz.threadPool.threadPriority = 5

#================================================================
# Configure JobStore
#================================================================
org.quartz.jobStore.misfireThreshold = 60000
org.quartz.jobStore.class = org.quartz.simpl.RAMJobStore
```

You'll recognize most of the settings in Listing 9.1 from the various quartz.properties files that you've seen in previous chapters. The only new properties are the ones added from Table 9.1.

Creating a Quartz RMI Server Startup Class

To run the Quartz RMI server, you need to create a startup class that obtains a Scheduler from the factory and starts running the Scheduler. This is true of Quartz with or without RMI. Because we are using RMI in this example, however, a few new steps must be carried out.

First, to make things less confusing, we rename our quartz.properties file server.properties and tell the Quartz RMI server to load that file instead of the default quartz.properties file. Changing the name makes things easier when trying to debug problems. This way, we can be sure that Quartz is loading the correct settings file.

The second change is that we load a new SecurityManager so that all the necessary permissions will be granted to the RMI server. We discussed the RMISecurityManager earlier in the chapter.

Other than these changes, the startup class shown in Listing 9.2 should look familiar.

Listing 9.2   The `QuartzRMIServer` Can Be Used to Start the Quartz RMI Server

```
package org.cavaness.quartzbook.chapter9;

import java.io.BufferedReader;
import java.io.InputStreamReader;
import java.util.Date;

import org.apache.commons.logging.Log;
import org.apache.commons.logging.LogFactory;
import org.quartz.Scheduler;
import org.quartz.SchedulerFactory;
import org.quartz.impl.StdSchedulerFactory;

public class QuartzRMIServer {

    public void run() throws Exception {
        Log log = LogFactory.getLog(QuartzRMIServer.class);

        // Use this properties file instead of quartz.properties
        System.setProperty("org.quartz.properties",
            "server.properties");

        // RMI with Quartz requires a special security manager
        if (System.getSecurityManager() == null) {
            System.setSecurityManager(new
                java.rmi.RMISecurityManager());
        }

        // Get a reference to the Scheduler
        Scheduler scheduler =
            StdSchedulerFactory.getDefaultScheduler();

        /*
         * Due to the server.properties file, our Scheduler will
         * be exported to RMI Registry automatically.
         */
        scheduler.start();

        log.info("Quartz RMI Server started at " + new Date());
        log.info("RMI Clients may now access it. ");

        System.out.println("\n");
        System.out.println(
            "The scheduler will run until you type \"exit\"");

        BufferedReader rdr = new BufferedReader(
                new InputStreamReader(System.in));

        while (true) {
            System.out.print("Type 'exit' to shutdown server: ");
            if ("exit".equals(rdr.readLine())) {
                break;
            }
        }

        log.info("Scheduler is shutting down...");
        scheduler.shutdown(true);
        log.info("Scheduler has been stopped.");
    }
```

```
    public static void main(String[] args) throws Exception {

        QuartzRMIServer example = new QuartzRMIServer();
        example.run();
    }
}
```

In Listing 9.2, after the RMISecurityManager has been set, a Scheduler is retrieved from the factory and the start() method is called. The server is designed to be run from the console so after the Scheduler is started, it runs until the user types exit from the console. The Scheduler then is shut down and stops serving remote clients.

Other than using the RMISecurityManager, notice that we didn't have to do anything special in the code with the Quartz Scheduler to use it as a remote Scheduler. That was all taken care of in the server.properties file. When the Scheduler is created, if the properties file tells it to, the Scheduler exports itself to the RMI Registry and makes it available to be called remotely.

Using the RMI Registry

The RMI Registry needs to be run for clients to get access to the server object. You can choose to run the Registry from the command line using Java's rmiregistry command, or you can allow Quartz to start the Registry automatically. The choice is up to you, but if you don't have a preference, it's probably easiest to just allow Quartz to start it when it needs it.

If you do start the Registry from the command line, make sure the port that you start it on is the same as the port specified in the properties file. When starting from the command line, you change to the <JAVA_HOME>/bin directory and type this:

```
rmiregistry <port>
```

If you don't specify a port number, the default 1099 is used. This happens to be the default that Quartz uses as well.

If you don't want to run the Registry from the command line, Quartz will start it automatically if you have the correct value for the property `org.quartz.scheduler.rmi.createRegistry`. From Table 9.1, the property has several possible values:

- `false (never)`
- `true (as_needed)`
- `always`

If you want Quartz to start the Registry, set the property to `true` or `always`.

Creating the RMI Client

You need to create a client that can invoke methods on the remote Quartz Scheduler. The client will communicate with the RMI Registry, locate the remote Scheduler object, and will then be capable of invoking methods on it. This includes methods to pause and stop the Scheduler, schedule and unschedule jobs, and perform all other methods that are available to remote clients.

Configuring the Quartz RMI Client

As with the server in Table 9.1, Table 9.2 lists all of the properties that must be set for the Quartz RMI client. Two of these properties must be set for both the server and the client.

For the client to locate the server object, it needs to know where the RMI Registry is running so that it can look up the object. The `org.quartz.scheduler.rmi.registryHost` and `org.quartz.scheduler.rmi.registryPort` should be the host and port of where the RMI Registry is running. If you configured the Quartz RMI server to start the Registry automatically, the RMI Registry is running on the same box as the RMI server.

Table 9.2   The Quartz RMI Properties Necessary for the Client

Property	Default
org.quartz.scheduler.rmi.registryHost	localhost
Notes: This is the host at which the RMI Registry is running.	
org.quartz.scheduler.rmi.registryPort	1099
Notes: This is the port on which the RMI Registry is listening (usually 1099).	
org.quartz.scheduler.rmi.proxy	false
Notes: If you want to connect to a remotely served scheduler, set the org.quartz.scheduler.rmi.proxy flag to true. You must also then specify a host and port for the RMI Registry process.	

Because you want the client to contact the remote Scheduler to schedule jobs, you need to set the property org.quartz.scheduler.rmi.proxy to true.

Listing 9.3 shows an example quartz.properties file that you can include with the RMI client to communicate with the server.

Listing 9.3   An Example quartz.properties File for Use with a Quartz RMI Client

```
#==============================================================
# Configure Main Scheduler Properties
#==============================================================
org.quartz.scheduler.instanceName = RMIScheduler
#org.quartz.scheduler.instanceId = AUTO

#==============================================================
# Configure RMI Properties
#==============================================================
org.quartz.scheduler.rmi.registryHost=localhost
org.quartz.scheduler.rmi.registryPort=1099
org.quartz.scheduler.rmi.proxy= true
```

Other than the three RMI properties, you've seen many example quartz.properties file like the one in Listed 9.3.

CLIENT AND SERVER INSTANCE NAMES MUST MATCH

The values for the property org.quartz.scheduler.instanceName in both the RMI client and server must match. Otherwise, the client will not be capable of looking up the server object from the Registry, and you'll receive an exception that the client could not get a handle to the remote Scheduler.

Creating the Quartz RMI Client Class

When you have the properties file for the client configured, you need to build a client Java class that will get a handle to the remote Scheduler and do something with it. There's not much to creating this class, but just as with the server class, we changed the quartz.properties file to be called client.properties and told the client to load the properties from this file. Again, this is done just to help us remember where the properties are coming from and to avoid any confusion. Other than this change, you've seen the code in Listing 9.4 many times before throughout the examples in previous chapters.

Listing 9.4   An Example Quartz RMI Client That Schedules a Job with a Remote Scheduler

```
package org.cavaness.quartzbook.chapter9;

import java.util.Date;

import org.apache.commons.logging.Log;
import org.apache.commons.logging.LogFactory;
import org.quartz.CronTrigger;
import org.quartz.JobDataMap;
import org.quartz.JobDetail;
import org.quartz.Scheduler;
import org.quartz.impl.StdSchedulerFactory;

public class RMITestClient {

    public void run() throws Exception {

        Log log = LogFactory.getLog(RMITestClient.class);

        // Use this properties file instead of quartz.properties
        System.setProperty("org.quartz.properties",
            "client.properties");

        // Get a reference to the remote scheduler
        Scheduler scheduler =
            StdSchedulerFactory.getDefaultScheduler();

        // Define the job to add
        JobDetail job = new JobDetail("remotelyAddedJob", "default",
            SimpleJob.class);
        JobDataMap map = new JobDataMap();
        map.put("msg", "Your remotely added job has executed!");
        job.setJobDataMap(map);
        CronTrigger trigger =
            new CronTrigger("remotelyAddedTrigger",
                "default", "remotelyAddedJob", "default", new
                    Date(), null, "/5 * * ? * *");
```

Listing 9.4   Continued

```
        // schedule the remote job
        scheduler.scheduleJob(job, trigger);

        log.info("Remote job scheduled.");
    }

    public static void main(String[] args) throws Exception {
        RMITestClient example = new RMITestClient();
        example.run();
    }
}
```

An interesting observation that seems almost magical is that we didn't have to tell the factory that we wanted a remote Scheduler. The factory determined this from the `client.properties` file that we told it to load. Specifically, setting this RMI property caused the factory to create a remote Scheduler:

```
org.quartz.scheduler.rmi.proxy = true
```

The following is a fragment of code from the `StdSchedulerFactory` that determines that the client wants to connect to a remote Scheduler:

```
if (rmiProxy) {

  if (autoId)
    schedInstId = DEFAULT_INSTANCE_ID;

  schedCtxt = new SchedulingContext();
  schedCtxt.setInstanceId(schedInstId);

  String uid =
QuartzSchedulerResources.getUniqueIdentifier(
schedName, schedInstId);

  RemoteScheduler remoteScheduler =
new RemoteScheduler(schedCtxt, uid, rmiHost, rmiPort);

  schedRep.bind(remoteScheduler);

  return remoteScheduler;
}
```

The fragment takes place in the `instantiate()` method on the `StdSchedulerFactory`. In this fragment, the factory checks to see if the `rmiProxy` was set to `true`, which it is for the client. If it is `true`, a new instance of `RemoteScheduler` is instantiated and returned. This is why our client didn't have to do anything special. The Scheduler instance that is returned to our client is really an instance of `RemoteScheduler`, but `RemoteScheduler` implements the Scheduler interface, so the client code is none the wiser.

Testing the RMI Server and Client

We've finally reached the time when we can run both the client and server and test the RMI configuration. The first thing to do is to start the Quartz RMI server. You shouldn't have to do anything special other than make sure the typical Quartz JARs and the `server.properties` file are included on the classpath. No additional JARs are necessary for RMI, but you need the ones that are required for any Quartz application.

Running the Quartz RMI Server

To run the Quartz RMI server, just run the `QuartzRMIServer` class as you would any other Java class. As we mentioned earlier, be sure to include all the required JARs in the classpath, as well as the `server.properties` file. The easiest way to accomplish this is to create a batch file (or shell script) with all of this in it. Listing 9.4 shows a sample batch file that you can use to start the server.

Listing 9.4   A Sample **startserver.bat** File Used to Start the Quartz RMI Server

```
java  org.cavaness.quartzbook.chapter9.QuartzRMIServer
```

You will need to include the necessary jars in the classpath for the command in Listing 9.4 to work correctly. These include quartz.jar, commons-logging.jar, commons-logging-api.jar, commons-collections3.1.jar, beanutils.jar, commons-beanutils-bean-collectons.jar, commons-beanutils-core.jar.

Running the Quartz RMI Client

When the server is running, you can then run the RMI client. The client can be run in the same way as the server, by creating a batch file or shell script. When you start the client, if all goes well, you should not only see the output from the client console that a remote job has been scheduled, but you should also see a message printed in the server console that it received the remote job to schedule and run.

Whereas the RMI client is designed to schedule its job and exit, the Quartz RMI server is designed to continue to run until you type `exit`. The server should write that it received a remote job to schedule and then go about its business of waiting for more clients to connect. This means that you can run the client multiple times, and this is exactly what you would want from a design like this.

You can just type `exit` when you're finished running the examples.

What's Up Next?

This chapter introduced a new way to interact with the Quartz Scheduler that wasn't possible before. Using Quartz with RMI enables you to build applications for which you can separate the components and distribute them across multiple machines. This is a powerful concept because it offers better scalability without additional development work.

The next chapter takes this concept to the next level by showing how it's possible to use Quartz within a J2EE application server. Interestingly, Java application servers all use a form of RMI as well to support remote method invocation.

## CHAPTER 10

USING QUARTZ
WITH J2EE

The Java 2 Platform, Enterprise Edition (J2EE) defines the standards for developing component-based enterprise applications. Whether you are inclined to use one of the open source J2EE servers, such as JBoss or Geronimo, or whether you prefer the comfort and safety of commercial support with ones such as WebSphere and WebLogic, Quartz can be used in several different deployment arrangements with all of them. This chapter demonstrates the various strategies for deploying Quartz with a J2EE application server and increasing the richness of J2EE with the Quartz framework.

If I Have J2EE,
Why Do I Need Quartz?

Since J2EE first came on the scene in the late 1990s, developers have been perplexed by some of the specification decisions and some of the seemingly obvious missing features. This is not necessarily a criticism of the specification writers, but more indicative of the problem that arises when many separate groups, all with differing opinions and agendas, try to agree on a single set of priorities—sort of like the United Nations, but not as nice. Many of the needed features showed up, but a few of the key ones were left out, to be added later. One of the key features that was deferred from the early specifications was a timer service.

I Need a Timer Service

Many business processes require asynchronous job scheduling. For example, Web sites usually need to send e-mails to registered users to alert them to new features or the latest specials. Medical claim–processing companies typically need to download medical data at night and do something with that data. A company that sells some type of product might have reports generated each night that show sales and commission information. All of these scenarios could benefit from a timer service that executes asynchronous jobs.

The Java/J2EE community has produced several attempts at solving the timer problem. Early on, vendors added propriety solutions within their J2EE servers. (For this chapter, the terms *J2EE server* and *J2EE container* are used interchangeably.) For example, the WebLogic product had some custom extensions, as did the IBM J2EE server. Unfortunately, they were not exactly compatible for moving components from one to another. Later, these vendors and others tried to develop a common set of timer components.

Starting with Java 1.3, Sun added the `java.util.Timer` and `java.util.TimerTask` classes to help add basic Timer functionality to the core language. Although the `Timer` and `TimerTask` can work for simple requirements, there is much more to true job scheduling than can be solved by two concrete classes. Hopefully, that's a point that you already understand.

Quartz/J2EE Deployment Models

Two basic strategies exist for architecting and deploying Quartz with J2EE. With one strategy, you can design Quartz to work outside the J2EE container as a standard J2SE client. As you'll see shortly, this is the simplest approach. The second strategy is to deploy Quartz as a J2EE client that resides within the J2EE container. In this scenario, the J2EE client is a Web Archive (WAR) file and is deployed like any other Web application. The strategy you choose depends on your exact needs. Each comes with a set of pros and cons.

Running Quartz as a J2SE Client

If you just need to invoke services on Enterprise JavaBeans (EJBs) or put messages inside a JMS queue or topic, the easiest way to configure Quartz with J2EE is to run Quartz outside the J2EE container as a stand-alone J2SE application. It then would function like any other Java application that lives outside the container but needs to call methods on distributed components within the container.

We've essentially been practicing this approach in the previous chapters, minus the part about calling EJBs. You can create a Quartz application that contains the Quartz libraries and job-scheduling information and connects to the J2EE server through the home and remote interfaces. You can then invoke methods on EJBs like any other distributed client. You can also create and insert JMS messages and have them processed by message-driven beans (MDB) running within the container. This approach is shown in Figure 10.1.

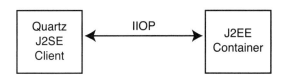

FIGURE 10.1   Quartz can work with J2EE as a stand-alone J2SE client.

This approach works nicely if you have existing J2EE components that you want Quartz to interoperate with, and you don't want to or can't make any changes to the server. To implement this approach, you just need to build a Quartz application, as we've done in previous chapters, and use the EJBInvokerJob that ships with Quartz. We discuss the EJBInvokerJob shortly.

Deploying Quartz Within the J2EE Server

Quartz can also be deployed directly within the container to do away with the external Quartz application. This is commonly referred to as using a J2EE client. You might choose this approach over the previous one for several reasons. One reason is that there's only one application to maintain, compared with two in the other approach. If the external Quartz client shuts down, the job-scheduling information is temporarily lost, and the business owners will not be thrilled. In other words, it's one failure point versus two. Another reason for deploying Quartz within the container is to have Quartz use some of the other resources that the container offers, such as mail sessions, data sources, and other resource adapters. If you are using the J2EE server in a clustered environment, it also makes sense to deploy Quartz within the container to make the clustering easier and more manageable. Figure 10.2 illustrates how Quartz can be deployed with the J2EE application.

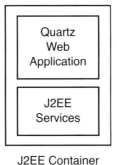

J2EE Container

FIGURE 10.2   Quartz can be deployed within a J2EE application.

When Quartz is deployed within a J2EE container, you must understand and deal with some complications. Before we get into those, let's talk about how to deploy Quartz as a J2SE client and access the container from outside the container.

Running Quartz as a J2SE Client

By far the easiest and simplest way to use Quartz with J2EE is to deploy it outside the container. What makes this approach easier is that you don't have to deal with many of the issues that will surface as Quartz attempts to create threads and execute within the container. It's also easier because deploying applications into a J2EE container can be frustrating, even with all of the latest tools and technologies such as XDoclet and administrative consoles.

Using the Quartz `EJBInvokerJob` to Call an EJB

The Quartz framework includes the `org.quartz.jobs.ee.ejb.EJBInvokerJob`, which enables you to schedule a job that can invoke an EJB method when triggered. The Job is easy to set up and can be used regardless of which deployment scenario you've chosen with Quartz. Suppose, for example, that you have a Stateless Session Bean (SLSB) like the one in Listing 10.1.

Listing 10.1   An Example Stateless Session Bean

```
import java.rmi.RemoteException;

import javax.ejb.EJBException;
import javax.ejb.SessionBean;
import javax.ejb.SessionContext;

public class TestBean implements SessionBean {

    /** The session context */
    private SessionContext context;

    public TestBean() {
        super();
    }

    // EJB Lifecycle Methods not shown for brevity

    public void helloWorld() throws EJBException {
        System.out.println("Hello World");
    }

    public void helloWorld(String msg) throws EJBException {
        System.out.println("Hello World - " + msg);
    }
}
```

With this EJB deployed and ready in your J2EE application server of choice, you can use the `EJBInvokerJob` to invoke one of the `helloWorld()` methods available to remote clients.

You set up the `EJBInvokerJob` just as you would for any other job. Listing 10.2 shows an example of using the `EJBInvokerJob` to invoke the `helloWorld()` on the SLSB.

Listing 10.2   A Simple Example Using the `EJBInvokerJob`

```
package org.cavaness.quartzbook.chapter10;

import java.util.Date;

import org.apache.commons.logging.Log;
import org.apache.commons.logging.LogFactory;
import org.quartz.JobDetail;
import org.quartz.Scheduler;
import org.quartz.SchedulerException;
import org.quartz.Trigger;
import org.quartz.TriggerUtils;
import org.quartz.impl.StdSchedulerFactory;
import org.quartz.jobs.ee.ejb.EJBInvokerJob;

public class Listing_10_2 {
    static Log logger = LogFactory.getLog(Listing_10_2.class);

    public static void main(String[] args) {
        Listing_10_2 example = new Listing_10_2();

        try {
            // Create a Scheduler and schedule the Job
            Scheduler scheduler = example.createScheduler();
            example.scheduleJob(scheduler);

            // Start the Scheduler running
            scheduler.start();

            logger.info("Scheduler started at " + new Date());

        } catch (SchedulerException ex) {
            logger.error(ex);
        }
    }

    // Schedule the EJBInvokerJob
    private void scheduleJob(Scheduler scheduler) throws SchedulerException {

        // Create a JobDetail for the Job
        JobDetail jobDetail = new JobDetail("HelloWorldJob",
                Scheduler.DEFAULT_GROUP,
                org.quartz.jobs.ee.ejb.EJBInvokerJob.class);

        loadJobDataMap(jobDetail);

        // Create a trigger that fires every 10 seconds, forever
        Trigger trigger = TriggerUtils.makeSecondlyTrigger(10);
        trigger.setName("helloWorldTrigger");
        // Start the trigger firing from now
        trigger.setStartTime(new Date());

        // Associate the trigger with the job in the scheduler
```

Listing 10.2   Continued

```
        scheduler.scheduleJob(jobDetail, trigger);
    }

    /*
     * Configure the EJB parameters in the JobDataMap
     */
    public JobDetail loadJobDataMap(JobDetail jobDetail) {
        jobDetail.getJobDataMap().put(EJBInvokerJob.EJB_JNDI_NAME_KEY,
                "ejb/HelloWorldSession");

        jobDetail.getJobDataMap().put(EJBInvokerJob.EJB_METHOD_KEY,
                "helloWorld");

        jobDetail.getJobDataMap().put(EJBInvokerJob.PROVIDER_URL,
                "t3://localhost:7001");

        jobDetail.getJobDataMap().put(
            EJBInvokerJob.INITIAL_CONTEXT_FACTORY,
                "weblogic.jndi.WLInitialContextFactory");

        return jobDetail;
    }

    /*
     * return an instance of the Scheduler from the factory
     */
    public Scheduler createScheduler() throws SchedulerException {
        return StdSchedulerFactory.getDefaultScheduler();
    }
}
```

As you can see from Listing 10.2, the EJBInvokerJob is configured like any other job. A JobDetail and trigger are created and registered with the Scheduler. Several JobDataMap parameters can be used for the job to function properly with various J2EE containers. Table 10.1 lists the JobDataMap parameters that the job supports.

The parameters you add to the JobDataMap depend on which J2EE server you're using and what its requirements are. For example, if you're using BEA WebLogic, you would need to specify at least the ones from Listing 10.1, obviously substituting values for your specific environment. If you were using WebSphere, most of the values would be different.

When we set up and run Listing 10.2 within our external Quartz application, every 10 seconds the helloWorld() method on the EJB is invoked. This approach is nice because we don't have to worry about deploying the Quartz application within the J2EE container. It enforces a separation of job information from business processing logic.

Table 10.1   The `EJBInvokerJob` **Uses Several Parameters, Depending on Your Specific J2EE Server**

Static Constant	String Value
`EJB_JNDI_NAME_KEY` **Notes:** JNDI name of the bean's home interface	`ejb`
`PROVIDER_URL` **Notes:** Vendor-specific URL that specifies where the server can be found	`java.naming.provider.url`
`INITIAL_CONTEXT_FACTORY` **Notes:** Vendor-specific context factory that is used to look up resources	`java.naming.factory.initial`
`EJB_METHOD_KEY` **Notes:** Name of the method to invoke on the EJB	`method`
`EJB_ARGS_KEY` **Notes:** `Object[]` of the args to pass to the method (optional—, if left out, there are no arguments)	`args`
`EJB_ARG_TYPES_KEY` **Notes:** `Class[]` of the args to pass to the method (optional—if left out, the types will be derived by calling `getClass()` on each of the arguments)	`argType`
`PRINCIPAL` **Notes:** The principal (user) to be used for the EJB method call	`java.naming.security.principal`
`CREDENTIALS` **Notes:** The credentials to be used for the EJB method call	`java.naming.security.credentials`

In the example in Listing 10.2, the `helloWorld()` method that was invoked on the EJB didn't defined any parameters. The `EJBInvokedJob` class enables you to pass arguments to an EJB method by specifying them using the EJB_ARGS_KEY and EJB_ARG_TYPES_KEY parameters shown in Table 10.1.

Listing 10.3 shows another simple example that passes an argument to a different version of `helloWorld()`EJB running on the Apache Geronimo J2EE server.

Listing 10.3 is very similar to Listing 10.2, except that it includes the parameters EJB_ARGS_KEY and EJB_ARG_TYPES_ KEY. Also, because it's running against the Geronimo J2EE application server, it needed to add the arguments for PRINCIPAL and CREDENTIALS.

Listing 10.3   A Simple Example Using the EJBInvokerJob

```
package org.cavaness.quartzbook.chapter10;

import java.util.Date;

import org.apache.commons.logging.Log;
import org.apache.commons.logging.LogFactory;
import org.quartz.JobDetail;
import org.quartz.Scheduler;
import org.quartz.SchedulerException;
import org.quartz.Trigger;
import org.quartz.TriggerUtils;
import org.quartz.impl.StdSchedulerFactory;
import org.quartz.jobs.ee.ejb.EJBInvokerJob;

public class Listing_10_3 {
    static Log logger = LogFactory.getLog(Listing_10_3.class);

    public static void main(String[] args) {
        Listing_10_3 example = new Listing_10_3();

        try {
            // Create a Scheduler and schedule the Job
            Scheduler scheduler = example.createScheduler();
            example.scheduleJob(scheduler);

            // Start the Scheduler running
            scheduler.start();

            logger.info("Scheduler started at " + new Date());

        } catch (SchedulerException ex) {
            logger.error(ex);
        }

    }

    // Schedule the EJBInvokerJob
    private void scheduleJob(Scheduler scheduler)
        throws SchedulerException {

        // Create a JobDetail for the Job
        JobDetail jobDetail = new JobDetail("HelloWorldJob",
                Scheduler.DEFAULT_GROUP,
                org.quartz.jobs.ee.ejb.EJBInvokerJob.class);

        // Load all of the necessary EJB parameters
        loadJobDataMap(jobDetail);

        // Create a trigger that fires every 10 seconds, forever
        Trigger trigger = TriggerUtils.makeSecondlyTrigger(10);

        trigger.setName("helloWorldTrigger");
        // Start the trigger firing from now
        trigger.setStartTime(new Date());

        // Associate the trigger with the job in the scheduler
        scheduler.scheduleJob(jobDetail, trigger);
    }
```

Listing 10.3   Continued

```
    /*
     * Configure the EJB parameters in the JobDataMap
     */
    public JobDetail loadJobDataMap(JobDetail jobDetail) {
        jobDetail.getJobDataMap().put(
            EJBInvokerJob.EJB_JNDI_NAME_KEY, "ejb/Test");

        jobDetail.getJobDataMap().put(EJBInvokerJob.EJB_METHOD_KEY,
                "helloWorld");

        Object[] args = new Object[1];
        args[0] = " from Quartz";
        jobDetail.getJobDataMap().put(
            EJBInvokerJob.EJB_ARGS_KEY, args);

        Class[] argTypes = new Class[1];
        argTypes[0] = java.lang.String.class;
        jobDetail.getJobDataMap().put(
            EJBInvokerJob.EJB_ARG_TYPES_KEY, argTypes);

        jobDetail.getJobDataMap().put(
            EJBInvokerJob.PROVIDER_URL, "127.0.0.1:4201");

        jobDetail.getJobDataMap().put(
            EJBInvokerJob.INITIAL_CONTEXT_FACTORY,
                "org.openejb.client.RemoteInitialContextFactory");

        jobDetail.getJobDataMap().put(
            EJBInvokerJob.PRINCIPAL, "system");

        jobDetail.getJobDataMap().put(
            EJBInvokerJob.CREDENTIALS, "manager");

        return jobDetail;
    }

    /*
     * return an instance of the Scheduler from the factory
     */
    public Scheduler createScheduler() throws SchedulerException {
        return StdSchedulerFactory.getDefaultScheduler();
    }
}
```

EJBInvokerJob PARAMETERS AND SERIALIZATION

Because of the typical serialization problems that are associated with Java and distributed applications, you should stick to passing Strings and primitives to your EJB methods. If you need to pass more complex types, your code must serialize the objects between client and server properly. For more in-depth information on Java serialization, check out Sun's Serialization specification at http://java.sun.com/j2se/1.5.0/docs/guide/serialization.

Because Quartz needs to get a reference to the home and remote interfaces for the EJB, you need to deploy some J2EE client JARs with your external Quartz application. The JARs you need to add depend on which J2EE container you're using. If you're using WebLogic, for example, you'll probably just put the weblogic.jar with the Quartz application. For Geronimo, several are involved. Check with the server documentation to be sure.

Running Quartz Within the J2EE Application Server

Running Quartz as a J2EE client is a little more involved than running Quartz as an external J2SE application. This is mostly because deploying applications within the container is somewhat more complicated. In addition, the J2EE specification puts some constraints on components within the container. One of the biggest guidelines that the specification gives involves who and what can create Java threads. Because it's the container's responsibility to manage all resources, it can't allow just anything or anyone to create threads. If it did, it would have a harder time managing the environment and keeping things stable. Quartz creates its own worker threads, so you need to follow some steps to make sure things work properly.

Assume that a stateless session bean such as the one from Listing 10.1 is already deployed in the container. The easiest way to deploy Quartz within the container is to build a WAR file that contains all the necessary files and then use the admin tools, or Eclipse, to deploy the Web application within the container.

The Web application directory structure is just like that of any other Web application. You need to add the following files to it:

- web.xml (put in WEB-INF)
- quartz.properties (put in WEB-INF/classes)
- quartz_jobs.xml (put in WEB-INF/classes)

- Quartz binary (put in WEB-INF/lib)
- Third-party libraries (put in WEB-INF/lib)

Because you are building a Web application, you need to add the requisite web.xml deployment descriptor. Listing 10.4 shows the web.xml for our client application that will be installed within the container.

Listing 10.4   The web.xml for the Quartz J2EE Client Application

```
<?xml version="1.0" encoding="UTF-8"?>

<web-app>
  <servlet>
    <servlet-name>QuartzServlet</servlet-name>
    <servlet-class>
      org.quartz.ee.servlet.QuartzInitializerServlet
    </servlet-class>
    <load-on-startup>1</load-on-startup>
  </servlet>

  <servlet-mapping>
    <servlet-name>QuartzServlet</servlet-name>
    <url-pattern>/servlet/QuartzServlet</url-pattern>
  </servlet-mapping>
</web-app>
```

The Quartz framework includes a Java servlet called QuartzInitializerServlet that, when invoked, initializes the Quartz Scheduler and loads job information. In Listing 10.4, we've set the <load-on-startup> parameter to have a value of 1 so the servlet will be loaded and initialized when the container is started. By using the servlet to start the Quartz Scheduler, we avoid the issues of thread permission because the container will allow servlets to create user threads.

QuartzInitializerListener ADDED TO QUARTZ

Recently, a new class called QuartzInitializerListener was added to Quartz that implements the javax.servlet.ServletContextListener interface. This class can be used as an alternative to the QuartzInitializerServlet mentioned earlier.

Next, you need to put the standard quartz.properties file into the WEB-INF/classes directory of the Web application.

There's nothing special about this version of the properties file; it's essentially what we did in past chapters. However, here we use the `JobInitializationPlugin` (this was shown in Chapter 8, "Using Quartz Plug-Ins," and is designed to load job information from an XML file). By default, the plug-in looks for a file called `quartz_jobs.xml` and loads the jobs found in the file. As Chapter 8 described, using this particular plug-in keeps you from having to write job-loading code and be forced to recompile when changes occur. The `quartz_jobs.xml` file for this example is shown in Listing 10.5.

Listing 10.5   The `quartz_jobs.xml` Used Within the J2EE Client

```xml
<?xml version='1.0' encoding='utf-8'?>

<quartz>
  <job>
    <job-detail>
        <name>HelloWorldJob</name>
        <group>DEFAULT</group>
        <job-class>org.quartz.jobs.ee.ejb.EJBInvokerJob</job-class>
        <volatility>false</volatility>
        <durability>false</durability>
        <recover>false</recover>

        <job-data-map allows-transient-data="true">
          <entry>
            <key>ejb</key>
            <value>ejb/Test</value>
          </entry>
          <entry>
            <key>java.naming.factory.initial</key>
            <value>org.openejb.client.RemoteInitialContextFactory</value>
          </entry>
          <entry>
            <key>java.naming.provider.url</key>
            <value>127.0.0.1:4201</value>
          </entry>
          <entry>
            <key>method</key>
            <value>helloWorld</value>
          </entry>
          <entry>
            <key>java.naming.security.principal</key>
            <value>system</value>
          </entry>
          <entry>
            <key>java.naming.security.credentials</key>
            <value>manager</value>
          </entry>
        </job-data-map>
    </job-detail>
```

Listing 10.5   Continued

```
    <trigger>
      <simple>
          <name>helloWorldTrigger</name>
          <group>DEFAULT</group>
          <job-name>HelloWorldJob</job-name>
          <job-group>DEFAULT</job-group>
          <start-time>2005-06-10 6:10:00 PM</start-time>
          <!- repeat indefinitely every 10 seconds ->
          <repeat-count>-1</repeat-count>
          <repeat-interval>10000</repeat-interval>
      </simple>
    </trigger>
  </job>
</quartz>
```

You can see from Listing 10.5 that we are still using the `EJBInvokerJob` by specifying it within the `quartz_jobs.xml` file.

SPECIFYING THE PLUG-IN IN `quartz.properties`

Chapter 8 stated that you need to specify the plug-in information for a Quartz plug-in within the `quartz.properties` file. For the `JobInitializationPlugin`, you must add the following line in the properties file:

```
org.quartz.plugin.jobInitializer.class =
org.quartz.plugins.xml.JobInitializationPlugin
```

After all these files have been configured, you can build the WAR file and deploy it within your container. When the container starts up, the servlet is loaded and initialized and starts the Scheduler. The Scheduler uses the `JobInitializerPlugin` to load job information from the `quartz_jobs.xml` file. From that point, the `EJBInvokerJob` invokes the `helloWorld()` method on the EJB.

Including J2EE Client JARs

When packaging the J2EE Client application, you need to package the J2EE client JARs necessary for your particular server. Each one is different, so check the documentation to be sure. You also need all the Quartz libraries that are required when building a stand-alone Quartz application.

Using the J2EE Container's DataSource

We have purposely not talked about JobStores or
DataSources up to this point. In Chapter 6, "JobStores and
Persistence," you learned that you can store your job information within memory, or, if you need job persistence between
application restarts, you can store the job information within a
relational database. Two types of JDBC JobStores exist:

- JobStoreTX–Manages its own transactions during
  persistence operations
- JobStoreCMT–Supports container-managed transactions
  (CMT) during persistence operations

If you are using a J2EE container and one of the two types
of JDBC JobStores, then you will want to use the container's
DataSource as well. Refer back to Chapter 6 for how to set up
the quartz.properties file when using JDBC JobStores
within a J2EE container.

Using Other J2EE Resources

When you deploy Quartz within the J2EE container, you can
take advantage of other resources available to the J2EE components. For example, if you need to send e-mails, one
approach would be to use the Quartz SendMailJob, which
relies on JavaMail. Another approach you can take if you
deploy Quartz within the container is to use the mail session
that should be readily available for all J2EE servers, assuming that you've set one up. That's another one of the benefits
of deploying Quartz as a J2EE client.

```
InitialContext initialContext = new InitialContext();
Session session = (Session)
initialContext.lookup(urlToMailSession);

Message msg = new MimeMessage(session);
// ... build up msg
Transport.send(msg);
```

The EJB 2.1 Specification: Finally Some Light

Chapter 22 of the EJB 2.1 specification discusses one of the new features to Enterprise JavaBeans, the Timer service. This service is a container-managed service that provides callbacks to components that need time-based events. This essentially means that EJBs can register themselves with the service and receive notifications when it's time for them to execute. The Timer service is implemented and managed by the EJB container. It's still pretty early to know how much functionality the J2EE vendors will add on top of these specifications. Some argue that the EJB Timer proposal is not currently sufficient, for the same reason that the `java.util.Timer` classes are not sufficient for a scheduling application. It would be nice to see the architects of the EJB specification add support for plugging in a framework such as Quartz to increase the flexibility of the Timer service.

## CHAPTER 11

CLUSTERING QUARTZ

Inevitably, all roads lead to clustering. Although a single Quartz instance gives you nice job-scheduling capabilities, it doesn't satisfy typical Enterprise requirements such as scalability and high availability. If you need failover capabilities and the ability to run an ever-increasing number of jobs, Quartz clustering should be part of your vernacular. This chapter shows you how to use the clustering capabilities of Quartz to better support your business needs and to ensure that all jobs execute, regardless of one machine's desire to break down at the worst moment.

What Does Clustering Mean to Quartz?

Clustering is the act of running multiple instances of a component or application that transparently work together to provide services. Clustering is an enterprise-wide phenomenon, not one limited to the Java world. When developing J2EE applications, for example, vendors provide the capability to cluster the application servers so that services such as EJB, JNDI, and Web Components can be made highly available. Then when a client or customer requests these services, they will be there.

This is exactly the same behavior that some users require of their Quartz applications. Users want to build and set up Quartz applications so that when a job absolutely needs to be executed, it gets executed. As the popularity of your Quartz application grows and an increasing demand is placed on it, a cluster of Quartz applications will provide better peace of mind that you'll be able to handle that demand and ensure that all goes as planned. And you get all of this with very little effort to set up and maintain.

The Benefits to Clustering Quartz Applications

Clustering Quartz applications provides two key benefits over nonclustered environments:

- High availability
- Scalability

HIGH AVAILABILITY

A highly available application is one that can service clients for a high percentage of the time. In some cases, this might mean 24 hours a day, 7 days a week. For other applications, it might just mean "most of the time." Availability is usually expressed as a percentage between 0 and 100 percent. An application might fail often but still achieve high availability. On the other hand, an application might go down once but then might stay down for a long time, for low availability. What counts is not how many times the application goes down, but the total amount of downtime. Obviously, as developers, we hope our applications never fail. But this does happen, and you must be prepared for it.

The level of availability for hardware and software is sometimes referred to as levels of nine. Levels of nine indicate the number of nine digits in the percentage of availability. For example, 99.999 is said to have five levels of nine because there are five digits. Table 11.1 shows the approximate percentage of downtime for a particular level.

Table 11.1   Application Availability Levels

Availability	Approximate Hours of Downtime Per Year
99%	87.6 hours
99.9%	8.8 hours
99.99%	.9 hours
99.999%	0.09 (about 5 minutes)

Looking at Table 11.1, you might come to the conclusion that four levels of nine (about an hour of downtime per year) is an awesome amount of availability—and, in general, that's true. However, if the application was a Quartz application designed to send out invoices and it was down for five minutes every day for 12 straight days when the invoices were supposed to go out, the business would lose a lot of revenue, and you would probably be looking for a new job (and I'm not talking about the Quartz kind of job, either). It's not just about the amount of downtime—it's also when that downtime strikes.

Part of what makes high availability possible is the concept of failover. Failover ensures that even if a system failure occurs, other redundant components or services can handle the requests and insulate the clients (or jobs) from the failures. The capability to fail over from a failed component or service to another functioning one increases the availability of the application. The switch or failover should be transparent.

SCALABILITY

Scalability means having the capability to dynamically add new resources such as hardware to the application environment, to increase the capacity of the application. In a scalable application, achieving this increase in capacity does not involve changing code or the design.

Achieving scalability is not done with magic. An application must be designed properly from the beginning; supporting extra capacity usually takes administrative effort in adding the new hardware (such as memory) or starting more instances of the application.

Load Balancing

As part of achieving good scalability, the capability to distribute work across the nodes in the cluster is very important. Spreading out work ensures that each node in the cluster is footing its share of the workload. Imagine if all the work was being given to one node in the cluster while the other nodes remained idle. If this pattern continued, eventually the over-worked node would not be able to handle the increased work, and this would result in a failure.

In the best scenario, work is spread evenly across all instances in the cluster. Several different algorithms can be used to distribute the work, including random, round-robin, and weighted round-robin, just to name a few.

Currently, Quartz provides a minimal load-balancing capability using a random algorithm. Each Scheduler instance in the cluster attempts to fire scheduled triggers as fast as the Scheduler permits. The Scheduler instances compete (using database locks) for the right to execute a job by firing its trigger. When a trigger for a job has been fired, no other Scheduler will attempt to fire that particular trigger until the next scheduled firing time. This mechanism works better than you might infer from its simplicity. This is because the Scheduler that is "most busy" will be the one least likely to find the next job to fire. Hence, it's possible to achieve something near to a true balancing of the load.

How Clustering Works in Quartz

Each node in a Quartz cluster is a separate Quartz application that is managed independently of the other nodes. This means that you must start and stop each node individually. Unlike clustering in many application servers, the separate Quartz nodes do not communicate with one another or with an administration node. (Future versions of Quartz will be designed so that nodes communicate with one another directly rather than through the database.) Instead, the Quartz applications are made aware of one another through the database tables.

QUARTZ CLUSTERING WORKS ONLY WHEN USING A JDBC JobStore
Because clustered nodes rely on the database to communicate the state of a Scheduler instance, you can use Quartz clustering only when using a JDBC JobStore. This means that you must be using either the JobStoreTX or the JobStoreCMT for job storage; you can't use RAMJobStore with clustering. A future release most likely will remove this requirement, and nodes will communicate directly with one another through a network protocol, possibly by using JGroups.

Figure 11.1 shows that each node communicates directly with the database and has no knowledge of others outside the database.

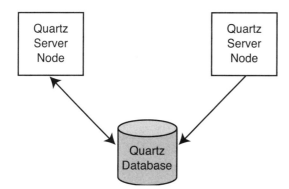

FIGURE 11.1   Each node in a Quartz cluster is aware of the other instances only via the database.

Quartz Scheduler on Startup in a Cluster

The Quartz Scheduler itself is not cluster-aware, but the JDBC JobStore configured for the Scheduler is. When the Quartz Scheduler is started, it calls the schedulerStarted() method on the JobStore, which, as the name implies, tells the JobStore that the Scheduler has been started. The schedulerStarted() method is implemented in the JobStoreSupport class.

The JobStoreSupport class uses a property setting from the quartz.properties file (discussed shortly) to determine whether the Scheduler instance is participating in a cluster. If a cluster is configured, a new instance of the class `ClusterManager` is created, initialized, and started. The `ClusterManager` is an inner class within the `JobStoreSupport` class. The `ClusterManager` class, which extends `java.lang.Thread`, runs periodically and performs a check-in function for the Scheduler instance. When the `clusterCheckin()` method is called, the `JobStoreSupport` updates the database table SCHEDULER_STATE for the Scheduler instance. The Scheduler also checks to see if any of the other cluster nodes have failed. The check-in occurs periodically based on a configuration property (discussed shortly).

Detecting Failed Scheduler Nodes

When a Scheduler instance performs the check-in routine, it looks to see if there are other Scheduler instances that didn't check in when they were supposed to. It does this by inspecting the SCHEDULER_STATE table and looking for schedulers that have a value in the LAST_CHECK_TIME column that is older than the property `org.quartz.jobStore.clusterCheckinInterval` (discussed in the next section). If one or more nodes haven't checked in, the running Scheduler assumes that the other instance(s) have failed.

RUNNING NODES ON SEPARATE MACHINES WITH UNSYNCHRONIZED CLOCKS

As you can ascertain by now, if you run nodes on different machines and the clocks are not synchronized, you can get unexpected results. This is because a timestamp is being used to inform other instances of the last time one node checked in. If that node's clock was set for the future, a running Scheduler might never realize that a node has gone down. On the other hand, if a clock on one node is set in the past, a node might assume that the node has gone down and attempt to take over and rerun its jobs. In either case, it's not the behavior that you want. When you're using different machines in a cluster (which is the normal case), be sure to synchronize the clocks. See the section "Quartz Clustering Cookbook," later in this chapter for details on how to do this.

Recovering Jobs from Failed Instances

When a Scheduler instance fails while it's executing a job, it's possible to get the job re-executed by another, working Scheduler. For this to happen, the job's recoverable property, configured in the `JobDetail` object, must be set to `true`.

If the recoverable property is set to `false` (the default), when a Scheduler fails while running a job, it won't be re-executed; instead, it will be fired by a different Scheduler instance upon the trigger's fire time, if any. How quickly a failed Scheduler instance is detected depends on the check-in interval of each Scheduler. This is discussed in the next section.

Configuring Quartz to Use Clustering

The steps for configuring a clustered environment for Quartz are much easier than for setting an equivalent environment for a J2EE cluster:

1. Configure each node's `quartz.properties` file.
2. Configure the JDBC `JobStore`.
3. Load the database with Scheduler information (jobs and triggers).
4. Start each Quartz node.

Configuring the Node's `quartz.properties` File

Just as when running Quartz in a nonclustered environment, each Quartz application requires a `quartz.properties` file. As mentioned in Chapter 3, "Hello, Quartz," if you don't specify one, the default `quartz.properties` file (within the `quartz.jar` file) gets used. It's best to always specify one because you will eventually need to modify one or more of the settings.

When using the clustered features of Quartz, you need to modify the `quartz.properties` file for each node. Listing 11.1 shows an example `quartz.properties` file that is used for a clustered instance. The properties are discussed after the listing.

Listing 11.1   Sample `quartz.properties` for Clustered Instance

```
#==============================================================
# Configure Main Scheduler Properties
#==============================================================
org.quartz.scheduler.instanceName = TestScheduler1
org.quartz.scheduler.instanceId = instance_one


#==============================================================
# Configure ThreadPool
#==============================================================
org.quartz.threadPool.class = org.quartz.simpl.SimpleThreadPool
org.quartz.threadPool.threadCount = 5
org.quartz.threadPool.threadPriority = 5


#==============================================================
# Configure JobStore
#==============================================================
org.quartz.jobStore.misfireThreshold = 60000
org.quartz.jobStore.class = org.quartz.impl.jdbcjobstore.JobStoreTX
org.quartz.jobStore.driverDelegateClass =
org.quartz.impl.jdbcjobstore.MSSQLDelegate
org.quartz.jobStore.tablePrefix = QRTZ_
org.quartz.jobStore.dataSource = myDS

org.quartz.jobStore.isClustered = true
org.quartz.jobStore.clusterCheckinInterval = 20000


#==============================================================
# Non-Managed Configure Datasource
#==============================================================
org.quartz.dataSource.myDS.driver = net.sourceforge.jtds.jdbc.Driver
org.quartz.dataSource.myDS.URL = jdbc:jtds:sqlserver://localhost:1433/quartz
org.quartz.dataSource.myDS.user = admin
org.quartz.dataSource.myDS.password = admin
org.quartz.dataSource.myDS.maxConnections = 10
```

CONFIGURING THE MAIN SCHEDULER PROPERTIES

These two properties should be configured in this section:

- `org.quartz.scheduler.instanceName`
- `org.quartz.scheduler.instanceId`

These properties are used in several places within the JDBC JobStore and database to uniquely identify the instance.

USE THE AUTO FEATURE FOR INSTANCE ID WHEN CLUSTERING

AUTO was created specifically for clustering. Unfortunately, in some of the earlier versions of the framework, the mechanism in version 1.4.5 didn't clean up old instance IDs in all cases. Version 1.5.1 has a facility for pluggable instance ID generators, one of which creates the ID based on the IP address of the node; this works great as long as you have only one Quartz cluster node on a given machine. AUTO should be used when clustering because many people deploy Quartz within an EAR that is distributed across a cluster of application servers. In this case, there must be a single quartz.properties file that is within the EAR and that is therefore the same for all nodes. If the instance ID was hard coded, the Quartz cluster wouldn't work because all nodes would have the same ID. AUTO thus solves the problem.

Some other serious clustering issues were introduced in Quartz 1.5.1. If you need to cluster Quartz, you probably should avoid that version.

Configuring the JobStore Section

To use clustering with Quartz, you are required to use either JobStoreTX or JobStoreCMT as the Scheduler's JobStore. Chapter 6, "JobStores and Persistence," detailed how to set up and use one of the two provided JDBC JobStores. From Listing 11.1, you can see that the same settings from Chapter 6 are shown, with two additional properties:

- org.quartz.jobStore.isClustered
- org.quartz.jobStore.clusterCheckinInterval

By setting the value of the org.quartz.jobStore.isClustered property to true, you are telling the Scheduler instance that it is participating in a cluster. This property is used throughout the scheduling framework to modify the default behavior when operating in a clustered environment.

The org.quartz.jobStore.clusterCheckinInterval property defines the frequency (in milliseconds) with which the Scheduler instance checks in with the database. The Scheduler checks to see if other instances haven't checked in as they should; that could indicate a failed Scheduler instance whereby the current Scheduler would take over any recoverable jobs that failed in progress. Upon check-in, the Scheduler also updates its own state record.

The smaller the `clusterCheckinInterval` is, the more often the Scheduler nodes check for failed Scheduler instances. The default value is set to 15000 (or 15 seconds).

Configuring the `JobStore` Data Source

Because you must use a JDBC `JobStore` (either `JobStoreTX` or `JobStoreCMT`) for clustering, you also need to configure a nonmanaged data source (by "nonmanaged," we mean that the data source is not managed by an application server). Look at Listing 11.1 for an example of setting up a nonmanaged data source for the `JobStoreTX`. Look at Chapter 6 for a list of available properties and their allowed values.

Loading the Database with Scheduler Information

As with all Quartz applications that use a database for Job storage, you must load job information into the database. We talked about the various methods of accomplishing this in Chapter 6.

One of the ways is to write a stand-alone Quartz application that is configured to use the database via one of the JDBC `JobStores`, creates a Scheduler instance, and schedules all of the job and trigger information. You might give this application the capability to clear the job information from the database by passing an argument into the command line. The problem with this approach is that maintaining the database becomes very cumbersome.

Another approach would be to use a query tool that comes with your specific RDBMS and load the information yourself manually. This makes updates and deletion quite easy, but it can be problematic loading the data for the first time unless you know what you're doing; we highly discourage this.

Some find using the Quartz Web Application, discussed in Chapter 13, "Quartz and Web Applications," to be a convenient method. Managing job information is easy and can even be done by nontechnical resources. See Chapter 13 for information on the Quartz Web Application and, if you choose, for information on integrating Quartz into your own GUI application.

Running the Quartz Cluster Nodes

Really no difference exists when starting Quartz applications in a cluster. Each instance (or node) must be started individually. On startup, the instance connects to the database, retrieves the Scheduler information, and starts scheduling jobs.

Because Quartz uses a random load-balancing algorithm, you will see jobs being executed by different instances in a random manner. No pattern or predetermined node executes a particular job or execution.

The next section discusses some of the more common problems and tasks when dealing with Quartz in a clustered environment.

Quartz Clustering Cookbook

This section is designed to provide a resource for developers looking to solve specific problems with clustering in Quartz.

Assigning Jobs to Specific Instances in the Cluster

Currently, no way exists to assign (pin) a job to a specific node in the cluster. If you need this behavior, you can create a non-clustered Quartz application running in parallel with a clustered node and use either a separate set of database tables or an XML file along with the `JobInitializationPlugin`.

Don't point a nonclustered instance to the same set of database tables being used by a cluster. You will get very erratic results.

Running Jobs on Every Node in the Cluster

As with the previous answer, there is currently no way to run an instance of a job on every node in a cluster. The best option is to use a nonclustered instance in parallel with each node in the cluster and either use a separate set of database tables or use an XML file along with the `JobInitializationPlugin` and the `RAMJobStore`.

Running Nodes on Separate Machines

Quartz doesn't really care if you run nodes on the same machine or on different ones. When clustering is done on separate machines, it is commonly referred to as *horizontal clustering*. When nodes are run from the same machine, it is referred to as *vertical clustering*. With vertical clustering, there is a single point of failure. This is bad news for highly available applications because if the machine crashes, all nodes are effectively stopped.

Using a Time Synch Service

When you are running a Quartz cluster on separate machines, the clocks should be synchronized to prevent weird and unpredictable behavior. We have already mentioned that if the clocks are not in synch, that Scheduler instances will become confused about the state of other nodes. There are several easy ways to ensure the clocks are in synch, and there should be no reason not to do this.

The easiest way to synch the computers' clocks is to use one of the Internet Time Servers (ITS). For information on how to set up your clock based on one of these internationally accepted standards, see http://tf.nist.gov/service/its.htm.

Retrieving a List of Executing Jobs from the Cluster

Currently there is no easy way to get a list of all jobs executing in the cluster without going to the database directly. If you ask a Scheduler instance, you will get only a list of jobs executing on that instance. You could write some JDBC code that hits the database and retrieves the information from the proper table. Of course, this goes outside of Quartz, but it will solve the problem. Another approach is to use Quartz's RMI features to connect to each node in turn, querying it for its currently executing jobs.

Running Clustered and Nonclustered Instances Together

Nothing prevents you from using clustered and nonclustered Quartz applications in the same environment. The only caution is not to mix these two environments in the same database. That is, the nonclustered environment should not go against the same set of database tables as the clustered applications; you will get erratic results, and both clustered and nonclustered Jobs could encounter problems.

If you do run a nonclustered Quartz application in parallel with a clustered node, try using the JobInitializationPlugin (along with an XML file) and the RAMJobStore. This will make your life much easier.

Using Global Listeners in a Clustered Environment

You can still use job and trigger listeners in a clustered environment. The only confusion comes in when you try to understand which Scheduler instance will receive the callback method.

The easiest way to remember this is that the Listener will be notified in the Scheduler instance where the job or trigger is executed. Because a job and trigger are executed on only a single node, the Listener is notified on that node.

## CHAPTER 12

QUARTZ COOKBOOK

The purpose of this chapter is to provide a set of examples and solutions for situations that are frequently encountered when building Quartz applications. This chapter can serve as a reference and supplement to the rest of the book material.

Working with the Scheduler

This section provides several examples of using the administrative functions of the Quartz Scheduler.

Creating and Starting the Scheduler

You can start the Quartz Scheduler in several ways, but the easiest is to use one of the two `SchedulerFactory` implementations. In particular, the `org.quartz.impl.StdSchedulerFactory` is easy to use and performs all the work of setting up the Scheduler—all you need to do is use the static `getDefaultScheduler()` method, as Listing 12.1 demonstrates.

Listing 12.1   Starting the Default Scheduler

```
public void startScheduler() {
  Scheduler scheduler = null;

  try {
    // Get a Scheduler instance from the Factory
    scheduler = StdSchedulerFactory.getDefaultScheduler();

    // Start the scheduler
    scheduler.start();
    logger.info("Scheduler started at " + new Date());

    // Schedule jobs and triggers

  } catch (SchedulerException ex) {
    // deal with any exceptions
    logger.error(ex);
  }

}
```

When you have an instance of the Scheduler from the factory, you can start the Scheduler and add any necessary jobs and triggers. You can add jobs and triggers either before or after you start the Scheduler.

The Quartz framework supports multiple configuration files, which enables you to create different versions of the Scheduler. As an example, one version of the configuration file might set up the Scheduler as a single instance using the RAMJobStore, whereas a different configuration file might configure the Scheduler to be part of a cluster and use one of the JDBCJobStores.

To specify a configuration file other than the default, you can use the initialize() method on the StdSchedulerFactory and specify the name of the configuration file as an argument. Listing 12.2 illustrates an example of this.

Listing 12.2   Starting a Scheduler Using a Different Quartz Configuration File

```
public static void main(String[] args) {

  Scheduler scheduler = null;

  try {
    StdSchedulerFactory factory =
            new StdSchedulerFactory();
    factory.initialize("myquartz.properties");
    scheduler = factory.getScheduler();
```

Listing 12.2   Continued

```
    scheduler.start();
    logger.info("Scheduler started at " + new Date());

    // Schedule jobs and triggers

} catch (SchedulerException ex) {
    // deal with any exceptions
    logger.error(ex);
    }
}
```

LOADING JOBS INTO THE SCHEDULER

These examples started the Scheduler but did not add any jobs to it. You can start the Scheduler first and then add your jobs, or you can choose to add the jobs first and then start the Scheduler. Either way works fine. Later in this chapter, we show some examples of doing it both ways.

Stopping a Scheduler

The Scheduler API includes two versions of the `shutdown()` method. One takes a Boolean argument, and one takes no arguments. The Boolean parameter tells the Scheduler to wait until executing jobs are finished.

Using the no-argument version is the same as passing `false` to the alternative method. If you don't care about stopping any currently executing jobs, just call this:

```
scheduler.shutdown();
```

Alternatively, use this:

```
scheduler.shutdown(false);
```

On the other hand, if you want the executing jobs to finish before stopping the Scheduler, pass `true` to the `shutdown` method:

```
scheduler.shutdown(true);
```

Pausing a Scheduler (Standby Mode)

To temporarily halt the firing of any triggers, you can call the standby() method on the Scheduler. The Scheduler and its resources are not destroyed, and the Scheduler can be restarted at any time. Listing 12.3 shows an example of using the standby() method.

Listing 12.3   Putting a Scheduler in Standby Mode

```
public void runScheduler() {
  Scheduler scheduler = null;

  try {
    // Get a Scheduler instance from the factory
    scheduler = StdSchedulerFactory.getDefaultScheduler();

    // Start the scheduler
    scheduler.start();

    // Pause the scheduler for some reason
    scheduler.standby();

    // Restart the scheduler
    scheduler.start();

  } catch (SchedulerException ex) {
    // deal with any exceptions
    logger.error(ex);
  }
}
```

When a Scheduler is put in standby mode, scheduled triggers will not fire. When the Scheduler is restarted using the start() method, all triggers that should have fired are processed based on the misfire settings.

Working with Jobs

This section provides examples for working with Quartz jobs.

Creating a New Job Class

Creating a new job class is simple. Just create a class that implements the org.quartz.Job interface. This interface requires that you implement the execute() method, which is called when the Scheduler determines that the job should execute.

Listing 12.4 demonstrates a simple job that checks a mail server for new mail messages for a specific user. When the Scheduler executes this job, the execute() method is called, and the code connects to a mail server and gets any mail messages. This job simply prints who the message is from and the subject of the mail message.

Listing 12.4   A Quartz Job That Checks a Mail Server for Mail Messages

```
package org.cavaness.quartzbook.chapter12;

import java.security.NoSuchProviderException;
import java.util.Properties;

import javax.mail.Folder;
import javax.mail.Message;
import javax.mail.MessagingException;
import javax.mail.Session;
import javax.mail.Store;

import org.quartz.Job;
import org.quartz.JobExecutionContext;
import org.quartz.JobExecutionException;

public class CheckEmailJob implements Job {

  String mailHost = "some.mail.host";
  String username = "aUsername";
  String password = "aPassword";

  // Default Constructor
  public CheckEmailJob() {
    super();
  }

  public void execute(JobExecutionContext context) throws JobExecutionException {

    checkMail();
  }

  protected void checkMail() {

    // Get session
    Session session = null;

    try {

      // Get system properties
      Properties props = System.getProperties();

      session = Session.getDefaultInstance(props, null);
```

Listing 12.4   Continued

```
      // Get the store
      Store store = session.getStore("pop3");
      store.connect(mailHost, username, password);

      // Get folder
      Folder folder = store.getFolder("INBOX");
      folder.open(Folder.READ_ONLY);

      // Get directory
      Message message[] = folder.getMessages();
      int numOfMsgs = message.length;

      if (numOfMsgs > 0) {
        for (int i = 0, n = numOfMsgs; i < n; i++) {
          System.out.println("(" + i + " of " + numOfMsgs + "): "
              + message[i].getFrom()[0] + "\t"
              + message[i].getSubject());
        }
      } else {
        System.out.println("No Messages for user");
      }

      // Close connection
      folder.close(false);
      store.close();
    } catch (NoSuchProviderException e) {
      // TODO Auto-generated catch block
      e.printStackTrace();
    } catch (MessagingException e) {
      // TODO Auto-generated catch block
      e.printStackTrace();
    }
  }

  public static void main(String[] args) {
    CheckEmailJob job = new CheckEmailJob();
    job.checkMail();
  }
}
```

Most of Listing 12.4 involves using the JavaMail API to access the mail server. In terms of implementing a new Quartz job class, very little has to be done. Essentially, you implement the job interface and the `execute()` method, and it's ready to be scheduled. This is shown in the next example.

HARD-CODING VS. PASSING IN JOB PARAMETERS

In Listing 12.4, the mail properties such as host, username, and password were hard-coded within the job class itself. This is rarely a good idea. Later in the chapter, we change the job to pass the parameters in the JobDataMap.

Scheduling a Quartz Job

As the previous example demonstrated, it's pretty straightforward to create a Quartz job. Fortunately, configuring a job
with the Scheduler isn't much more difficult. Listing 12.5 shows
an example of scheduling the CheckEmailJob from the
previous listing.

Listing 12.5   Example Showing How to Schedule the **CheckEmailJob**

```
package org.cavaness.quartzbook.chapter12;

import org.apache.commons.logging.Log;
import org.apache.commons.logging.LogFactory;
import org.quartz.JobDetail;
import org.quartz.Scheduler;
import org.quartz.SchedulerException;
import org.quartz.Trigger;
import org.quartz.TriggerUtils;
import org.quartz.impl.StdSchedulerFactory;

public class Listing_12_5 {
  static Log logger = LogFactory.getLog(Listing_12_5.class);

  public static void main(String[] args) {
    Listing_12_5 example = new Listing_12_5();
    example.runScheduler();
  }

  public void runScheduler() {
    Scheduler scheduler = null;

    try {
      // Get a Scheduler instance from the Factory
      scheduler = StdSchedulerFactory.getDefaultScheduler();

      // Start the scheduler
      scheduler.start();

      // Create a JobDetail for the Job
      JobDetail jobDetail = new JobDetail("CheckEmailJob",
          Scheduler.DEFAULT_GROUP, CheckEmailJob.class);

      // Create a trigger that fires every 1 hour
      Trigger trigger = TriggerUtils.makeHourlyTrigger();

      trigger.setName("emailJobTrigger");

      // Start the trigger firing from now
      // trigger.setStartTime(new Date());

      // Associate the trigger with the job in the scheduler
      scheduler.scheduleJob(jobDetail, trigger);
```

Listing 12.5   Continued

```
      } catch (SchedulerException ex) {
        // deal with any exceptions
        logger.error(ex);
      }
    }

  }
```

The code in Listing 12.5 obtains the Scheduler from the StdSchedulerFactory and starts it. It then creates a Job-Detail for the CheckEmailJob and creates a trigger for the job to fire every hour, starting immediately.

Firing a Job One Time

The org.quartz.TriggerUtils class is convenient and contains many useful methods. One of the most useful methods is the one that can schedule a fire-once immediate trigger. Listing 12.6 demonstrates how to fire the CheckEmailJob only once.

Listing 12.6   Using a Fire-Once Trigger for the CheckEmailJob

```
package org.cavaness.quartzbook.chapter12;

import org.apache.commons.logging.Log;
import org.apache.commons.logging.LogFactory;
import org.quartz.JobDetail;
import org.quartz.Scheduler;
import org.quartz.SchedulerException;
import org.quartz.Trigger;
import org.quartz.TriggerUtils;
import org.quartz.impl.StdSchedulerFactory;

public class Listing_12_6 {
  static Log logger = LogFactory.getLog(Listing_12_6.class);

  public static void main(String[] args) {
    Listing_12_6 example = new Listing_12_6();
    example.runScheduler();
  }

  public void runScheduler() {
    Scheduler scheduler = null;

    try {
      // Get a Scheduler instance from the Factory
      scheduler = StdSchedulerFactory.getDefaultScheduler();

      // Start the scheduler
      scheduler.start();
```

Listing 12.6   Continued

```
        // Create a JobDetail for the Job
        JobDetail jobDetail = new JobDetail("CheckEmailJob",
            Scheduler.DEFAULT_GROUP, CheckEmailJob.class);

        // Create a trigger that fires every 1 hour
        Trigger trigger = TriggerUtils.makeImmediateTrigger(0, 0);
        trigger.setName("emailJobTrigger");

        // Associate the trigger with the job in the scheduler
        scheduler.scheduleJob(jobDetail, trigger);

    } catch (SchedulerException ex) {
        // deal with any exceptions
        logger.error(ex);
    }
  }
}
```

Listing 12.6 uses the static makeImmediateTrigger() method on
the TriggerUtils clas and passes 0 for the repeatCount and 0
for the repeatInterval so that the trigger fires only once.

Replacing an Existing Scheduled Job

Quartz provides the flexibility to modify jobs that are already
scheduled. It supports this by allowing the JobDetail to be
replaced with a modified JobDetail. To show an example of
this, let's update our CheckEmailJob class from Listing 12.4.
The version that was shown in Listing 12.4 hard-coded the mail
properties within the job class. It would be better if those properties were passed in so they could be changed at will; let's
change the CheckEmailJob to allow for that. Listing 12.7 shows
an updated version of that job.

Listing 12.7   An Updated CheckEmailJob That Allows Properties to Be Passed In

```
package org.cavaness.quartzbook.chapter12;

import java.util.Properties;

import javax.mail.Folder;
import javax.mail.Message;
import javax.mail.MessagingException;
import javax.mail.NoSuchProviderException;
import javax.mail.Session;
import javax.mail.Store;
```

Listing 12.7 Continued

```java
import org.quartz.Job;
import org.quartz.JobDataMap;
import org.quartz.JobExecutionContext;
import org.quartz.JobExecutionException;

public class CheckEmailJob implements Job {
  public static String HOST_KEY = "mailHost";
  public static String USERNAME_KEY = "username";
  public static String PASSWORD_KEY = "password";

  String mailHost = "some.mail.host";
  String username = "aUsername";
  String password = "aPassword";

  public CheckEmailJob() {
    super();
  }

  public void execute(JobExecutionContext context) throws JobExecutionException {
    loadMailProperties(context.getJobDetail().getJobDataMap());
    checkMail();
  }

  protected void loadMailProperties(JobDataMap map) {
    if (map.getString(HOST_KEY) != null) {
      mailHost = map.getString(HOST_KEY);
    }

    if (map.getString(USERNAME_KEY) != null) {
      username = map.getString(USERNAME_KEY);
    }

    if (map.getString(PASSWORD_KEY) != null) {
      password = map.getString(PASSWORD_KEY);
    }
  }

  protected void checkMail() {
    // Get session
    Session session = null;

    try {
      // Get system properties
      Properties props = System.getProperties();

      session = Session.getDefaultInstance(props, null);

      // Get the store
      Store store = session.getStore("pop3");
      store.connect(mailHost, username, password);

      // Get folder
      Folder folder = store.getFolder("INBOX");
      folder.open(Folder.READ_ONLY);

      // Get directory
      Message message[] = folder.getMessages();
      int numOfMsgs = message.length;
```

Listing 12.7   Continued

```
    if (numOfMsgs > 0) {
      for (int i = 0, n = numOfMsgs; i < n; i++) {
        System.out.println("(" + i + " of " + numOfMsgs + "): "
            + message[i].getFrom()[0] + "\t"
            + message[i].getSubject());
      }
    } else {
      System.out.println("No Messages for user");
    }

    // Close connection
    folder.close(false);
    store.close();
  } catch (NoSuchProviderException e) {
    // TODO Auto-generated catch block
    e.printStackTrace();
  } catch (MessagingException e) {
    // TODO Auto-generated catch block
    e.printStackTrace();
  }
}

public static void main(String[] args) {
  CheckEmailJob job = new CheckEmailJob();
  job.checkMail();
}
}
```

The main difference between the CheckEmailJob from Listing 12.7 and the version in 12.4 is the loadMailProperties() method. This method is called when the job is first executed and checks the JobDataMap to see if the mail properties were set within the map. If so, those are used. If not, the defaults within the job class are used.

Listing 12.8 shows how the properties can be set up within the JobDataMap and passed to the job. This listing also shows how you can change the job by replacing the JobDetail with a modified instance.

Listing 12.8   An Example Showing How to Update a Scheduled Job

```
package org.cavaness.quartzbook.chapter12;

import org.apache.commons.logging.Log;
import org.apache.commons.logging.LogFactory;
import org.quartz.JobDetail;
import org.quartz.Scheduler;
import org.quartz.SchedulerException;
import org.quartz.Trigger;
import org.quartz.TriggerUtils;
import org.quartz.impl.StdSchedulerFactory;
```

Listing 12.8   Continued

```
public class Listing_12_8 {
  static Log logger = LogFactory.getLog(Listing_12_8.class);

  public static void main(String[] args) {
    Listing_12_8 example = new Listing_12_8();
    example.runScheduler();
  }

  public void runScheduler() {
    Scheduler scheduler = null;

    try {
      // Get a Scheduler instance from the Factory
      scheduler = StdSchedulerFactory.getDefaultScheduler();

      // Start the scheduler
      scheduler.start();

      // Create a JobDetail for the Job
      JobDetail jobDetail = new JobDetail("CheckEmailJob",
          Scheduler.DEFAULT_GROUP, CheckEmailJob.class);

      // Set the properties used by the job
      jobDetail.getJobDataMap().put(CheckEmailJob.HOST_KEY, "host1");
      jobDetail.getJobDataMap().put(CheckEmailJob.USERNAME_KEY, "username");
      jobDetail.getJobDataMap().put(CheckEmailJob.PASSWORD_KEY, "password");

      // Create a trigger that fires at 11:30pm every day
      Trigger trigger = TriggerUtils.makeDailyTrigger(23, 30);
      trigger.setName("emailJobTrigger");

      // Associate the trigger with the job in the scheduler
      scheduler.scheduleJob(jobDetail, trigger);

      // Update the Job with a different mail host
      jobDetail.getJobDataMap().put(CheckEmailJob.HOST_KEY, "host2");
      scheduler.addJob(jobDetail, true);

    } catch (SchedulerException ex) {
      // deal with any exceptions
      logger.error(ex);
    }
  }
}
```

The code in Listing 12.8 shows two things. First, it shows how you can pass mail properties to the job class through the JobDataMap. Second, it illustrates how you can use the addJob() method to update the JobDetail of an already scheduled job. The addJob() method takes a Boolean argument that tells the Scheduler whether to replace the scheduled JobDetail with the one being passed in. The job name and group must match the one within the Scheduler for it to be replaced with the new one. Typically, your code would retrieve the existing job, modify the contents of its JobDataMap, and then resave it.

Updating an Existing Trigger

You might also need to update an existing trigger for a job. You can replace a trigger with a different one as long as it's for the same job. You can replace a trigger by using the rescheduleJob() method on the Scheduler:

```
Trigger newTrigger = // Create a new Trigger

// Replace the old trigger with a new one
sched.rescheduleJob(jobName, Scheduler.DEFAULT_GROUP, newTrigger);
```

Listing Jobs in the Scheduler

If you were building a GUI for Quartz, you might need to list the jobs registered with the Scheduler. Listing 12.9 presents an approach for doing just that.

Listing 12.9   An Example of Listing the Jobs Within the Scheduler

```
package org.cavaness.quartzbook.chapter12;

import org.apache.commons.logging.Log;
import org.apache.commons.logging.LogFactory;
import org.quartz.JobDetail;
import org.quartz.Scheduler;
import org.quartz.SchedulerException;
import org.quartz.Trigger;
import org.quartz.TriggerUtils;
import org.quartz.impl.StdSchedulerFactory;

public class Listing_12_9 {
  static Log logger = LogFactory.getLog(Listing_12_9.class);

  public static void main(String[] args) {
    Listing_12_9 example = new Listing_12_9();
    example.runScheduler();
  }

  public void runScheduler() {
    Scheduler scheduler = null;

    try {
      // Get a Scheduler instance from the Factory
```

Listing 12.9 Continued

```
    scheduler = StdSchedulerFactory.getDefaultScheduler();

    // Start the scheduler
    scheduler.start();

    // Create a JobDetail for the Job
    JobDetail jobDetail = new JobDetail("CheckEmailJob",
        Scheduler.DEFAULT_GROUP, CheckEmailJob.class);

    // Create a trigger that fires at 11:30pm every day
    Trigger trigger = TriggerUtils.makeDailyTrigger(23, 30);
    trigger.setName("emailJobTrigger");

    // Associate the trigger with the job in the scheduler
    scheduler.scheduleJob(jobDetail, trigger);

    String[] jobGroups = scheduler.getJobGroupNames();
    int numOfJobGroups = jobGroups.length;

    for (int i = 0; i < numOfJobGroups; i++) {
      System.out.println("Group: " + jobGroups[i]
          + " contains the following jobs");

      String[] jobsInGroup = scheduler.getJobNames(jobGroups[i]);
      int numOfJobsInGroup = jobsInGroup.length;

      for (int j = 0; j < numOfJobsInGroup; j++) {
        System.out.println("- " + jobsInGroup[j]);
      }
    }
  } catch (SchedulerException ex) {
    // deal with any exceptions
    logger.error(ex);
  }
 }
}
```

Listing 12.9 registers a single job, the CheckEmailJob from Listing 12.7, and then demonstrates how to loop through the JobGroups and list the jobs within each group. In a GUI, this list could be presented in a list box or a drop-down list.

Listing Triggers Within the Scheduler

You can also list the triggers in a manner similar to that in Listing 12.9. The code would look very similar, but with triggers instead.

```
String[] triggerGroups = sched.getTriggerGroupNames();
int numOfTriggerGroups = triggerGroups.length;
```

```
for (i = 0; i < numOfTriggerGroups; i++) {
    System.out.println("Group: "
        + triggerGroups[i]
        + " contains the following triggers");

    String{[] triggersInGroup = sched.getTriggerNames(triggerGroups[i]);
    int numOfTriggersInGroup = triggersInGroup.length;
    for (j = 0; j < numOfTriggersInGroup; j++) {
        System.out.println("- " + triggersInGroup[j]);
    }
}
```

If you need to list the triggers of a single job, you can use
the getTriggersOfJob() method found on the Scheduler. This
method returns a Trigger[] of the triggers associated with
the job.

## CHAPTER 13

QUARTZ AND WEB APPLICATIONS

Up to this point, our interaction with the Quartz framework has primarily been through the command line. For users such as my old college computer science professor (who would tell me every day, "GUIs are for wimps!"), command-line usage is very acceptable. When applications are developed and finished, however, they are often turned over to end users or support teams. Putting GUI front ends on top of command-line applications can be quite helpful and much appreciated. This chapter describes how to use Quartz within Web applications to make scheduling and maintaining jobs easier.

Using Quartz Within a Web Application

By now, you've seen many examples of Quartz running as a stand-alone application in a J2SE environment. In Chapter 10, "Using Quartz with J2EE," you also learned that Quartz can function well running within a J2EE environment. But what we haven't shown you is how to deploy Quartz within a Java Web application (normally abbreviated as Web app). That is the sole intent of this chapter.

You might want to integrate Quartz within a Web application for several reasons. A few of the more obvious ones are listed here:

- To schedule and launch jobs using a GUI interface
- To improve job management and monitoring
- To make it easier for multiple users to schedule jobs
- To schedule jobs from within your own Web applications

The primary use of Quartz within a Web app is, of course, to allow easier scheduling and maintenance of jobs through a GUI interface. Other secondary reasons include better management of running and scheduled jobs, as well as quicker notification when things go wrong. In general, the same reasons that you would want to put a GUI around any software application can be generalized for applications using Quartz: to make it easier to use the application.

Integrating Quartz

Fortunately, two things make it easy to integrate Quartz into a Web application. First, the list of third-party libraries the Quartz framework requires is pretty straightforward. Most of the third-party dependencies already are included in any Java Web application, especially ones built with open source frameworks such as Apache Struts. When deploying Quartz within a Web application, Quartz requires the following third-party libraries:

- Commons BeanUtils
- Commons Collections
- Commons Logging
- Commons Digester

If you've built Java Web applications before, you've seen all these listed here. A few other JARs might be necessary, depending on your exact deployment of Quartz. For example, if Quartz stores its job information in a database, the Standard JDBC APIs library (`jdbc2_0-stdext.jar`) is required, along with possibly the Java Transaction API (`jta.jar`).

You might also need some optional libraries, depending on the totality of your requirements. For example, if your application needs to send e-mails, you'll need the activation and JavaMail libraries. But this is true whether you are deploying Quartz within a Web application or just as a stand-alone application.

Structure of a Web Application

Over the past several years, the Servlet and JSP specifications have improved and allowed for better portability between tool vendors. This has had a calming effect on the Java development community and allows Web developers to focus on the "real" business needs and not on what has to be done to get the application to deploy and run.

Installing the Quartz Libraries

As in any other Java Web application, the Servlet specification instructs that all JARs (third-party or otherwise) must be placed into WEB-INF/lib. Therefore, one of the first steps is to put the quartz.jar file and its dependent JARs into the WEB-INF/lib directory.

JAR VERSION AND LOCATION DO MATTER

You must be careful about not only which JAR files you put in a Web application, but also which version of the JAR you are using and exactly where you put it. As the development community continues to mature, more continuous integration is occurring across independent projects. So issues such as one project depending on an out-of-date version of another project are becoming less frequent. Be sure to check the dependencies before upgrading to newer versions of libraries.

The other thing to keep in mind is that it's extremely important (and sometimes confusing) where you install libraries. Fortunately, Web container vendors are starting to adhere to specifications more closely, and developers are becoming more educated. For Web applications, you almost always want to install any third-party library (specific to your application) into the WEB-INF/lib directory. Issues with XML parsers and encryption packages such as Sun Java Secure Socket Extensions (JSSE) still pop up, but these are becoming rare as commercial and open source vendors update their releases.

Choosing a Web Application Framework

It's entirely up to you which Java Web application framework you choose to integrate with Quartz. So many frameworks are available that it can be quite overwhelming. To say that one particular framework is better than another is very subjective because a lot has to do with your requirements and skill set. However, a few Web frameworks have proven themselves over time. One example is the Apache Struts framework (formerly known as Jakarta Struts). For the purpose of this section, we will use the Struts framework to demonstrate how to integrate with Quartz.

Using Quartz with the Struts Framework

The first step is to download Apache Struts and create your Web application directory structure. The Struts framework is available from the Apache Struts site, at http://struts.apache.org. You're welcome to grab the source code and build from that, although the binary download of the latest version should be sufficient.

Because Quartz does not directly depend on the Struts framework, you don't have to worry about the version of Struts that you use. Just grab the latest version that's available. You should realize, however, that the Struts and Quartz frameworks share some third-party dependencies. In fact, the required libraries we listed earlier for Quartz are all required by the Struts framework. Just be careful about mixing up different versions, as the note in the last section warned.

Creating Your Web Application Directory Structure

After you download Struts, you can create your directory structure and install the necessary files. For this example, we're going to create a fictitious Web application called Job Management Console. Because this is just a pretend application, we won't be building it to completion. Instead, we use it to explain several key points of integration with Quartz and leave the rest for you to explore. For now, assume that the boss has given us a task to build a GUI around our Job Scheduling framework (which, of course, would be based on Quartz). Figures 13.1 and 13.2 show the login and main screen of the Job Management Console application.

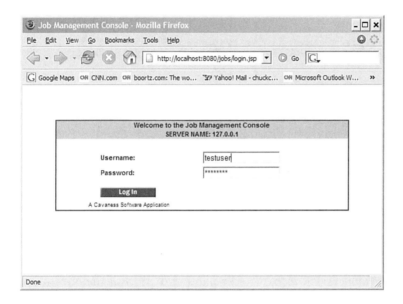

FIGURE 13.1   The login screen for our Job Management Console application.

When the user presses the Login button, the application should take the user to the Dashboard screen, which is shown in Figure 13.2.

Figure 13.2 shows the Dashboard of the console, where all users are taken after they log in.

The Dashboard page shown in Figure 13.2 is pretty simple but is good enough for our purposes.

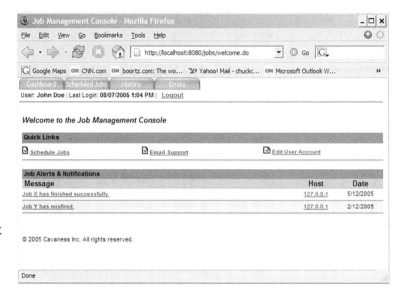

FIGURE 13.2
The Job Management Console Dashboard is the main screen for users.

Creating the Job Management Console Project Structure

The project structure for the Job Management Console is very standard among Java Web applications, and most Java Web developers will recognize the purpose of most of the directories shown. The tags directory underneath WEB-INF will house the .tld files, used by applications to reference the custom tag libraries. The Struts framework provides several tag libraries that can be used to make JSP development easier; the .tld directories hold the descriptor files for those tags. Figure 13.3 shows the project structure for the application.

FIGURE 13.3
The project structure for the Job Management Console.

Initializing Quartz Within the Web Application

When Quartz is used from the command line, a Java class is used to create a `SchedulerFactory` and instantiate a Scheduler instance. Because Quartz will now be running within a Web application, you don't have easy access to the `main()` method because the application is started by the container, and `main()` is buried in code, possibly even behind an actual executable. Fortunately, the solution is easy: All you have to do is ensure that when the container first starts the Web application, you have some code that performs the factory-creation logic. That is to say, when the container first loads the web application, you need to create a `SchedulerFactory` and start the Scheduler.

> ### To Start() OR NOT TO Start()
>
> Depending on your requirements, you might want the Scheduler to start immediately when the Web application is first loaded. However, you also might need the scheduler to be ready to run but not start until some other action is taken. Maybe in your Job Management Console application, for example, the scheduler shouldn't start until the user gets to the Dashboard screen and presses the Start button. If this is the case, the factory can be obtained, but the Scheduler should not be started until you're ready.

The `QuartzInitializerServlet` to the Rescue

The Quartz framework includes a Java servlet called `org.quartz.ee.servlet. QuartzInitializerServlet`, which extends a standard `HttpServlet`. You can use this servlet in your Web application, and it will create a `StdSchedulerFactory` instance and make it available to the rest of your application. In general, it does what the `main()` method did in the command-line version of our Quartz application.

THE QuartzInitializerServlet WAS CHANGED IN QUARTZ 1.5

In the 1.5 release of Quartz, the QuartzInitializerServlet was modified to store the StdSchedulerFactory instance in the ServletContext of the Web application. This allows your application to access the factory from anywhere there's an HttpServletRequest or HttpSession object available, and have access to the Scheduler instance by calling getScheduler() on the factory.

A new servlet initialization parameter called start-scheduler-on-load also is available. This parameter specifies whether the scheduler should be started from the QuartzInitializerServlet or somewhere else. If it is not specified or is set to true, the scheduler will be started from the QuartzInitializerServlet. Otherwise, your application will have to get the Scheduler instance and call the start() method.

When the container loads the QuartzInitializerServlet, the servlet's init() method is called. The servlet reads several initialization parameters, creates an instance of the StdSchedulerFactory class, and initializes the Scheduler using the specified (or default) Quartz properties file.

After the factory is created, the init() method determines whether the Scheduler should be started immediately or whether the application should decide when to start it. Listing 3.1 shows the init() method of the QuartzInitializerServlet.

Listing 13.1   The init() Method of the QuartzInitializerServlet Class

```
public void init(ServletConfig cfg) throws ServletException {
  super.init(cfg);

  log("Quartz Initializer Servlet loaded, initializing Scheduler...");

  StdSchedulerFactory factory;
  try {

    String configFile = cfg.getInitParameter("config-file");
    String shutdownPref = cfg.getInitParameter("shutdown-on-unload");

    if (shutdownPref != null)
      performShutdown = Boolean.valueOf(shutdownPref).booleanValue();

    // get Properties
    if (configFile != null) {
      factory = new StdSchedulerFactory(configFile);
    } else {
      factory = new StdSchedulerFactory();
    }

    // Should the Scheduler being started now or later
```

Listing 13.1   Continued

```
String startOnLoad =
  cfg.getInitParameter("start-scheduler-on-load");

/*
 * If the "start-scheduler-on-load" init-parameter is not specified,
 * the
 * scheduler will be started. This is to maintain backwards
 * compatability.
 */

if (startOnLoad == null ||
  (Boolean.valueOf(startOnLoad).booleanValue())) {
  // Start now
  scheduler = factory.getScheduler();
  scheduler.start();
  log("Scheduler has been started...");
} else {
  log("Scheduler has not been started. Use scheduler.start()");
}

log(
  "Storing the Quartz Scheduler Factory in the servlet context at key: " +
      QUARTZ_FACTORY_KEY);
cfg.getServletContext().setAttribute(QUARTZ_FACTORY_KEY, factory);

} catch (Exception e) {
  log("Quartz Scheduler failed to initialize: " + e.toString());
  throw new ServletException(e);
}
}
}
```

The QuartzInitializerServlet is part of the Quartz JAR
file. As long as you have the quartz.jar file in the WEB-INF/
lib of the Web application, the servlet is available for you to
use within your application.

Configuring the Web Deployment Descriptor

The Java Servlet specification specifies that every Web application must contain a Web deployment descriptor. The descriptor
(web.xml) contains the following types of information:

- Initialization parameters
- Session configuration
- Servlet/JSP definitions
- Servlet/JSP mappings
- MIME type mappings
- Welcome file list

■ Error pages

■ Security

Because the QuartzInitializerServlet is a Java servlet, it must be configured within the deployment descriptor for the container to load it. Listing 13.2 illustrates how to set up the QuartzInitializerServlet within the web.xml file.

Listing 13.2 The QuartzInitializerServlet Requires Modification to the web.xml File

```
<web-app>
 <servlet>
  <servlet-name>QuartzInitializer</servlet-name>
  <display-name>Quartz Initializer Servlet</display-name>

  <servlet-class>
    org.quartz.ee.servlet.QuartzInitializerServlet
  </servlet-class>

  <load-on-startup>1</load-on-startup>

  <init-param>
    <param-name>config-file</param-name>
    <param-value>/some/path/my_quartz.properties</param-value>
  </init-param>

  <init-param>
    <param-name>shutdown-on-unload</param-name>
    <param-value>true</param-value>
  </init-param>

  <init-param>
    <param-name>start-scheduler-on-load</param-name>
    <param-value>true</param-value>
  </init-param>

 </servlet>

 <!- other web.xml items here ->

</web-app>
```

The QuartzInitializerServlet supports three Quartz-specific initialization parameters.

THE config-file INITIALIZATION PARAMETER

The config-file parameter is used to specify a path and a file-name for the Quartz properties file. The StdSchedulerFactory uses this file to configure the Scheduler instance. This parameter is optional; if it is not specified, the default `quartz.properties` file is used. The easiest way to use this parameter (assuming that you want to provide your own properties file) is to put your properties file in the `WEB-INF/classes` directory and specify the `init-param` as follows:

```
<init-param>
  <param-name>config-file</param-name>
    <param-value>/my_quartz.properties</param-value>
</init-param>
```

THE `shutdown-on-unload` INITIALIZATION PARAMETER

The `shutdown-on-unload` parameter is used to cause the `scheduler.shutdown()` method to be called when the container unloads the servlet. A container unloads the servlet when it is shutting down and, in some conditions, when it is being reloaded in a hot-deploy environment. This parameter is optional and defaults to `true`.

THE `start-scheduler-on-load` INITIALIZATION PARAMETER

The `start-scheduler-on-load` parameter is used to tell the servlet to call the `start()` method on the Scheduler instance. If it is not started, the Scheduler will need to be started by the application at a later time, and no jobs will run until the `start()` method is called. The parameter is optional and defaults to `true` if it is not specified. This parameter was added in release 1.5 and might not be present in earlier versions.

Accessing the `SchedulerFactory` and `Scheduler`

Starting with Quartz 1.5, the `QuartzInitializerServlet` will automatically store the `StdSchedulerFactory` instance in the `ServletContext` at a predetermined key.

QuartzInitializerServlet IN EARLIER VERSIONS OF QUARTZ

The QuartzInitializerServlet was available in earlier versions of the framework. In those versions, however, the StdSchedulerFactory wasn't stored in the ServletContext. The Scheduler was initialized and started, all from the servlet's init() method. To retrieve the Scheduler instance from your code, you needed to use one of the get methods of the StdSchedulerFactory class to access the Scheduler that the servlet created. The change to access the Scheduler from the ServletContext was added in version 1.5.

You can see this from the end of the init() method in Listing 13.1. After the factory is stored within the ServletContext, there are many ways to gain access to it. The easiest way, especially if you are using the Struts framework, is to use the request object. Listing 13.3 shows a Struts Action class called StartSchedulerAction. When this action is invoked (presumably with a URL such as /startscheduler.do), the SchedulerFactory is retrieved, and the method getScheduler() can be called.

Listing 13.3 The SchedulerFactory and Scheduler Can Be Easily Accessed

```
import javax.servlet.ServletContext;
import javax.servlet.http.HttpServletRequest;
import javax.servlet.http.HttpServletResponse;

import org.apache.struts.action.Action;
import org.apache.struts.action.ActionForm;
import org.apache.struts.action.ActionForward;
import org.apache.struts.action.ActionMapping;
import org.cavaness.jobconsole.web.QuartzFactoryServlet;
import org.cavaness.jobconsole.web.WebConstants;
import org.quartz.Scheduler;
import org.quartz.impl.StdSchedulerFactory;

public class StartSchedulerAction extends Action {
    public ActionForward execute(ActionMapping mapping,
    ActionForm form, HttpServletRequest request,
    HttpServletResponse response) throws Exception {

        // Retrieve the ServletContext
        ServletContext ctx =
            request.getSession().getServletContext();

        // Retrieve the factory from the ServletContext
        StdSchedulerFactory factory =
            (StdSchedulerFactory)
            ctx.getAttribute(
            QuartzFactoryServlet.QUARTZ_FACTORY_KEY);
```

Listing 13.3   Continued

```
        // Retrieve the scheduler from the factory
        Scheduler scheduler = factory.getScheduler();

        // Start the scheduler
        scheduler.start();


        // Forward to success page
        return mapping.findForward(WebConstants.SUCCESS);
    }
}
```

When the Scheduler is retrieved from the
SchedulerFactory, you can use the methods on the Scheduler
instance as normal. In Listing 13.3, the Scheduler is started
using the start() method that you've become accustomed to.

The benefit of storing the StdSchedulerFactory in the
ServletContext is that it prevents you from having to create
it repeatedly. In fact, you can make it even easier to access
the Scheduler by putting all the logic of accessing the
ServletContext and creating the Scheduler in a utility class.
Listing 13.4 shows a class called ActionUtil that makes it easier to get a reference to the Scheduler object.

Listing 13.4   The ActionUtil Class Is Convenient for Accessing the Scheduler

```
import javax.servlet.ServletContext;
import javax.servlet.http.HttpServletRequest;

import org.quartz.Scheduler;
import org.quartz.SchedulerException;
import org.quartz.impl.StdSchedulerFactory;

public class ActionUtil {

    public static Scheduler getScheduler(HttpServletRequest request)
        throws SchedulerException {

        ServletContext ctx =
            request.getSession().getServletContext();

        StdSchedulerFactory factory =
            (StdSchedulerFactory) ctx.getAttribute(
            QuartzFactoryServlet.QUARTZ_FACTORY_KEY);

        return factory.getScheduler();
    }
}
```

You can use the `ActionUtil getScheduler()` method to conveniently retrieve the Scheduler instance. The following code fragment shows the `StartSchedulerAction` class from Listing 13.3 using the `ActionUtil getScheduler()` method:

```
public class StartSchedulerAction extends Action {
    public ActionForward execute(ActionMapping mapping,
    ActionForm form, HttpServletRequest request,
    HttpServletResponse response) throws Exception {

        // Retrieve the scheduler from the factory
        Scheduler scheduler = ActionUtil.getScheduler();

        // Start the scheduler
        scheduler.start();

        // Forward to success page
        return mapping.findForward(WebConstants.SUCCESS);
    }
}
```

The `ActionUtil` shown in Listing 13.4 is not part of the Quartz framework yet, but it's possible that it will be added in the future. You can add the same thing in your application as needed.

Using a `ServletContextListener`

It's worth mentioning that you can configure and integrate Quartz within a Web application in another way. Starting with version 2.3 of the Servlet API, you can create listeners that get callbacks from the servlet container at certain times during the life cycle of the container. One of the listener interfaces is called `javax.servlet.ServletContextListener` and contains two methods:

```
public void contextInitialized(ServletContextEvent sce);
public void contextDestroyed(ServletContextEvent sce );
```

The container calls these two methods when the container is started and shut down, respectively. It's possible to initialize the Quartz Scheduler in the `contextInitialized()` method and shut it down from the `contextDestroyed()` method. Listing 13.5 illustrates this.

Listing 13.5 A ServletContextListener Can Also Be Used to Initialize Quartz

```java
import javax.servlet.ServletContext;
import javax.servlet.ServletContextEvent;
import javax.servlet.ServletContextListener;

import org.apache.commons.logging.Log;
import org.apache.commons.logging.LogFactory;
import org.quartz.SchedulerException;
import org.quartz.impl.StdSchedulerFactory;

public class QuartzServletContextListener implements ServletContextListener {
    private static Log logger = LogFactory
            .getLog(QuartzServletContextListener.class);

    public static final String QUARTZ_FACTORY_KEY =
        "org.quartz.impl.StdSchedulerFactory.KEY";

    private ServletContext ctx = null;

    private StdSchedulerFactory factory = null;

    /**
     * Called when the container is shutting down.
     */
    public void contextDestroyed(ServletContextEvent sce) {
        try {
            factory.getDefaultScheduler().shutdown();
        } catch (SchedulerException ex) {
            logger.error("Error stopping Quartz", ex);
        }

    }

    /**
     * Called when the container is first started.
     */
    public void contextInitialized(ServletContextEvent sce) {

        ctx = sce.getServletContext();

        try {

            factory = new StdSchedulerFactory();

            // Start the scheduler now
            factory.getScheduler().start();

            logger.info("Storing QuartzScheduler Factory at"
                    + QUARTZ_FACTORY_KEY);

            ctx.setAttribute(QUARTZ_FACTORY_KEY, factory);

        } catch (Exception ex) {
            logger.error("Quartz failed to initialize", ex);
        }
    }
}
```

As we did for the `QuartzInitializerServlet`, we need to add some configuration information to the Web deployment descriptor (`web.xml`) for the listener. For our listener, we need to add a `<listener>` element to the deployment descriptor. It is shown in this snippet:

```
<web-app>
  <listener>
    <listener-class>
      org.cavaness.jobconsole.web.QuartzServletContextListener
    </listener-class>
  </listener>
  <!-Other deployment descriptor info not shown ->
</web-app>
```

New `QuartzInitializerListener` Added to Quartz

A `ServletContextListener` has been added to the Quartz framework because of requests from the user community. The code from Listing 13.5 should be considered an example in case you need to develop your own listener.

Introducing the Quartz Web Application

The early developers of the Quartz framework realized that a GUI would be necessary for a certain group of users. Several years ago, a Web application was created that could be used to manage the Quartz framework. There has been quite a bit of development over the years, but, arguably, it has been sporadic.

Lately there has been an increased call for the application to be updated and supported, and it's starting to draw new developers who are willing to work on it and keep it up-to-date. The application is known as the Quartz Web application.

Screenshots of the Quartz Web Application

The upper-left side of the main screen in the Quartz Web application presents a list of features that are available (see Figure 13.4).

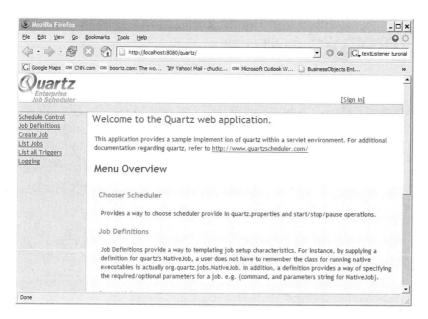

FIGURE 13.4   The main screen of the Quartz Web application

Figure 13.5 shows the Scheduler Control screen, which enables you to start, stop, and pause the Scheduler.

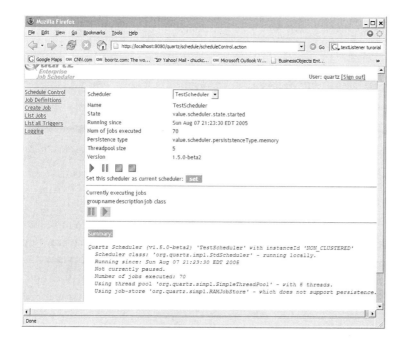

FIGURE 13.5
The Scheduler Control screen contains Scheduler-management features.

Downloading and Building the Quartz Web Application

The Quartz Web application is part of the Quartz source repository on OpenSymphony. It used to be housed on SourceForge, but it has recently moved over to its new home. The old site was located at http://sourceforge.net/projects/quartz; the new site (including the Quartz Web application) can be found at www.opensymphony.com/quartz/cvs.action.

Currently, there is no binary release of the Web application, and the standard Quartz download does not include the Web application, although the maintainers of the application have said they will have a build set up early 2006. For now, you need to download the Quartz source tree and build the Web application using the Ant build file located in the quartz/ webapp directory.

To download Quartz from CVS, you need an account on the java.net site because anonymous access is not permitted. From a command line where you want to download the source tree to, type this:

```
cvs -d :pserver:[username]@cvs.dev.java.net:/cvs login
cvs -d :pserver:[username]@cvs.dev.java.net:/cvs checkout quartz
cvs -d :pserver:[username]@cvs.dev.java.net:/cvs checkout opensymphony
```

QUARTZ REQUIRES OPENSYMPHONY SOURCE

OpenSymphony projects are practicing continuous integration. This means that projects have tighter but supportive dependencies on one another. You also must download the OpenSymphony source for Quartz to build successfully. Use the previous checkout command and substitute opensymphony for quartz. You should execute this command from the same place you executed the checkout for Quartz.

After you have downloaded the Quartz and OpenSymphony source, you can build Quartz from the quartz directory, but you also can build the Web application from the webapp directory underneath quartz. Change directories to webapp and type **ant**.

Installing the Quartz Web Application

When you have successfully built the Web application, there should be a `quartz.war` file created in the `webapp/dist` directory. Deploy this Web Archive (WAR) file into a container of your choice.

NOT ALL CONTAINERS ARE CREATED EQUAL

We should point out that although the various Servlet and JSP specifications are designed to make it easier to move applications from one container to another, vendors sometimes fall short. At a minimum, we can say that each vendor interprets the specifications differently.

Some Quartz users have reported issues with deploying the Quartz Web application as a WAR file into WebLogic 8.1 and particular versions of WebSphere. If you're using Tomcat, you generally won't have many problems, but you might face some challenges with other containers. If you do encounter some trouble, try deploying the application in an exploded format instead of as a WAR.

Configuring and Running the Quartz Web Application

Now that the WAR file is deployed, fire it up in your Web browser. For Tomcat, the default URL is http://localhost:8080/quartz/. From the home page, you have options to manage the Scheduler, jobs, triggers, and logging.

All the menu options on the home page are secured. A new security filter was added in the latest release to mimic container-managed security. This means that you can call `HttpServletRequest.getRemoteUser()` and `HttpRequest.isUserInRole()` just like you can with container-managed security. Users are defined in the `SecurityFilter-config.xml` file. By default, it contains one user, `quartz`, with the password `quartz`. You can add your users to the `SecurityFilter-config.xml` file or simply extend `org.securityfilter.realm.SecurityRealmInterface` to provide a Security Realm to suit your needs.

Start by selecting the Scheduler Control menu item and, when prompted, sign in as user quartz. A test Scheduler is preconfigured with the Quartz Web application, and it is your only choice on this page. Take a look inside `quartz\webapp\` `config\resources` to see how the Scheduler is configured. There you'll find the now familiar `quartz.properties` file. The name in the dropdown list on the Scheduler Controller page is the `org.quartz.scheduler.instanceName` property from `quartz.properties`.

Click the Job Definitions menu next. There you see three jobs: `NativeJob`, `NoJob`, and `SendMailJob`. If you looked around in the `\webapp\config\resources` folder, you've already guessed where jobs are defined: `JobDefinitions.xml`. This is loaded by the `ContextLoaderServlet` when the Quartz Web application starts. You can edit the `JobDefinitions.xml` file or provide your own job-definition files by changing the `ContextLoaderServlet` `<init-param>` in the `web.xml` file.

If you're ready to run a job, you can select the Create link to the left of `NativeJob` on the Job Definitions page. You want to pick a native application that makes it very plain to see that your job has run. If you are on the Windows platform, you can use `Notepad.exe`. Start by giving the job a name—possibly Native Job Test. The name must be unique within the Scheduler. Next, type **notepad** in the command parameter and click Save. You should now see the Job Detail properties you just created.

Click the List Jobs menu item to see all the `JobDetails` on the Scheduler. Click the Execute link to the left of your `JobDetail`. A Notepad window pops open—not very practical, but you can imagine the possibilities. Have you been wondering as you read this book how you could leverage Quartz for non-Java jobs? Now you have your answer.

Now would be a good time to explore the Logging menu. Click Logging and scroll to the bottom of the listing. There you will find an entry for the job you just executed, along with other activity that has been occurring since you started your Scheduler.

Clicking the List all Triggers menu option shows you triggers that the Job Initializer loaded. Notice that there is no option to add a trigger from the Quartz Web application. Triggers must be declared within the `job.xml` files, which are also in the `resources` folder. The list of `job.xml` files is declared in the Job Initializer section of the `quartz. properties` file.

That's all there is to the Quartz Web application. All that is left to do is add your own jobs and triggers.

## CHAPTER 14

USING QUARTZ WITH WORKFLOW

Quartz does a fabulous job of what it was designed to do. Unfortunately, the jobs required to run a business are often a little more complicated than a single job or task can be. Every year millions of dollars are spent on understanding, designing, and constructing business processes for organizations. The Quartz framework includes some simple facilities that can be used to chain multiple jobs together to construct a simplified business process model. This chapter discusses how you can use Quartz to connect jobs. For true workflow operability, you need something more than what comes with the Quartz framework. This chapter looks at how you can extend the Quartz framework to achieve workflow for your jobs.

What Is Workflow?

The Web is full of definitions and examples of what one person or group thinks workflow is. Some define workflow as "the automation of the back office." Others use the phrase, "business processing modeling," and charge a lot of money for consulting fees explaining it to you. For the purposes of this chapter, we use the following definition of workflow:

> A workflow is a set of interdependent tasks that occur in a specific sequence.

As we get further into the chapter, this definition will become clearer.

What Does Workflow Have to Do with Quartz?

If you're asking, "What does workflow have to work Quartz?" the answer is, "Quite a bit." Even for simple tasks such as performing automated builds or just sending e-mails, workflow has a place. Quartz supports some basic approaches to chaining jobs together. This chapter discusses those and shows how to integrate Quartz with a popular open source workflow solution.

Job Chaining in Quartz

Job chaining is a topic that gets raised from time to time on the Quartz users' forum. In fact, it has been asked enough that it's part of the Quartz FAQ (see www.opensymphony.com/quartz/faq.html#chaining). Whether they realize it not, most of the users who are asking whether Quartz supports job chaining are really asking, "How can I add workflow to Quartz?" But before we dive deep into OSWorkflow, let's look at how you might accomplish job chaining with the facilities that come in the Quartz framework.

Job Chaining Isn't Workflow

For clarity, we should make the distinction that job chaining is one Quartz job either conditionally or unconditionally scheduling another job when the first one finishes. Using the Quartz framework alone to accomplish this is laden with problems and limitations. It's worth going through the exercise, however, so that you can fully understand those limitations.

We're going to make some of you mad with this statement, but as you'll learn from this material, job chaining in Quartz is not workflow. It might have some resemblance to workflow, and it might smell like workflow or feel like workflow, but it's definitely not workflow as you'll soon come to know it. You can think of it as the "lazy man's workflow"—sort of workflow on a shoestring budget. In all seriousness, workflow systems such as OSWorkflow offer much more functionality than you'll get out of Quartz job chaining. This is not a knock on Quartz: Quartz was designed for job scheduling, and it does that very well. Workflow frameworks such as OSWorkflow are designed to do workflow. Both are great tools.

Quartz takes two main approaches to job chaining. One uses Quartz listeners; the other uses the JobDataMap.

Job Chaining with Listeners

The first approach to job chaining is to use Quartz listeners. This is done by creating either a JobListener or a TriggerListener that, when notified by the Scheduler, schedules the next job for execution. The method jobWasExecuted() on the JobListener or the triggerComplete() method on the TriggerListener can be used as the location to "chain" the next job. Let's suppose that you have a job called ImportantJob that performs some important logic for your business. You create it like any other Quartz job that you created so far. Listing 14.1 shows the outline of the job that represents some important job your Quartz application needs to perform.

Listing 14.1   ImportantJob Represents a Job That You Might Need to Perform for Your Business

```java
public class ImportantJob implements Job {

    public void execute(JobExecutionContext context) {
        // Do something important in this Job
    }
}
```

Notice that there's nothing special about the job in Listing 14.1. Let's further suppose that you needed to chain a second job to the completion of the ImportantJob shown in Listing 14.1. You could choose any job, but let's make it one that prints some details about the job that ran before it. Call it PrintJobResultJob (see Listing 14.2).

Listing 14.2   PrintJobResultJob Prints Information About the Chained Job That Ran Before It

```java
public class PrintJobResultJob implements Job {
    Log logger = LogFactory.getLog(PrintJobResultJob.class);

    public void execute(JobExecutionContext context) {

        // Get the JobResult for the previous chained Job
        JobResult jobResult =
            (JobResult) context.getJobDataMap().get("JOB_RESULT");

        // If no Job was chained before this one, do nothing
        if (jobResult != null) {
            logger.info(jobResult);
        }
    }
}
```

The PrintJobResultJob is designed to look in its JobDataMap and see if a JobResult object is present. The class JobResult is not part of the Quartz framework, but you can easily create it to represent the result of a job execution. In many instances, creating something like a JobResult class can be helpful. Listing 14.3 shows the JobResult class for our example.

Listing 14.3   The JobResult Represents the Result of a
Job Execution

```
public class JobResult {

    private boolean success;
    private String jobName;
    private long startedTime;
    private long finishedTime;

    public JobResult(){
        startedTime = System.currentTimeMillis();
    }

    // getters and setters not shown in this listing

    public String toString() {
        StringBuffer buf = new StringBuffer();
        buf.append(jobName);
        buf.append(" executed in ");
        buf.append(finishedTime - startedTime);
        buf.append(" (msecs) ");

        if (success) {
            buf.append("and was successful. ");
        } else {
            buf.append("but was NOT successful. ");
        }

        return buf.toString();
    }
}
```

The JobResult class in Listing 14.3 contains several pieces
of information about the result of a job execution: the time it
started, the time it finished, and a flag that indicates whether
the execution was successful. You can obviously put whatever
fields you need in your version; this is just a simple example.

The next step in this job-chaining example is to create the
listener class to perform the actual chaining. For this example,
we're going to use a JobListener, but a TriggerListener
would work as well. Listing 14.5 shows the job-chaining
JobListener.

Listing 14.5   A Nonglobal JobListener That Performs Job Chaining

```java
public class JobChainListener implements org.quartz.JobListener {
    Log logger = LogFactory.getLog(JobChainListener.class);

    public Class nextJobClass;

    public String listenerName;

    public JobChainListener() {
        super();
    }

    public JobChainListener(String listenerName, Class nextJob) {
        setName(listenerName);
        this.nextJobClass = nextJob;
    }

    public String getName() {
        return listenerName;
    }

    public void setName(String name) {
        this.listenerName = name;
    }

    public void jobToBeExecuted(JobExecutionContext context) {
        // Do nothing in this example
    }

    public void jobExecutionVetoed(JobExecutionContext context) {
        // Do nothing in this example
    }

    public void jobWasExecuted(JobExecutionContext context,
            JobExecutionException jobException) {
        Scheduler scheduler = context.getScheduler();

        try {
            // Create the chained JobDetail
            JobDetail jobDetail =
                new JobDetail("ChainedJob", null,
                    nextJobClass);

            // Create a one-time trigger that fires immediately
            Trigger trigger =
                TriggerUtils.makeSecondlyTrigger(0, 0);
            trigger.setName("FireNowTrigger");
            trigger.setStartTime(new Date());

            // Update the JobResult for the next Job
            JobResult jobResult =
                (JobResult) context.getJobDataMap().get(
                    "JOB_RESULT");
            jobResult.setFinishedTime(System.currentTimeMillis());
            jobResult.setSuccess(true);

            // Pass JobResult to next job through its JobDataMap
            jobDetail.getJobDataMap().put(
                "JOB_RESULT", jobResult);
```

Listing 14.5   Continued

```
                // Schedule the next job to fire immediately
                scheduler.scheduleJob(jobDetail, trigger);

                logger.info(nextJobClass.getName() +
                    " has been scheduled executed");

        } catch (Exception ex) {
            logger.error("Couldn't chain next Job", ex);
            return;
        }
    }
}
```

As you can see from Listing 14.5, the work of chaining the next job is done in the jobWasExecuted() method. As you learned in Chapter 7, "Implementing Quartz Listeners," the Scheduler calls the jobWasExecuted() method when a job is finished executing. This makes the perfect method to chain the jobs together. In the jobWasExecuted() method from Listing 14.5, several things are going on.

First, a new JobDetail and trigger are created for the chained job. Then the JobResult is retrieved from the JobDataMap of the first job, and the finishedTime and success fields are set. For the chained (next) job to have access to the JobResult object, it is

---

PASSING DATA FROM ONE JOB TO ANOTHER

The idea of a JobResult was used in this example to illustrate that although passing data from one job to the chained job is possible, it can be cumbersome. In the case of the current example, the data is passed in the listener. This is the only place it can happen because this is where the chaining occurs. If you need to chain three jobs, entanglement just gets worse.

---

loaded into the JobDataMap of the chained job.

The last part of Listing 14.5 schedules the new job with the Scheduler. Because the trigger for the new job was set to fire right away, the PrintJobResultJob job will execute immediately. Looking back at Listing 14.2, you can see that when the execute() method on the PrintJobResultJob class is called, it retrieves the JobResult object and calls the toString()

method. Again, this is a very simple example to show you how to chain jobs. Your jobs would obviously have more complicated logic than those shown here. The job chaining, however, would work the same.

So the good news is that it's not that difficult to use a listener class to chain jobs. The bad news is that there are some serious design issues with this approach. First, although we were smart enough to pass in the name of the next job to the listener class, there's a fairly tight coupling in this code. The listener needs to be told about the chained job at creation, so the listener becomes tightly coupled to a specific chained job for the life cycle of the listener. You would need to set up a listener for each chained job—and what about when you need to chain more than two jobs? Things can get out of hand very quickly.

VARIATIONS ON THE LISTENER APPROACH

Of course, there are some variable ways in which you can implement your listener to function. For example, you could create a single `JobDetail` instance, set its `durability` flag to `true`, and prestore it in the Scheduler. Then the listener would not need to create the `JobDetail` and trigger each time; it would only need to create a `JobDataMap`, place the `JobResult` within it, and call `scheduler.triggerJob(jobName, groupName, jobDataMap)`; the existing job would be executed and passed the `JobResult`.

Job Chaining with the `JobDataMap`

Another approach for chaining jobs is to use the `JobDataMap` to store the next job to execute. In the earlier listener example, we used the `JobDataMap` to store and pass the `JobResult`, but this new approach gets rid of the listener and uses the `JobDataMap` to do it all.

Because we've ridden ourselves of the listener class, this means that the job itself must handle the chaining of the next job. The behavior can be abstracted to a base job class, if you want. The example here doesn't do that, however, to keep it as simple as possible.

Listing 14.5 shows the new `ImportantJob` class. After it completes, the next job in the chain gets scheduled. You might even decide to schedule the next job based on some flag or condition of the last execution. For example, if some flag were set to true, you would execute Job A; if the flag were set to false, you would execute Job B.

The next job in the chain is stored in the JobDataMap using a key of your choice. In this example, we used the value NEXT_JOB. One of the problems with this approach is that something must store the next job in the JobDataMap before the job execution.

Listing 14.5   Job Chaining Can Also Be Done Using the JobDataMap

```
public class ImportantJob implements Job {
    static Log logger = LogFactory.getLog(JobChainListener.class);

    public void execute(JobExecutionContext context) {

        // Do something important in this Job

        // Set some condition based on this Job execution
        boolean success = true;

        // schedule the next Job if condition was successful
        if (success) {
            scheduleNextJob(context);
        } else {
            logger.info("Job was NOT chained");
        }
    }

    protected void scheduleNextJob(JobExecutionContext context) {
        JobDataMap jobDataMap = context.getJobDataMap();

        String nextJob = jobDataMap.getString("NEXT_JOB");
        if (nextJob!= null && nextJob.length() > 0) {

            try {
                Class jobClass = Class.forName(nextJob);
                scheduleJob(jobClass, context.getScheduler());
            } catch (Exception ex) {
                logger.error("error scheduling chained job", ex);
            }
        }
    }

    protected void scheduleJob(Class jobClass, Scheduler scheduler) {
        JobDetail jobDetail =
            new JobDetail(jobClass.getName(), null, jobClass);

        // Create a fire now, one time trigger
        Trigger trigger = TriggerUtils.makeSecondlyTrigger(0, 0);
        trigger.setName(jobClass.getName() + "Trigger");
        trigger.setStartTime(new Date());

        // Schedule the next job to fire immediately
        try {
            scheduler.scheduleJob(jobDetail, trigger);
```

Listing 14.5   Continued

```
            } catch (SchedulerException ex) {

                logger.error("error chaining Job "
                    + jobClass.getName(), ex);

                }
            }

        }
```

After the name of the job is retrieved from the JobDataMap, a JobDetail and trigger are created, and the job is scheduled. As with the listener example from before, the code that schedules the first job needs to add the initial chained job to the JobDataMap for all this to work. This can be done when the job is first added to the Scheduler and the Scheduler is started. Listing 14.6 shows this.

Listing 14.6   The First Chained Job Needs to Be Configured When the First Job Is Scheduled

```
public class NewScheduler {
    static Log logger = LogFactory.getLog(NewScheduler.class);

    public static void main(String[] args) {

        try {
            // Create and start the Scheduler
            Scheduler scheduler =
                StdSchedulerFactory.getDefaultScheduler();
            scheduler.start();

            JobDetail jobDetail =
                new JobDetail("ImportantJob", null,
                    ImportantJob.class);

            // Set up the first chained Job
            JobDataMap dataMap = jobDetail.getJobDataMap();
            dataMap.put("NEXT_JOB",
                "org.cavaness.quartzbook.chapter14.ChainedJob");

            // Create the trigger and scheduler the Job
            Trigger trigger =
                TriggerUtils.makeSecondlyTrigger(10000, 0);
            trigger.setName("FireOnceTrigger");
            trigger.setStartTime(new Date());

            scheduler.scheduleJob(jobDetail, trigger);

        } catch (SchedulerException ex) {
            logger.error( ex );
        }
    }
}
```

The code in Listing 14.6 is used to schedule the first job and, at the same time, set up the next job in the chain. If there were a third job, it would have to be set up in the `JobDataMap` for the second job. You can obviously see how unwieldy this approach becomes when you have more than two jobs in a chain. OSWorkflow helps with this and a whole mess of other problems.

Using the `JobInitializationPlugin` with Job Chaining

If you are specifying your job information in the `quartz_jobs.xml` file and are using the `JobInitializationPlugin` to load that information, this approach might not be so bad. That's because you can specify the job chain very easily in the XML file. For example, consider the `quartz_jobs.xml` in Listing 14.7.

Listing 14.7   Job Chaining Is a Little More Manageable When Using the `JobInitializationPlugin`

```xml
<?xml version='1.0' encoding='utf-8'?>

<quartz>
  <job>
    <job-detail>
      <name>ImportantJob</name>
        <job-class>
          org.cavaness.quartzbook.chapter14.ImportantJob
        </job-class>

        <job-data-map allows-transient-data="true">
          <entry>
            <key>NEXT_JOB</key>

<value>org.cavaness.quartzbook.chapter14.ChainedJob</value>
          </entry>
        </job-data-map>
    </job-detail>

    <trigger>
        <simple>
        <name>FireOnceTrigger</name>
          <group>DEFAULT</group>
          <job-name>ImportantJob</job-name>
          <job-group>DEFAULT</job-group>
          <start-time>2005-07-19 8:31:00 PM</start-time>
          <repeat-count>0</repeat-count>
        </simple>
    </trigger>
  </job>
</quartz>
```

The result of the job information in Listing 14.7 is identical to that of the previous example, only better. If you needed to change which job gets chained to the `ImportantJob`, you would only need to change the XML file. In the previous job-chaining examples, code would have had to be changed and recompiled.

Quick Introduction to OSWorkflow

Like Quartz, OSWorkflow is an open source project built entirely in Java and is also part of the OpenSymphony family of projects. Many workflow projects are available, both commercial and open source. OSWorkflow shares many similarities in design with Quartz, and the integration between the two frameworks makes it a no-brainer for us.

OSWorkflow operates on the principle of a finite state machine. A workflow consists of a set of states, with a start state and one or more end states. To move from one state to another, a transition needs to occur. There might be multiple transitions out of a particular state—in fact, you can have multiple transitions out of a state at the same time. The transition that is chosen depends on the environment, the inputs to the state, and some conditional information that we discuss later.

NO SUBSTITUTION FOR THE OSWORKFLOW DOCUMENTATION

The material on OSWorkflow in this chapter should not replace a thorough review of the documentation that is available on the OSWorkflow site. We are primarily concerned with explaining how to use OSWorkflow with Quartz. For the examples in this chapter, we don't use very many of the available features of OSWorkflow because we are interested only in giving you an overall taste of what OSWorkflow can do. We do not have time to explore many other features, so be sure to read the documentation and tutorials available on the OSWorkflow Web site.

Workflow Descriptor File

One of the key components of OSWorkflow is the workflow descriptor, which is sometimes called the workflow definition; we use the two terms interchangeably here. The workflow descriptor defines all the aspects of a particular workflow. The descriptor is implemented as an XML file, and the framework includes a DTD for validation. Much of your time working with OSWorkflow will involve understanding the layout and rules for the descriptor file. You can view the DTD for version 2.7 at www.opensymphony.com/osworkflow/workflow_2_7.dtd.

OSWorkflow Concepts

To help the discussion, we'll create a fictitious workflow and use it throughout the remainder of this chapter. When created, this workflow will scan a directory looking for files. In the medical field, these could be electronic orders from customers or patient information.

If any files are present when we check, the workflow process reads them and stores the information in a database. The last step in the workflow generates an e-mail with a count of records that were inserted into the database. You can imagine that if we were running a worldwide business, we would expect that files could be dropped at any time of the day or night. That's why Quartz is so perfect for the scheduling portion.

We want to build a system using Quartz and OSWorkflow that will check for these files periodically and, when one or more is received, process the file(s) through a specific workflow. Figure 14.1 shows the workflow that we want to use.

FIGURE 14.1   An example workflow for processing electronic data files

As you can see from the workflow in Figure 14.1, several steps make up the workflow itself. It's a good idea to develop a set of generic steps that can be reused in many different workflows. Let's look at a quick series of definitions and explanations for the example workflow.

First, a workflow descriptor (definition) file has the following format:

```xml
<?xml version="1.0" encoding="UTF-8"?>
<!DOCTYPE workflow PUBLIC
   "-//OpenSymphony Group//DTD OSWorkflow 2.7//EN"
   "http://www.opensymphony.com/osworkflow/workflow_2_7.dtd">

<workflow>
  <initial-actions>
    ...
  </initial-actions>

  <steps>
    ...
  </steps>
</workflow>
```

We now go through the important parts of the workflow.

Workflow Step

A workflow consists of a number of states or steps. Each step is given a name of your choosing. In OSWorkflow, the transition from one step to another is a result of an action. The following XML fragment illustrates a step:

```xml
<step id="1" name="Read Files">
 <actions>
  <action id="1" name="Read the records from the files" auto="true">

  <results>
    ...
  </results>
  </action>

 </actions>
</step>
```

Workflow Action

Simply put, the goal of any workflow engine is to progress the workflow from the start to the finish. That means we need a way to transition the workflow from one step to another. In OSWorkflow, actions are used to determine which transition path is chosen and, therefore, which step is transitioned to. A single step in the workflow might have multiple paths (or transitions) that it can perform based on the result of the action. Several factors can be used to help determine which path the workflow takes, including external events and input from users. Workflow actions use conditions and functions to determine the action result and, therefore, which transition to take. Each action must have at least one unconditional result and might have zero or more conditional results. This helps ensure that a workflow will transition out of the step, even if none of the conditional results causes a transition. In general, an action will result in a single transition out of a step. As we discuss later, this is not entirely true because you can cause a split to occur where multiple transitions out of a step take place. Eventually, these multiple transitions must join back into a single path. The following XML fragment provides an example of a workflow action element:

```
<action id="1" name="Start Workflow">
 <results>
  <unconditional-result old-status="Finished" status="Queued" step="1"/>
 </results>
</action>
```

Special types of actions called *initial actions* are used to start a workflow by specifying the first step to execute. Here's an example of an `initial-actions` element:

```
<initial-actions>
 <action id="1" name="Start Workflow">
  <results>
    <unconditional-result old-status="Finished"
      status="Queued" step="1" />

  </results>
 </action>
</initial-actions>
```

ACTION RESULT

An action result tells the workflow what tasks to do next. OSWorkflow provides both conditional and unconditional results. A result can have multiple condition elements that evaluate to true or false. The first condition within the result element that evaluates to true is executed and determines the next step. Unconditional results will execute if it's the only one present or if none of the conditional ones resulted in a true value.

Three types of supported workflow result elements exist, regardless of whether they are conditional or unconditional:

- Transition to a single step
- Split into two or more steps
- Join multiple steps back into a single step

You will use a combination of these to build your workflows.

WORKFLOW FUNCTIONS

In OSWorkflow, most of its power and flexibility comes from the use of functions and conditions. Functions are logic that can be performed during a transition from one step to another; they are where most of the work takes place, especially for our Quartz + OSWorkflow integration approach. OSWorkflow includes functions to call EJB methods, functions that use the Java Message Service (JMS), functions that send e-mails, and many more. The function support that we are interested in is the one that can call an ordinary Java class.

OSWorkflow includes the function interface com.opensymphony.workflow.FunctionProvider. All we need to do is create a Java class that implements the FunctionProvider interface, which contains a single method:

```
public void execute(java.util.Map transientVars,
                java.util.Map args,
                com.opensymphony.module.propertyset.PropertySet ps)
        throws WorkflowException;
```

After creating the `FunctionProvider` class, we set up the function in the workflow like this:

```
function type="class">
  <arg name="class.name">
    org.cavaness.quartzbook.chapter14.ReadFileFunction
  </arg>
</function>
```

When the workflow gets to the step and action with this function definition, it calls our Java class and invokes the function's `execute()` method. This is really powerful because you can easily integrate new and legacy systems into your workflow.

AUTO ACTIONS

If you are building workflows with steps that you want to automatically transition without user input, you can use the `auto` property on an action to force the action to occur. This means that the workflow, once started, will run through its steps automatically and will not wait for an external event to cause it to transition.

Workflow GUI Designer

We don't use the GUI designer here, but it's worth noting that the OSWorkflow team has built a graphical tool to create and edit workflow definitions. The tool is a rich client that can be launched using Sun's Java Web Start technology. Figure 14.2 shows a screenshot of the GUI tool with the example workflow loaded.

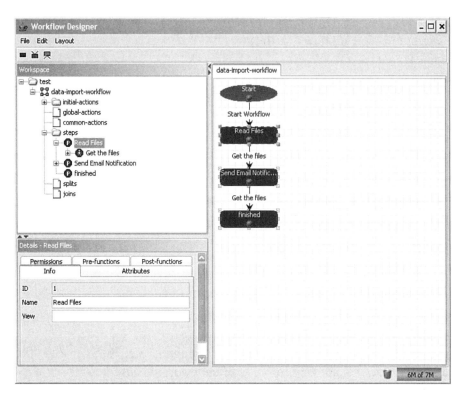

FIGURE 14.2   The OSWorkflow Designer is a nice tool for creating and modifying workflows.

Integration of Quartz with OSWorkflow

The first step in integrating OSWorkflow with Quartz is to change the way you think about jobs. You need to think in a totally different way when incorporating OSWorkflow into your Quartz applications. That's not to say that your current thinking is bad or incorrect, but using workflow with Quartz forces you to develop some new ideas about what constitutes a job. What you used to think of as a job will now become an OSWorkflow function. You can think of the logic that you had in your old jobs essentially as steps in the workflow. You'll still need and use Quartz jobs, but when integrating workflow with the Quartz framework, a Quartz job will initiate the workflow. When the workflow is running, the job will wait for it to finish.

Earlier in this chapter, when we talked about chaining jobs, each job represented a separate task. Job X executed and performed a task, and then called on Job Y to perform a somewhat related but separate task. There must have been some dependency between the two tasks, or you wouldn't have chained them together.

When adding workflow to this process, those individual jobs turn into steps within the workflow, and you need to create only a single job. When notified by the Scheduler, that job starts the workflow and then waits for the workflow to complete. This has some serious implications. The good news is tha by using OSWorkflow, you end up with fewer Quartz jobs because what used to be jobs are now steps (actually functions). The bad news is that if you have lots of jobs already created, it might take some work to convert jobs into OSWorkflow functions.

Downloading and Installing OSWorkflow

You can download the full distribution of OSWorkflow from its home on the OpenSymphony site at www.opensymphony.com/osworkflow. Grab the OSWorkflow binary from the distribution's root directory and also the third-party libraries within the `<OSWORKFLOW_DISTRIBUTION>/lib/core` directory. Drop these binaries into the `lib` directory of your project. This should be the same directory where the Quartz binary is already located.

You must create a couple configuration files and place them in your `classes` directory. The first configuration file you need to create is called `osworkflow.xml`. This file is loaded at OSWorkflow startup and configures the runtime environment. The file for our example is shown in Listing 14.8.

Listing 14.8 The `osworkflow.xml` File Is Used to Configure the Runtime Environment for OSWorkflow

```
<osworkflow>
  <persistence
    class="com.opensymphony.workflow.spi.memory.MemoryWorkflowStore"/>
  <factory class="com.opensymphony.workflow.loader.XMLWorkflowFactory">
    <property name="resource" value="workflows.xml" />
  </factory>
</osworkflow>
```

If you review the OSWorkflow documentation, you will find that you can choose from different types of persistence stores and workflow factories. The ones used in Listing 14.8 are the simplest and work fine for our examples.

The workflow factory class configured in Listing 14.8 is called the `XMLWorkflowFactory`, and it includes a property called `resource`. The `XMLWorkflowFactory` is used to load a resource file that contains all the available workflows. In this case, the `resource` property has a value of `workflows.xml`. You are allowed to have as many different workflows as you want. Each workflow will reside in a separate XML file, but you need some way of specifying the list of workflows that are available to the OSWorkflow engine. Because we have specified the factory as an `XMLWorkflowFactory`, the framework looks in the `workflows.xml` file to get the list of available workflows to load. Listing 14.9 shows the `workflows.xml` file for our example.

Listing 14.9 The `workflows.xml` File Defines the List of Workflows Available to the Application

```
<workflows>
  <workflow
    name="data-import"
    type="resource"
    location="data-import-workflow.xml"/>
</workflows>
```

Listing 14.9 lists only one workflow: `data-import`, which will be used to reference when we start the workflow. The actual workflow definition is stored in the file `data-import-workflow.xml`. Listing 14.10 shows the `data-import` workflow.

Listing 14.10   The data-import Workflow Is Defined in an XML File

```xml
<?xml version="1.0" encoding="UTF-8"?>
<!DOCTYPE workflow PUBLIC
                "-//OpenSymphony Group//DTD OSWorkflow 2.7//EN"
                "http://www.opensymphony.com/osworkflow/workflow_2_7.dtd">
<workflow>
    <initial-actions>
        <action id="1" name="Start Workflow">
            <results>
                <unconditional-result old-status="Finished" status="Queued"
                    step="1" />
            </results>
        </action>
    </initial-actions>

    <steps>
        <step id="1" name="Read Files">
            <actions>
                <action id="2" name="Get the files" auto="true">
                    <pre-functions>
                        <function type="class">
                            <arg name="class.name">
                                org.cavaness.quartzbook.chapter14.ReadFileFunction
                            </arg>
                        </function>
                    </pre-functions>

                    <results>
                        <unconditional-result old-status="Finished"
                            status="Underway" step="2" />
                    </results>
                </action>
            </actions>
        </step>


        <step id="2" name="Send Email Notification">
            <actions>
                <action id="3" name="Get the files" auto="true">
                    <pre-functions>
                        <function type="class">
                            <arg name="class.name">
                                org.cavaness.quartzbook.chapter14.SendEmailFunction
                            </arg>
                        </function>
                    </pre-functions>

                    <results>
                        <unconditional-result old-status="Finished"
                            status="Underway" step="3" />
                    </results>
                </action>
            </actions>
        </step>

        <step id="3" name="finished" />
    </steps>
</workflow>
```

The workflow definition in Listing 14.10 contains two steps: "read files" and "send e-mail notification. When the workflow is started, the initial-actions section is executed, and it calls step 1. When step 1 is entered, the execute() method in org.cavaness.quartzbook.chapter14.ReadFileFunction is called. Listing 14.11 shows this function.

Listing 14.11　The Workflow Engine Calls the ReadFileFunction During step 1

```
public class ReadFileFunction implements FunctionProvider {
    static Log logger = LogFactory.getLog(ReadFileFunction.class);

    public void execute(Map transientVars, Map args, PropertySet ps)
            throws WorkflowException {
        logger.info("Entered " + this.getClass().getName());

        // Read the files and process the data
        String dirName = (String)transientVars.get("SCAN_DIR");
        if ( dirName == null ) {
            throw new InvalidInputException( "Scan dir not set" );
        }

        File dir = new File( dirName );
        File[] files = dir.listFiles();

        int fileCount = files.length;
        ps.setInt( "FILE_COUNT", fileCount );
    }
}
```

When the execute() method of the ReadFileFunction completes, the workflow transitions to step 2. In step 2, the org.cavaness.quartzbook.chapter14.SendEmailFunction is called and given a chance to execute. The SendEmailFunction is shown in Listing 14.12.

Listing 14.12　The SendEmailFunction Is Called During Step 2 of the Workflow

```
public class SendEmailFunction implements FunctionProvider {
    static Log logger = LogFactory.getLog(SendEmailFunction.class);

    public void execute(Map transientVars, Map args, PropertySet ps)
            throws WorkflowException {
        logger.info("Entered " + this.getClass().getName());

        int fileCount = ps.getInt("FILE_COUNT");
        logger.info( "File count " + fileCount );

        // Email creation code not shown
    }
}
```

We've obviously left out the implementation for our functions; it wouldn't have added anything to the discussion. We assume that you know how to send an e-mail using JavaMail.

Creating a Workflow Job

Finally, we need to show the Quartz job that starts the workflow process. When the Scheduler calls it, the Quartz job looks up the name of the workflow and starts it running. If no workflow name has been configured in the JobDataMap, the job exits.

Listing 14.13 shows the WorkflowJob.

Listing 14.13   The Quartz WorkflowJob **Is Designed to Call an** OSWorkflowJob

```
public class WorkflowJob implements Job {
    static Log logger = LogFactory.getLog(WorkflowJob.class);

    /**
     * Called by the scheduler to execute a workflow
     */
    public void execute(JobExecutionContext context)
            throws JobExecutionException {
        JobDataMap jobDataMap = context.getJobDataMap();

        String wfName = jobDataMap.getString("WORKFLOW_NAME");
        if (wfName != null && wfName.length() > 0) {
            try {
                executeWorkflow(wfName, jobDataMap);
            } catch (Exception ex) {
                logger.error(ex);
                    throw new
                        JobExecutionException(ex.getMessage());
            }
        } else {
            logger.error("No Workflow name in JobDataMap");
        }
    }

    protected void executeWorkflow(String workflowName,
        JobDataMap jobDataMap) throws WorkflowException {

        // Create the inputs for the workflow from JobDataMap
        Map workflowInputs = new HashMap();
        Iterator iter = jobDataMap.keySet().iterator();
        while (iter.hasNext()) {
            String key = (String) iter.next();
            Object obj = jobDataMap.get(key);
            workflowInputs.put(key, obj);
        }
```

Listing 14.13   Continued

```
        // Create and execute the workflow
        Workflow workflow = new BasicWorkflow("someuser");
        workflow.setConfiguration(new DefaultConfiguration());

        long workflowId =
            workflow.initialize(workflowName, 1, workflowInputs);

        workflow.doAction(workflowId, 1, workflowInputs);
    }
}
```

The workflow is actually started in the executeWorkflow()
method in Listing 14.13. A new instance of a workflow object is
created. It's initialized with the name of the workflow that was
read from the JobDataMap. The initialize() and doAction()
methods on the workflow instance take a java.util.Map as the
third argument. The values in the Map are passed to each function in the workflow through the transientVars parameter. If
you look back at Listing 14.11, you can see how the SCAN_DIR
is being pulled from the transientVars. This data was origi-
nally in the JobDataMap.

In this example, we take the JobDataMap from the Quartz
job and pass the values into the workflow. This is one of the
ways in which integration between the two frameworks is easy
and straight-forward.

Finally, Listing 14.14 shows the Scheduler code that is used
to schedule the WorkflowJob and store the workflow name and
SCAN_DIR into the JobDataMap.

Listing 14.14   The WorkflowJob Is Scheduled as Normal, but the Workflow Name Must Be Stored in the JobDataMap

```
public class WorkflowScheduler {
    static Log logger = LogFactory.getLog(WorkflowScheduler.class);

    public static void main(String[] args) {

        try {
            // Create and start the Scheduler
            Scheduler scheduler =
                StdSchedulerFactory.getDefaultScheduler();
            scheduler.start();

            JobDetail jobDetail =
                new JobDetail("WorkflowJob", null,
                    WorkflowJob.class);
```

Listing 14.14   Continued

```
            // Store the scan directory and workflow name
            JobDataMap dataMap = jobDetail.getJobDataMap();
            dataMap.put("SCAN_DIR", "c:\\quartz-book\\input");
            dataMap.put("WORKFLOW_NAME", "data-import");

            // Create a simple trigger
            Trigger trigger =
                TriggerUtils.makeSecondlyTrigger(30000, -1);
            trigger.setName("WorkflowTrigger");
            trigger.setStartTime(new Date());

            // schedule the job
            scheduler.scheduleJob(jobDetail, trigger);

        } catch (SchedulerException ex) {
            logger.error(ex);
        }
    }
}
```

You should see no surprises in Listing 14.14. The only
thing of interest is that we store the workflow name in the
JobDataMap. As with the job-chaining example earlier in this
chapter, if you wanted to use the JobInitializationPlugin,
you could easily specify the name of the workflow within
the file.

Conclusion

What have you learned in this chapter? First, job chaining can
be done with the Quartz framework. You can use either of the
presented approaches, but the approach without the listener
implementation probably will give you fewer headaches. The
other lesson I hope you take away is that job chaining is not
workflow. It might seem like workflow, and you might not be
convinced of this yet, but go back through the examples and try
to build one of your own. Be sure to read the OSWorkflow documentation and find out about the features that we didn't mention. You should see that workflow is much more than Job
chaining.

Finally, you should have learned that using OSWorkflow
with Quartz is really pretty easy. All it takes is a few binaries, a

few configuration files, and some workflow functions. Tie all that together with a workflow definition file, and off you go. Before you know it, you will have built a library of reusable functions and a bunch of workflows to run your business. Pretty soon, you'll have a nice little application that you can be proud of.

QUARTZ CONFIGURATION REFERENCE

This appendix is designed to be used as a quick reference for configuring a Quartz application. Although this information is available in the Quartz documentation, this appendix provides a quicker way of looking up configuration properties and their possible values.

The Main Quartz Properties

Table A.1 lists the main scheduler properties. They are used to declare and identify the Scheduler and other top-level settings.

Table A.1   The Main Quartz Scheduler Properties

Name	Required	Type	Default Value
org.quartz.scheduler.instanceName	No	String	'QuartzScheduler'
org.quartz.scheduler.instanceId	No	String	'NON_CLUSTERED'
org.quartz.scheduler.instance IdGenerator.class	No	String	org.quartz.simpl. SimpleInstanceIdGenerator
org.quartz.scheduler.threadName	No	String	instanceName + '_QuartzSchedulerThread'
org.quartz.scheduler.idleWaitTime	No	Long	30000
org.quartz.scheduler.dbFailure RetryInterval	No	Long	15000
org.quartz.scheduler.classLoad Helper.class	No	String	org.quartz.simpl.Cascading ClassLoadHelper
org.quartz.context.key.SOME_KEY	No	String	None
org.quartz.scheduler.user TransactionURL	No	String	'java:comp/ UserTransaction'
org.quartz.scheduler.wrapJob ExecutionInUserTransaction	No	Boolean	false
org.quartz.scheduler.job Factory.class	No	String	.quartz.simpl.Simple JobFactory

org.quartz.scheduler.instanceName

Each Quartz Scheduler must be identified by a given name. The name serves as a mechanism for client code to distinguish Schedulers when multiple instances are used within the same program. If you are using the clustering features, you must use the same name for every instance in the cluster that is "logically" the same Scheduler.

org.quartz.scheduler.instanceId

Each Quartz Scheduler must be assigned a unique ID. The value can be any string but must be unique for all schedulers. You may use the value AUTO as the instanceId if you want the ID to be generated for you. Starting with version 1.5.1, you can customize how instance IDs are automatically generated. See the instanceIDGenerator.class property, which is described next.

org.quartz.scheduler.instanceIdGenerator.class

Starting with version 1.5.1, this property enables you to customize how instanceIDs are generated. This property can be used only if the property org.quartz.scheduler.instanceId is set to AUTO. Defaults to org.quartz.simpl.SimpleInstanceIdGenerator, which generates an instance ID based on host name and time stamp.

org.quartz.scheduler.threadName

This can be any String that is a valid name for a Java thread. If this property is not specified, the thread will receive the Scheduler's name (org.quartz.scheduler.instanceName) plus the appended string '_QuartzSchedulerThread'.

org.quartz.scheduler.idleWaitTime

This property sets the amount of time in milliseconds that the Scheduler will wait before it requeries for available triggers when the Scheduler is otherwise idle. Normally, you should not have to tune this parameter, unless you're using XA transactions and are having problems with delayed firings of triggers that should fire immediately.

org.quartz.scheduler.dbFailureRetryInterval

This property sets the amount of time in milliseconds that the Scheduler will wait between retries when it has detected a loss of connectivity within the JobStore (such as to the database). This parameter is not used when using RamJobStore.

org.quartz.scheduler.classLoadHelper.class

This defaults to the most robust approach, which is to use the org.quartz.simpl.CascadingClassLoadHelper class—which, in turn, uses every other ClassLoadHelper class until one works. You will probably not need to specify any other class for this property, except maybe within application servers. All the current possible `ClassLoadHelper` implementations can be found in the `org.quartz.simpl` package.

org.quartz.context.key.SOME_KEY

This property is used to add a name-value pair that will be placed into the "Scheduler context" as strings. (see `Scheduler.getContext()`). So for example, the setting `org.quartz.context.key.MyEmail = myemail@somehostcom` would perform the equivalent of `scheduler.getContext().put("MyEmail"," myemail@somehost.com")`

org.quartz.scheduler.userTransactionURL

This should be set to the JNDI URL where Quartz can locate the application server's `UserTransaction` manager. The default value (if not specified) is `java:comp/UserTransaction`, which works for almost all application servers. Websphere users might need to set this property to `jta/usertransaction`. This is used only if Quartz is configured to use JobStoreCMT, and `org.quartz.scheduler.wrapJobExecutionInUserTransaction` is set to `true`.

org.quartz.scheduler.
wrapJobExecutionInUserTransaction

Set this property to `true` if you want Quartz to start a `UserTransaction` before calling `execute` on your job. The transaction will commit after the job's `execute` method completes and after the `JobDataMap` is updated (if it is a `StatefulJob`). The default value is `false`.

org.quartz.scheduler.jobFactory.class

This is the class name of the `JobFactory` to use. The default is `org.quartz.simpl.SimpleJobFactory`. You can also try the value `org.quartz.simpl.PropertySettingJobFactory`. A job factory is responsible for producing instances of job classes. The `SimpleJobFactory` class calls `newInstance()` on the job class. The `PropertySettingJobFactory` also calls `newInstance()` but reflectively sets the job's bean properties using the contents of the `JobDataMap`.

Configuring the Quartz ThreadPool

Table A.2 lists the available properties for configuring the Quartz ThredPool. Only a few of the properties are required, and the rest have reasonable defaults.

Table A.2   The Properties for Configuring the Quartz ThreadPool

Name	Required	Type	Default Value
`org.quartz.threadPool.class`	Yes	`String`	`null`
`org.quartz.threadPool.threadCount`	Yes	`Integer`	`-1`
`org.quartz.threadPool.threadPriority`	No	`Integer`	`5`
`org.quartz.threadPool.makeThreadsDaemons`	No	`boolean`	`false`
`org.quartz.threadPool.threadsInheritGroupOf-` `InitializingThread`	No	`boolean`	`True`
`.quartz.threadPool.threadsInheritContext-` `ClassLoaderOfInitializingThread`	No	`boolean`	`false`

org.quartz.threadPool.class

This is used to specify the class name of the `ThreadPool` implementation you want to use. The `ThreadPool` that ships with Quartz is `org.quartz.simpl.SimpleThreadPool` and should be sufficient in most situations. It has very simple behavior and is very well tested. It provides a fixed-size pool of threads that "live" the lifetime of the Scheduler.

org.quartz.threadPool.threadCount

This specifies the number of threads that are available for concurrent execution of jobs. It can be set to a positive integer between 1 and 100. Values greater than 100 are allowed but might be impractical. If you have only a few jobs that fire a few times a day, one thread is plenty. If you have tens of thousands of jobs, with many firing every minute, you probably want a thread count more like 50 or 100.

org.quartz.threadPool.threadPriority

This is used to specify the priority that the worker threads run at. The value can be any integer between 1 and 10. The default is 5, which equates to Thread.NORM_PRIORITY.

org.quartz.threadPool.makeThreadsDaemons

Set this to true to have the threads in the pool created as daemon threads. The default is false.

org.quartz.threadPool. threadsInheritGroupOfInitializingThread

Set this to true if you want new threads to inherit the group of its parent thread. The default is true.

org.quartz.threadPool.threadsInheritContext- ClassLoaderOfInitializingThread

Set this to true if you want new threads to inherit the ClassLoader of the parent creating thread. The default is false.

Configuring Quartz Listeners

Configuring Quartz listeners in the properties file involves specifying a name, the class name, and any other properties to be set on the instance. The listener class must have a no-arg constructor; the properties will be set reflectively. Only primitive data type values (including Strings) are supported.

Configuring a `JobListener`

To configure a `JobListener`, you must specify the class that implements the listener interface:

```
org.quartz.jobListener.NAME.class =
➡com.foo.SomeListenerClass
```

NAME can be any name that you want to provide for the listener but should match the value returned from the `getName()` call to the class. You can provide properties for the listener that will be set reflectively:

```
org.quartz.jobListener.NAME.propName = propValue
org.quartz.jobListener.NAME.prop2Name = prop2Value
```

Configuring a `TriggerListener`

The process of configuring a `TriggerListener` is very similar to that of a `JobListener`. In fact, aside from switching `jobListener` for `triggerListener`, it's the same.

```
org.quartz.triggerListener.NAME.class =
     com.foo.SomeListenerClass
```

You also provide the properties in the same way:

```
org.quartz.triggerListener.NAME.propName = propValue
org.quartz.triggerListener.NAME.prop2Name = prop2Value
```

For more information on Quartz `Listeners`, see Chapter 7, "Implementing Quartz Listeners."

Configuring Quartz Plug-Ins

The process of configuring Quartz plug-ins is very similar to that of configuring listeners, as described earlier. When you have a class that implements the `SchedulerPlugin` interface, you configure the plug-in by adding a line similar to this:

```
org.quartz.plugin.NAME.class = com.foo.MyPluginClass
```

Here, `NAME` is a name that you assign to the plug-in. You can pass parameters to a plug-in instance by providing configuration lines like these:

```
org.quartz.plugin.NAME.propName = propValue
org.quartz.plugin.NAME.prop2Name = prop2Value
```

The `NAME` for the parameters must match the `NAME` assigned to the plug-in. For more information on Quartz plug-ins, see Chapter 8, "Using Quartz Plug-Ins."

Configuring Quartz RMI Settings

When using Quartz via RMI, you need to start an instance of Quartz with it configured to "export" its services via RMI. You can then create clients that connect to the server by configuring a Quartz scheduler to "proxy" its work to the server. Table A.3 lists the available RMI settings.

Table A.3   The Properties for Using RMI with Quartz

Name	Required	Type	Default Value
org.quartz.scheduler.rmi.export	No	Boolean	false
org.quartz.scheduler.rmi.registryHost	No	String	localhost
org.quartz.scheduler.rmi.registryPort	No	Integer	1099
org.quartz.scheduler.rmi.createRegistry	No	String	never
org.quartz.scheduler.rmi.serverPort	No	Integer	Random
org.quartz.scheduler.rmi.proxy	No	Boolean	False

org.quartz.scheduler.rmi.export

Set this to `true` if you want the Quartz Scheduler to export itself via RMI as a server.

org.quartz.scheduler.rmi.registryHost

This is the host at which the RMI Registry can be found. The default is localhost.

org.quartz.scheduler.rmi.registryPort

This is the port on which the RMI Registry is listening. The default is 1099.

org.quartz.scheduler.rmi.createRegistry

Set this property according to how you want Quartz to create an RMI Registry. Use false or never if you don't want Quartz to create a registry (for example, if you already have an external registry running). Use true or as_needed if you want Quartz to first attempt to use an existing registry and then fall back to creating one. Use always if you want Quartz to attempt to create a registry and then fall back to using an existing one. If a registry is created, it will be bound to a port number in the given org.quartz.scheduler.rmi.registryPort property, and org.quartz.rmi.registryHost should be localhost.

org.quartz.scheduler.rmi.serverPort

This indicates the port on which the Quartz Scheduler service will bind and listen for connections. By default, the RMI service randomly selects a port as the scheduler is bound to the RMI registry.

org.quartz.scheduler.rmi.proxy

Set this property to true if you want to connect to a remotely served Scheduler. You must also then specify a host and port for the RMI Registry process, which is typically localhost port 1099. Do not specify true for both org.quartz.scheduler.rmi.export and org.quartz.scheduler.rmi.proxy in the same config file; if you do, the `export` option will be ignored. A value of `false` for both `export` and `proxy` properties is, of course valid, if you're not using Quartz via RMI.

For more information on using Quartz with RMI, see Chapter 10, "Using Quartz with J2EE."

Configuring `JobStore` Settings

You configure the `JobStore` by providing a fully qualified class that implements the `JobStore` interface. For example, the following tells a Quartz application to use the `RAMJobStore`:

```
org.quartz.jobStore.class = org.quartz.simpl.RAMJobStore
```

Besides the `RAMJobStore`, Quartz provides two types of JDBC `JobStore`s:

- `JobStoreTX`
- `JobStoreCMT`

Configuring the `JobStoreTX` JobStore

You can select the `JobStoreTX` class by setting the class name like this:

```
org.quartz.jobStore.class =
    org.quartz.impl.jdbcjobstore.JobStoreTX
```

Table A.4 lists the available properties for configuring a Quartz `JobStore`. Only a few of the properties are required, and the rest have reasonable defaults.

Table A.4   The Properties for Configuring the **Quartz** JobStore

Name	Required	Type	Default Value
org.quartz.jobStore.driverDelegateClass	Yes	String	null
org.quartz.jobStore.dataSource	Yes	String	null
org.quartz.jobStore.tablePrefix	No	String	QRTZ_
org.quartz.jobStore.useProperties	No	Boolean	false
org.quartz.jobStore.misfireThreshold	No	Integer	60000
org.quartz.jobStore.isClustered	No	Boolean	false
org.quartz.jobStore.clusterCheckinInterval	No	Long	15000
org.quartz.jobStore.maxMisfiresToHandleAtATime	No	Integer	20
org.quartz.jobStore.dontSetAutoCommitFalse	No	Boolean	false
org.quartz.jobStore.selectWithLockSQL	No	String	"SELECT * FROM {0}LOCKS WHERE LOCK_NAME = ? FOR UPDATE"
org.quartz.jobStore.txIsolationLevelSerializable	No	Boolean	false

org.quartz.jobStore.driverDelegateClass

Quartz can use most of the popular database platforms by using a delegate. These are the allowed values for the org.quartz.jobStore.driverDelegateClass property:

- org.quartz.impl.jdbcjobstore.StdJDBCDelegate
- org.quartz.impl.jdbcjobstore.MSSQLDelegate
- org.quartz.impl.jdbcjobstore.PostgreSQLDelegate
- org.quartz.impl.jdbcjobstore.WebLogicDelegate (for WebLogic drivers)
- org.quartz.impl.jdbcjobstore.oracle.OracleDelegate
- org.quartz.impl.jdbcjobstore.oracle.WebLogicOracleDelegate
- org.quartz.impl.jdbcjobstore.oracle.weblogic.WebLogicOracleDelegate
- org.quartz.impl.jdbcjobstore.CloudscapeDelegate
- org.quartz.impl.jdbcjobstore.DB2v6Delegate
- org.quartz.impl.jdbcjobstore.DB2v7Delegate
- org.quartz.impl.jdbcjobstore.HSQLDBDelegate
- org.quartz.impl.jdbcjobstore.PointbaseDelegate

org.quartz.jobStore.dataSource

The value for this property must be the name of one the DataSources defined in the DataSource configuration section later in this appendix.

org.quartz.jobStore.tablePrefix

The table prefix property is a string equal to the prefix given to Quartz's tables that were created in your database. You can have multiple sets of Quartz tables within the same database if they use different table prefixes.

org.quartz.jobStore.useProperties

The "use properties" setting instructs the JDBC JobStore that all values in JobDataMaps will be Strings and, therefore, can be stored as name-value pairs instead of storing more complex objects in their serialized form in the BLOB column. This can be helpful because you avoid the class-versioning issues that can arise from serializing your non-String classes into a BLOB.

org.quartz.jobStore.misfireThreshold

Set this property to the number of milliseconds the Scheduler will tolerate a trigger to pass its next-fire time before it is considered misfired. The default value is 60000 (60 seconds).

org.quartz.jobStore.isClustered

Set this to true to turn on clustering features. This property must be set to true if you are using multiple instances of Quartz and the same set of database tables.

org.quartz.jobStore.clusterCheckinInterval

Set the frequency (in milliseconds) at which this instance checks in with the other instances of the cluster. This value affects the quickness of detecting failed instances.

org.quartz.jobStore.maxMisfiresToHandleAtATime

This is the maximum number of misfired triggers the JobStore will handle in a given pass. Handling many (more than a couple dozen) at once can cause the database tables to be locked long enough to hamper the performance of firing other (not yet misfired) triggers.

org.quartz.jobStore.dontSetAutoCommitFalse

Setting this parameter to true tells Quartz not to call setAutoCommit(false) on connections obtained from the DataSource(s). This can be helpful in a few situations, such as if you have a driver that complains if it is called when it is already off. This property defaults to false because most drivers require setAutoCommit(false) to be called.

org.quartz.jobStore.selectWithLockSQL

This must be a SQL string that selects a row in the LOCKS table and places a lock on the row. If it is not set, the default is SELECT * FROM {0}LOCKS WHERE LOCK_NAME = ? FOR UPDATE, which works for most databases. The {0} is replaced during runtime with the TABLE_PREFIX that you configured earlier.

org.quartz.jobStore.txIsolationLevelSerializable

A value of true tells Quartz (when using JobStoreTX or CMT) to call setTransactionIsolation(Connection.TRANSACTION_SERIALIZABLE) on JDBC connections. This can be helpful to prevent lock timeouts with some databases under high load and long-lasting transactions.

Configuring JobStoreCMT

The JobStoreCMT provides an alternate JobStore that can work with a relational database. You can choose the JobStoreCMT by selecting it with the org.quartz.jobStore.class property:

```
org.quartz.jobStore.class =
➥org.quartz.impl.jdbcjobstore.JobStoreCMT
```

When using the JobStoreCMT, a few additional properties can be set. These are shown in Table A.5.

Table A.5   The Properties for Configuring the Quartz JobStoreCMT

Name	Required	Type	Default Value
org.quartz.jobStore.nonManagedTXDataSource	Yes	String	null
org.quartz.jobStore.dontSetNonManagedTX-ConnectionAutoCommitFalse	No	Boolean	false
org.quartz.jobStore.txIsolationLevelReadCommitted	No	Boolean	false

org.quartz.jobStore.nonManagedTXDataSource

JobStoreCMT requires a (second) datasource that contains connections that will not be part of container-managed transactions. The value of this property must be the name of one of the datasources defined in the configuration properties file. This datasource must contain non-CMT connections—in other words, connections for which it is legal for Quartz to directly call commit() and rollback() on.

org.quartz.jobStore.dontSetNonManagedTXConnectionAutoCommitFalse

This is the same as org.quartz.jobStore.dontSetAutoCommitFalse, except that it applies to the nonManagedTXDataSource.

org.quartz.jobStore.
txIsolationLevelReadCommitted

When set to `true`, this property tells Quartz to call
`setTransactionIsolation(Connection.TRANSACTION_READ_`
`UNCOMMITTED)` on the non-managed JDBC connections. This
can be helpful to prevent lock timeouts with some databases
(such as DB2) under high load and long-lasting transactions.

For more information on JDBC `JobStores`, see Chapter 6,
"JobStores and Persistence."

Configuring Quartz Datasources

If you're using the JDBC `JobStore`, you'll need to define a
datasource for its use. If you're using the `JobStoreCMT`, you'll
actually need to define two datasources.

Datasources can be configured in three ways:

- The pool properties are specified in the `quartz.`
  `properties` file so that Quartz can create the
  `Datasource` itself.

- The JNDI location of an application server managed
  `Datasource` can be specified so that Quartz can use it.

- A custom-defined `org.quartz.utils.`
  `ConnectionProvider` implementation can be used.

Each datasource that you define must be given a name, and
the properties you define for each must contain that name. The
`dataSource`'s `NAME` can be anything you want; it has no meaning and simply identifies the `datasource` when it is assigned to
the JDBC `JobStore`.

When configuring a `datasource` using `quartz.`
`properties` to define all the pool properties, the properties in
Table A.6 are available for use.

Table A.6   The Properties for Configuring the Quartz Datasource

Name	Required	Type	Default Value
org.quartz.dataSource.NAME.driver	Yes	String	Null
org.quartz.dataSource.NAME.URL	Yes	String	null
org.quartz.dataSource.NAME.user	No	String	""
org.quartz.dataSource.NAME.password	No	String	""
org.quartz.dataSource.NAME.maxConnections	No	Integer	10
org.quartz.dataSource.NAME.validationQuery	No	String	null
org.quartz.jobStore.clusterCheckinInterval	No	Long	15000

org.quartz.dataSource.NAME.driver

This must be the Java class name of the JDBC driver for your database.

org.quartz.dataSource.NAME.URL

This is the connection URL (host, port, and so on) for connection to your database.

org.quartz.dataSource.NAME.user

This is the username to use when connecting to your database.

org.quartz.dataSource.NAME.password

This is the password to use when connecting to your database.

org.quartz.dataSource.NAME.maxConnections

This is the maximum number of connections that the DataSource can create in its pool of connections.

org.quartz.dataSource.NAME.validationQuery

This is an optional SQL query string that the DataSource can use to detect and replace failed/corrupt connections. For example, an Oracle user might choose `select table_name from user_tables`, which is a query that should never fail unless the connection is actually bad.

When you're using the `Datasource` defined in an application server, the properties in Table A.7 are available.

Table A.7   The Properties for Configuring Quartz to Use a `Datasource` from an Application Server

Name	Required	Type	Default Value
`org.quartz.dataSource.NAME.jndiURL`	Yes	String	null
`org.quartz.dataSource.NAME.java.naming.factory.initial`	No	String	null
`org.quartz.dataSource.NAME.java.naming.provider.url`	No	String	null
`org.quartz.dataSource.NAME.java.naming.security.principal`	No	String	null
`org.quartz.dataSource.NAME.java.naming.security.credentials`	No	String	null

`org.quartz.dataSource.NAME.jndiURL`

This is the JNDI URL for a `DataSource` that is managed by your application server.

`org.quartz.dataSource.NAME.java.naming.factory.initial`

This is the (optional) class name of the JNDI `InitialContextFactory` that you want to use.

`org.quartz.dataSource.NAME.java.naming.provider.url`

This is the (optional) URL for connecting to the JNDI context.

`org.quartz.dataSource.NAME.java.naming.`
`security.principal`

This is the (optional) user principal for connecting to the
JNDI context.

`org.quartz.dataSource.NAME.java.naming.`
`security.credentials`

These are the (optional) user credentials for connecting to the
JNDI context.

Configuring a Datasource Using a Custom ConnectionProvider

Starting with Quartz 1.5.1, you can create a custom
ConnectionProvider and configure Quartz to use it by providing the class name within the properties file:

```
org.quartz.dataSource.myConnProvider.connectionProvider.class =
➥com.foo.MyConnectionProvider
```

After instantiating the class, Quartz can automatically set
configuration properties on the instance, bean style.

```
org.quartz.dataSource.myConnProvider.someStringProperty = someValue
org.quartz.dataSource.myConnProvider.someIntProperty = 5
```

BOOKS ONLINE

ENABLED

THIS BOOK IS SAFARI ENABLED

INCLUDES FREE 45-DAY ACCESS TO THE ONLINE EDITION

The Safari® Enabled icon on the cover of your favorite technology book means the book is available through Safari Bookshelf. When you buy this book, you get free access to the online edition for 45 days.

Safari Bookshelf is an electronic reference library that lets you easily search thousands of technical books, find code samples, download chapters, and access technical information whenever and wherever you need it.

TO GAIN 45-DAY SAFARI ENABLED ACCESS TO THIS BOOK:

- Go to **http://www.prenhallprofessional.com/safarienabled**

- Complete the brief registration form

- Enter the coupon code found in the front of this book on the "Copyright" page

PRENTICE
HALL

If you have difficulty registering on Safari Bookshelf or accessing the online edition, please e-mail customer-service@safaribooksonline.com.

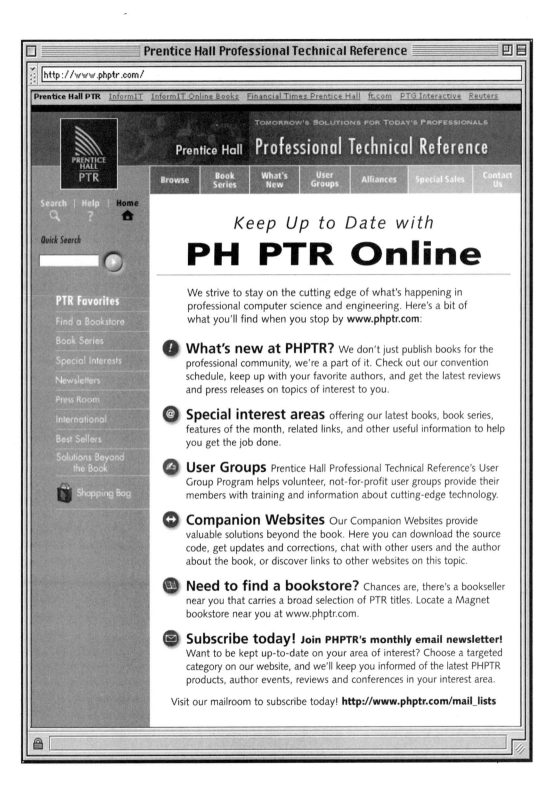